Old Plantations and Historic Homes around

MIDDLEBURG, VIRGINIA

and the Families Who Lived and Loved within Their Walls

Volume II

Old Plantations and Historic Homes around
MIDDLEBURG, VIRGINIA

and the Families Who Lived and
Loved within Their Walls

Volume II

Audrey Windsor Bergner

Howell Press
Charlottesville, Virginia

Designed by Lisa Wayand
Edited by Dara Powers Parker

Library of Congress Cataloging-in-Publication Data

Bergner, Audrey Windsor, 1929–
    Old plantations and historic homes around Middleburg, Virginia: and the families who lived and loved within their walls / Audrey Windsor Bergner
       p. cm.
    Includes bibliographical references and index.
    ISBN 1-57427-142-3 (alk. papers)
    1. Historic sites—Virginia—Middleburg Region. 2. Plantations—Virginia—Middleburg Region—History. 3. Dwellings—Virginia—Middleburg Region—History. 4. Plantation life—Virginia—Middleburg Region—History. 5. Middleburg Region (Va.)—History. 6. Middleburg Region—Social life and customs. 7. Middleburg Region (Va.)—Bibliography. I. Title
F234.M48B47 2003
975.5´28—dc21   00-060291

ISBN 1-57427-142-3

Printed in China

12 11 10 09 08 07 06 05 04 03   10 9 8 7 6 5 4 3 2 1

Howell Press, Inc.
1713-2D Allied Lane, Charlottesville, VA 22903
(434) 977-4006, www.howellpress.com

TABLE OF CONTENTS

ACKNOWLEDGMENTS

*N*o one is an island, and this writer is very grateful to the many gracious people who helped create this history of the Piedmont and its people. Some are current owners of these old homes, some are descendants of those who once owned them, others simply care about preserving a heritage.

They have opened their doors, their old records, diaries, pictures, memories, and often their hearts, so that these tales could be told.

Mrs. Athelstan Spilhaus of Aspen Hill
Mrs. Jean Gold, Ms. Ellen Goldberg, and Mr. Dan Haendel
    of Briar Patch
Mr. and Mrs. William Albers of Exning
Mrs. Douglas Robin of The Dairy Barn
Mr. and Mrs. Arthur Osteen of The Carriage House
Mr. and Mrs. Henry Otis Chapman of The Log Cabin
Mrs. Benjamin Evans of Groveton Farm
Mr. and Mrs. Edward MacMahon of Creek Hill
Mr. and Mrs. Anthony Siriani of Fairview
Col. and Mrs. James Burton of Mercer House
Mr. and Mrs. Gerald Keatinge of The Miller's House
Mr. George Wiltshire of Mosby Spring Farm
Mr. and Mrs. John Gulick of Mount Buclah
Mr. and Mrs. Richard Collette of Mount Defiance
Mr. and Mrs. Ralph Feneis of Mount Harmony
Mr. and Mrs. Horace Figuers of Noland Ferry House
Mr. and Mrs. James Whitner of Old Welbourne
Mr. and Mrs. Nathaniel Morison of Welbourne Plantation
Mr. and Mrs. William Tayloe of Welbourne's Old
    Church House
Mr. and Mrs. Stanley Dees of Crednal
Mrs. Dorothy Mace of Poor House Farm
Ms. Karen Casey of Pot House
Mr. and Mrs. Thomas Slater of Rose Hill
Mr. and Mrs. George Morison of Stoke
Mr. and Mrs. Paul Ziluca of Trappe Spring
Mr. Ken Tomlinson and Ms. Lisa Campbell of Vine Hill

To other members of Piedmont families who have been so supportive of this endeavor, my sincere appreciation, especially:
Mrs. Janet Dulany Roszel Tayloe,
Mr. J. MacKenzie Tabb III,
Mr. Thomas Underwood Dudley IV,
Mrs. Claree Noland Doty,
Mr. Stephen Roszel VI, and Mr. Roger Roszell;
Mr. Richard Lundgren and Mr. Robert Humphrey;
Mrs. Sarah Douglass, Mrs. Mildred Gulick,
Mrs. Betty Furr, Mrs. Joan Furr, and Mrs. Patricia Boatright;
Mr. David Boyce and Mr. Clifford "Okie" Turner;
and Ambassador George C. McGhee.

To Mr. Howard Allen for the beautiful cover picture of Welbourne Plantation; Mr. Eugene Scheel for his excellent articles on Loudoun County history; the ever-helpful staff of the Thomas Balch Library; Mrs. Lina Burton for excellent indexing; Mr. George Devorshak for keeping my testy computer going; and Mr. Tucker Withers, for just being Tucker.

To Mr. James Poston, photographer and friend, for his reproduction of old pictures and total dedication to this project; Mr. Ross Howell, a true Virginia gentleman and fine publisher; And especially to my dear Andrew for his love, support, encouragement, and a thousand missed dinners.

Thank you all. I am ever grateful. Together we have preserved another small part of the history of this "gentle valley" called the Piedmont.

8

PREFACE

"It is good to love one's Native Land"
~John Eston

Someone once said that it takes an expatriate, or someone who returns to a place they once loved, to appreciate its beauty. And perhaps there is some truth to that. By seeing things through a new, or at least a different perspective, perhaps created by time or distance, one becomes a quintessential observer, where the seemingly mundane becomes a marvel.

So I roam the shaded, winding, rock-walled byways of this little corner of Northern Virginia, watching Black Angus cows and thoroughbred horses lazily grazing in verdant fields; corn and golden wheat growing tall under a summer sun; and young, white-tailed, spotted fawns bounding across an open meadow where centuries-old homes stand back from roads once roamed by Indian tribes who left their names on our landscape.

These scenes speak of a time when the Piedmont was a large, open canvas, painted slowly and painstakingly in brilliant colors and broad strokes by strong men and women.

As the picture on the canvas evolves, this little town of Middleburg becomes a microcosm of other towns all across Virginia. It survived Indian attacks and epidemics, bears and wild boars, devastating droughts when crops dried up on barren land, and deep winter snows when cattle froze in the fields. It sent two thousand of its sons to fight a Revolution…an incredible number from such a sparsely settled area. Its people created laws by which to live, churches in which to worship, farms, mills, and a way of life around the four "Sacraments of the South": kinship, civility, hospitality, and tradition.

Nicholas Cresswell, a Tory Englishman, who traveled around America at a time when anger against the crown erupted into Revolution, spent almost two years in Loudoun County and wrote these words in 1777:

> The inhabitants…are the most hospitable people on earth. If a stranger went amongst them, no matter of what country, if he behaved decently, had a good face, a good coat and a tolerable share of good nature, he would dance with the women and drink with the men, and be entertained with the greatest friendship as long as he pleased to stay.[1]

The Southern states were the richest of the thirteen colonies at this point in history, and the following decades became known as the "Golden age of Virginia." Giants walked its paths…Washington, Jefferson, Madison, Mason, and Monroe, Virginians all, left a lasting imprint upon the land and the nation.

Meanwhile, many New England fortunes arose from the African slave trade, at the same time as many Southerners, though dependent upon it in an agrarian society, espoused the "Back to Africa" movement. Slavery is often stated as the cause of that terrible conflict called the Civil War, but since only sixteen percent of Virginians owned slaves,[2] this was not the only or even the prime reason for secession. It was, rather, a belief in the right of Virginians to determine their own destiny. Barbara Holland, a noted author, put it best:

I can't recall meeting anyone who considered himself first and foremost a Marylander or a Pennsylvanian. Virginia's different. It always was. Lee was not alone in fighting a war for his country…and then, forced to choose, chose Virginia instead. They had no choice. America was their country…but Virginia was their mother, their home, their heart, the mystic dirt of love.[3]

Incredible phrase, that "mystic dirt of love." It summons up not just romantic images of gallant, young, gray-coated cavalry officers with plumed hats riding thoroughbred horses, but also that of dirt-poor farmers, carpenters, stonemasons, blacksmiths, and cobblers who plodded through mud and muck, from Bull Run to Gettysburg, who gave their livelihoods, and their lives, for something they believed in.

Names like Stonewall Jackson, Jefferson Davis, Robert E. Lee, J.E.B. Stuart, and John Singleton Mosby stand tall in Piedmont lore. But memories of other, simpler men, who fought for what they believed in, that "mystic dirt of love," are not forgotten in the Piedmont.

The inherently unfair Lincolnian "Emancipation" of slaves in the South, while not freeing those in Northern states, the desolation that followed defeat, and the subsequent vulnerability to Reconstruction agents and the hated "carpetbaggers," along with punitive tariff duties imposed upon Southern states, effectively destroyed Virginia's economy for the next half-century. Many of its farms and plantations were sold for pennies on the dollar, leased to tenants and sharecroppers, or simply abandoned.

Middleburg owes much of its resurgence to New York horse lovers (the "Second Northern Invasion" it was called—though this time the Yankees were welcomed!) who poured into the Piedmont, bought up and restored its old manor homes, revitalized its economy, and turned the countryside into "The Heart of the Virginia Hunt Country."

Thanks to them—and to a few descendants of the old families who spend their lives preserving, against all odds, a treasured old home place—many of those historic homes survive today.

Some of them speak of Englishmen torn between loyalty to a distant king and independence. Some speak of day-in, day-out, backbreaking farm labor and of religious preachers who swept through the Piedmont after the Revolution like avenging angels with sermons of fire and brimstone.

Others tell of white children, indentured for simply being born poor; of weary travelers heading west in Conestoga wagons who found succor at a wayside inn; of once-wealthy young aristocrats who ended their days in the almshouse; and of slaves[4] yearning for an elusive thing called freedom, yet remained loyal to their former owners long after emancipation.

Some homes recall Klan activities, hidden "likker" stills during Prohibition years, or politicians and presidents. Others honor the glory days that ended at Appomattox and that resilient quality called pride, which is so much a part of the Southern psyche.

Today, at a time when the most basic coordinates of life, our sense of continuity, of time, place, and belonging, have vanished in much of America, and anomie undermines urban life, there's a special significance in a small Southern town where heritage and intangible "sense of belonging" is imbibed along with mothers' milk.

That heritage has often been told by people far more talented than I…who have, "turned the South into the most fertile ground our literature has ever known…and the flow of fiction from and about the region was nothing less than historic."[5] Walter Percy, back in 1962, said that so much good writing came from the South "because we lost the war…because defeat forced the white South to confront human fallibility in ways the rest of the nation never did."[6]

Perhaps that's true. Southerners were forced to confront and were penalized for problems that were prevalent in other parts of the country.

But today, a century and a half later, bugles echo across rounded hillsides on crisp golden mornings, calling scarlet-coated riders and hounds to the chase; deer romp across meadows, cattle graze lazily in fields, summer corn grows high…and old homes of the eighteenth and nineteenth centuries, and their families, are still treasured.

Here are their stories.

—Audrey Windsor Bergner 2003

ARCHITECTURAL NOTES

Early manor homes around the Piedmont generally fall into three architectural styles:

GEORGIAN (prior to 1781).
Brick, wood, or stone. Two- or three-storied construction featuring center halls with doors at front and back and high ceilings to allow breezes to flow through; fireplaces; symmetric six-over-six windows; a wide, winding staircase to upper floors; and fairly steep tin or slate roofs.

FEDERAL (1781-1820).
Basically Georgian in design, with four large rooms on both lower and upper floors, they tend to have somewhat plainer exterior elevations, lower pitched roofs, and fan lights over exterior doors. Again, each room features a fireplace with beautifully carved mantles and surrounds.

GREEK REVIVAL (1820-1860).
Many early homes around the Piedmont were re-vamped during this period, with smooth plaster over exterior brick or stone walls and Doric, Ionic, or Corinthian pillars, which came to symbolize the typical Southern Plantation home. The Custis-Lee mansion in Arlington, built in 1826, reflects the Greek Revival style, as do some homes around the Piedmont, including magnificent Oatlands and Welbourne.

Many Colonial-era homes, however, began as simple log or stone cabins with just one or two rooms on ground level and a narrow staircase leading up to a sleeping area. The basement kitchen, or "keeping room," held a large fireplace where all the cooking, and much of the living, occurred.

As crops and cattle brought prosperity to the Piedmont, labor and craftsmen became more available. So over time, many a small cabin, such as those at Crednal and The Miller's House, became the nucleus of a larger home featuring fine, hand-carved mantels, balustrades, and cornices, which spoke of a rising economy and an appreciation of fine craftsmanship.

Quakers, however, tended to remain in their strong, rough-hewn stone homes, which are prized today for their rugged authenticity.

Later additions to early Georgian- and Federal-style homes—of porches, second-floor balconies, and gingerbread trim on eaves and gables—occurred during the Victorian era and have fortunately been removed during renovation.

In many instances, the exact date of construction of a home, even that of its additions or original owner, has been lost to history. Building permits were not required in early times, family lore is sometimes unreliable, and even when a date appears on a chimney or mantle, the original part of the house often preceded it.

As an elderly retainer on an old farm once said, "this house was built so doggoned long ago that there ain't nobody 'members when she was built."

Where concrete evidence is lacking, and with no pretence to expertise in eighteenth- and nineteenth-century construction techniques, I have relied on tax and tithe rolls, contemporary references, family letters and records, cemetery inscriptions (where old family graveyards exist), and the opinions of those far more knowledgeable than I.

And as the old retainer might have said, "Even then, ain't nobody will ever know fer sure."

Aspen Hill as it appears today. Originally this was the rear of the home, but now it serves as the entryway.

ASPEN HILL

he year was 1719. King George I reigned on England's throne when Catherine Culpeper, Lady Fairfax, gave her son Thomas five million acres of land in the northern neck of the Virginia Colony. It was a wilderness occupied only by Indian tribes, however, and thus brought no wealth to the coffers of young Lord Fairfax, so he offered large grants of this virgin territory to English and Virginia gentlemen, whose young sons would settle here, build homes, farms, inns, and mills and create a civilization out of a wilderness.

One of those Virginia gentlemen was Rawleigh Chinn[1] who in 1731 received a grant of 3,300 acres around Middleburg. That grant, on the south side of Goose Creek, ran all the way from what is now Parson's Road on the east to Millville Road on the west.

Rawleigh was quite a man. An attorney by profession, he married Esther Ball—sister of Mary Ball, mother of George Washington—who bore him four sons. But Rawleigh was also a lover whose eye was drawn to yet another Ball sister, the beautiful Margaret Ball Downman, by whom he sired three more sons "on the wrong side of the blanket" as they say.

Give Rawleigh his due, however. He was fair to all seven of his sons, for each received five hundred acres of his land grant in what was then Prince William County. (Part of Prince William was later subdivided into Loudoun and Fauquier Counties). The first Chinn son to settle in the Piedmont was Joseph and his wife (and first cousin), Priscilla Downman.

They opened an inn, or "ordinary" as it was called, in a small stone building now known as the famed Red Fox Inn. Joseph's brothers, Elijah, Charles, Rawleigh, Jr., and Christopher soon followed. Upon Christopher's early death, his land was acquired by his brother Charles. So it is with Charles that we begin the story of Aspen Hill.

Land speculation was rampant in the 1700s. It was also the key to power in the Piedmont, and two prominent families competed for that power: the Powells, led by Leven Powell, and the Chinns, led by Charles Chinn. Leven, who later founded the town of Middleburg, purchased not only Joseph Chinn's five hundred acres, but much of the surrounding area. Charles Chinn, however, was the largest landowner west of town and charged that the land Leven purchased on the west was actually his land. And thus began a battle that would rage through the courts for almost forty years.

And that brings us to Aspen Hill. Upon Leven Powell's death in 1810, he provided generously for his sons. Yet his only daughter, Sarah Harrison Chilton, was given nothing except part of the Aspen Hill land "for her use and benefit" during her lifetime, and this seems an interesting provision. Certainly the Chiltons were a prominent and respected family,[2] so why then would Leven Powell, who left so much wealth to his sons, cut off his only daughter with just twenty-five pounds per year and unsecured property? Perhaps the answer lies in the fact that the land dispute with the Chinns was not resolved until three years after his death, so Leven couldn't give Sarah the property outright. Or, perhaps since the Chiltons were wealthy, Leven felt that Sarah did not need property. Or,

Opposite top: The hand-chiseled ceiling beams, dating from the mid-1700s, in the living room at Aspen Hill were recently uncovered during renovation.

Below: Aspen Hill as it appeared circa 1900 when the front door faced the highway.

possibly, like many men of his time, Leven hoped to establish a dynasty based on huge land holdings, and this was his way of keeping the land intact within the Powell family.[5]

In any case, buildings and gardens and orchards dating back prior to 1766 stood on the land by this time.[4] Sarah and William Chilton enlarged the original house in 1810 into a traditional Georgian design, with two large rooms with fireplaces downstairs, plus a central hall staircase, and upper sleeping area. It was not a manor house by any means—for that would have been far more pretentious. But still, it was a fine home, built of stone, then stuccoed with the fine smooth finish preferred by Englishmen over the rough stone texture favored by German settlers.

There were apple orchards, barns, stables, slave quarters, store rooms, a corn crib, meat house, and spring house, though only one of those original buildings has survived. This surviving building has been

J. MacKenzie Tabb, Nina Carter Tabb, and their son, J. MacKenzie Tabb II, in 1916.

Above: The guest house.

Opposite: Nina Carter Tabb and Mrs. Wallace Simpson, the future duchess of Windsor, at the races, circa 1930.

converted into a charming guest house, and although its original purpose cannot be ascertained, since it sits close to the main house, it may well have been servants' quarters. (For those who love the trivia of antebellum Virginia, in polite society slaves who worked in the house were always referred to as "servants," while others were simply "field hands.")

After Sarah Powell Chilton's death, the house and lands were conveyed to her brother Cuthbert Powell of Llangollen in September of 1838. Just two months later, he sold the entire 374 acres to Samuel Rector. And that too is another old name around Middleburg.

In 1763, Henry Rector, founder of the local Rector family, received a grant of 273 acres right down the old Belhaven Road (now Route 50) from Aspen Hill. A century later, in 1863, Henry's grandson, Caleb Rector, welcomed Col. John Mosby there, and Henry's great-grandsons, Caleb-Clinton and Richard, served in Virginia's 6th Cavalry while Thomas, Edward, and Welby Rector all served with Mosby's Rangers.[5]

Meanwhile, the name of the old Belhaven Road, which lay just twenty feet from Aspen Hill's door, had changed to Ashby Gap Road and was surfaced with sand and gravel in 1856. It served as a perfect spot for travelers on horseback, carriage, or Conestoga wagon to find shelter and supper at the Rector's Inn. Meanwhile, another great stone barn and three hundred more acres were added to their holdings.

Aspen Hill's oral history includes many tales. One concerns a Confederate officer who raced up on horseback one day and begged to be hidden from pursuing Yankees. He was quickly tied to a rope and lowered into the nearby well, but sadly, by the time Union troops departed and he was hauled to the surface, the poor officer had drowned. Legend has it that his bones are still in that well.

Samuel Rector's son Walter remained at Aspen Hill with his wife, Sarah, until 1905 when the property, which now covered 525 acres, was sold (for nineteen thousand dollars) to their cousins, Amos and Laura Payne. Their daughter Golda described it this way:

> The house was surrounded by trees, most of which were Aspens. There was a stone wall around it and a brick path led to the front door. There was a long porch across the front with rockers, a big red barn, a corn crib and a spring house with a room above it which was used as a school room.

Four years later, the Paynes conveyed Aspen Hill to Henry and Nellie MacKenzie Bangs whose nephew, MacKenzie Tabb, married Nina Dulany Carter in October of 1911.[6] A newspaper clipping of the time tells of that event:

> Society all over the State is deeply interested in the approaching wedding of Miss Nina Dulany Carter, daughter of Colonel Richard Welby Carter, dec'd and Mrs. Welby Carter to John MacKenzie Tabb of Baltimore which will be celebrated on Saturday evening, Oct. 28th at Crednal,[7] the Carter home near Middleburg. Miss Carter is one of the most beautiful girls in Virginia…and many guests from Richmond will go to Middleburg for the wedding and a perfect round of entertaining will be done this week in honor of the bride and her attendants.[8]

The young Tabbs took up residence at Aspen Hill, which they referred to simply as "The Aspens," but sadly, MacKenzie died just five years later. And it was a strange occurrence indeed. Like most well-to-do young men of the time, "Mac" Tabb was an avid horseman. One October day in 1916, he and a friend were staying at a Warrenton hotel while attending the three-day Fall Horse Show. Upon returning to the hotel, they drank water from a pitcher in their hotel room and soon after became deathly ill. MacKenzie Tabb died of typhoid a few days later.

Nina was left with her two-year-old son, Mackenzie Tabb, Jr.,[9] a home at Aspen Hill,[9] several hundred acres of farmland, a herd of cattle, sheep, some old family silver, and not much else. But she did have an impeccable background and social connections. Nina used those gifts to become a society columnist,

reporting on parties, galas, and Hunt events from Richmond to Washington and, by the early 1930s, had her own column in *The Washington Times* entitled "Turf and Field."

She was not as quick about paying her bills, however. The local grocery, run by Arthur and Donald Gartrell, kept tabs for their customers that would be paid when the crops came in or cattle were sold at market. The biggest tab belonged to Nina Carter Tabb. As the Depression deepened during the 1930s and Nina's bills kept piling up, the Gartrell brothers needed cash, but were loathe to confront her. Finally, Winnie Gartrell (Arthur's wife) drove over to Aspen Hill one morning. Nina's black maid, a Mrs. Davis, informed her that Mrs. Tabb was still in bed but would receive her upstairs. No one knows exactly what was said, but Winnie Gartrell left with two lambs as partial payment of Nina's account.

Then Mrs. Wallace Simpson arrived in town for the races. Well, you knew that Nina had social connections, right? So where else would the future Duchess of Windsor stay but at Aspen Hill? And though she arrived with a man who was not her husband, it did not apparently pose a problem for she was, by all accounts, well received.

By 1940, after MacKenzie Tabb, Jr., a Virginia Military Institute graduate, had settled in Richmond, Nina sold Aspen Hill. Frank and Helen Schaefer acquired it but conveyed the house and a small amount of acreage to Minna Reese Whitney. Mrs. Whitney, her son John, and two beautiful daughters, Louise and

Wendy, remained at Aspen Hill for almost twenty years[10] and converted the nearby stone servants' quarter[11] into the charming guest cottage of today.

In 1953, Frank Schaefer, who owned the remaining Aspen Hill acreage, began subdividing it into twelve residential lots in which homes sold for fifteen thousand dollars! Today, these homes are in the quarter-million-and-up range.

Now, there is a feeling among those who love old homes, that they attract unusual people. And that is certainly true in regard to the most recent owner of Aspen Hill, who was not only a brilliant raconteur, but a genuine Renaissance character. His name was Athelstan Spilhaus. He was "an inventor, scientist, author, artist, sculptor, professor, dean and advisor to presidents. He was also father of the Sea Grant College Program whose goal was to marshal the total intellectual strength of outstanding American universities in pursuit of the vast bounties of the world's oceans."

So reads the accolade given by the Virginia Laureate Society to Athel Spilhaus when he was elected as one of only fifteen Virginians to receive such an honor for outstanding lifetime achievement. This was a Renaissance man indeed, who with a keen sense of

humor and a delicious smile, offered a business card which read, "Retired Genius."

But the brilliance of Athel Spilhaus was no accident of fate. His grandfather, Sir Thomas Muir, of the famed Scots family, had come to South Africa at the behest of Cecil Rhodes to set up an educational system for the English colony. Athel's mother, Nellie Muir, became the first woman member of the South African Parliament in 1947, and his father, Karl Spilhaus, was the leading merchant of Cape Town who helped invent an early primitive type of refrigeration to ship meat to England.

Athel was just a child when World War I erupted, and families with German names like Spilhaus became persona non grata in Cape Town. So Karl Spilhaus moved his family to a remote farm fifty miles from the nearest railroad station for the duration of the war. Not even basic amenities existed in such a barren, parched place. No electricity, no indoor plumbing, no rain for months on end, and certainly no toys. So Athel and his four siblings created their own toys out of river mud.

Athel compensated for this loss in adulthood by amassing the largest toy collection in the United States! Thousands of toys forced the construction of

first one addition to the old Aspen Hill house, then another, and another, and still another. The toys walk, they talk, and include everything from eighteenth-century clockwork automatons (complex engineering designs with springs and pulleys) to ship models, dolls, and even the original RCA dog listening to "his master's voice" on an old Victrola.

Why did this brilliant man devote a lifetime to collecting toys? Well, he said, "I love history and humor, engineering, scientific ideas and good art…and they all come together in a toy." Perhaps, but in the background is a little boy who created toys out of river mud in a forsaken part of the South African outback.

Since Athel's death in 1998, his delightful wife, Kathy, has enhanced the toy collection and graciously sends it on tours for others to enjoy. But she too has a passion, illustrated in the old basement kitchen where the huge fireplace of 1755 serves as background for her collection of antique cooking implements, from cherry stoners and corn scrapers to a primitive revolving fan designed to keep the flies away from the cook.

The old front door, which once stood just twenty feet from the old Ashby Gap Road, is still there, but guests today drive along a winding path that leads to the north side of the house, and enter a huge gourmet kitchen where two Corgies yelp their welcome. But Kathy Spilhaus has also restored the original rooms of Aspen Hill revealing hand-chiseled ceiling beams, which had long been hidden by a false ceiling.

Ancient pine floors and mantles shine again, old clocks and chandeliers gleam, and fine antique furniture and paintings fill the charming front rooms, which are the same today as they were two-and-a-half centuries ago.

If those walls could talk, they'd tell exciting, or sometimes sad tales, of Sarah Powell and William Chilton; of simple farmers like the Rectors who suffered through Civil War; of socialites like Nina Carter Tabb and the future Duchess of Windsor; of the beautiful Whitney sisters who entranced their beaus; and of an incredible man named Athel Spilhaus who dreamed dreams and achieved goals far beyond the ken of most of us.

Sadly, however, the beauty and primordial connection which binds men to nature and certain trees has been broken, for there are no longer any Aspens at Aspen Hill.

Above, top and bottom: Athel and Kathy Spilhaus in one of the four rooms added to display their famous toy collection. Athel was a Renaissance Man: scientist, sculptor, author, advisor to presidents, and self-described "Retired Genius."

Opposite: The original basement kitchen at Aspen Hill, with thick-beamed ceiling, now displays Kathy Spilhaus' collection of antique cooking instruments.

This lovely scene of Briar Patch in wintertime illustrates its stages of development. On the left is the original log cabin, which was later joined to the large mansion on the right. The covered verandah, which in the summer holds wicker rockers and pots of geraniums, was added after the Civil War.

20

BRIAR PATCH

Whether surrounded by a blanket of winter white or by summer sun dancing on pots of crimson geraniums along the verandah, historic Briar Patch always extends a warm welcome. That welcome is due to the kindness and smile of a lady who has called it home since 1965.

For thirty-five years, she has opened her heart and home to every benefit, political rally, and dramatic and social endeavor that touched the Middleburg community. Her name is Jean Gold, and her home is filled with French antiques, colorful chintzes, glowing fires, wonderful old prints and paintings, unusual memorabilia, and books. Books everywhere!

There's a sense of serenity at Briar Patch; it's almost as though it has chosen to remember the good times and forget other parts of its past. Back in 1805, it was just a simple, one-room log cabin with a sleeping loft above. Sadly, its builder left no clue—no initials on the chimney or carved onto the ceiling beams—as to his identity, though it was most likely a tenant house on Charles Fenton Mercer's 1,300-acre plantation.[1]

It was the fascinating DiZerega family who purchased Mercer's home on the hillside over Aldie and its acreage in 1842.[2] And it was also the DiZeregas who owned Hillcrest (as Briar Patch was then known) in the early 1850s.[3] The family began in Loudoun County in 1842 with Augustus DiZerega, owner of a clipper ship line, and his wife, Eliza Uytendelle, daughter of Baron von Britten of Denmark. They returned to New York in 1855, but some of their sons remained in Aldie.

Hillcrest grew during those years, acquiring a drawing room, library, and dining room, as well as seven bedrooms in the main house, and two cottages, a studio and ten-stall stable, a dairy barn, and fenced fields for cattle and horses. By the 1860s, the log cabin had become a plantation.

Then disaster struck. Civil War erupted and the little village of Aldie was alternately occupied by Union and Confederate troops for four long years. But the DiZeregas were not living there then! Alfred DiZerega, a New Yorker by birth, had joined the U.S. Navy and was stationed in New Orleans, a vital

Above: The original keeping room at Briar Patch with its extensive ceiling beams, old stone fireplace, deep-shuttered windows, and 250-year-old gleaming pine floors, is now a charming conversation area.

Opposite and right: Stable and silo stand witness to earlier times when farming was an essential part of life in Loudoun County, while the old well pump is the reminder of water buckets laboriously hauled up to house.

position since control of the Mississippi was essential for Union troops and supplies.

Alfred leased Hillcrest to William Adam, and it was Adam who was there on that hot July 17th in 1863 when Gen. Alfred Pleasanton's Federal troops crossed over the little stone bridge in Aldie.[4] A mile down the road, Pleasanton's forces ran into fifty Rebels commanded by Capt. Reuben Boston, holding

22

the knoll at Hillcrest with carbines and three cannons. It was a fierce battle. Smoke and dust swirled around the mansion, cannons roared, and bullets hit its walls. Outnumbered, the Confederates were driven off the hillside and finally surrendered. It was the first time that any of Gen. J.E.B. Stuart's men had ever surrendered.[5]

While in New Orleans, Alfred DiZerega met and married Alice Almeda Gasquet, and at war's end, they returned to Hillcrest where several children soon joined their family. Augustus, their first son, married Agnes Green and purchased Sleepy Hollow[6] in Aldie. Another son, Gasquet, married Fredericka Foote Hauser of Prince William County, and upon his father's demise, became the new owner of Hillcrest.

But the years after Appomatox held almost all Southerners in the grip of poverty. With no money to pay field hands, buy or plant seed, harvest crops, or get them to the Washington markets, times were tough. Hillcrest began its decline as repairs to leaking roofs, broken fences, mildewed walls, barns, and stables soon became impossible.

By 1912, Gasquet took a job as postmaster of Aldie. Perhaps he was appointed because he was one of the few men in the area to own one of those new Ford machines called an automobile. But a few years later, during the terrible influenza epidemic of 1919 that killed more people than all the guns and cannons of World War I, he died. He was just forty years old. His wife, Frederica, was left to carry on both farm and family at Hillcrest.

Frederica had retained her Louisiana roots, however, so a few years later their daughter, also named Frederica, married Henry Crabites of New Orleans.

Above top: Bright, cheerful ambiance welcomes guests to the 1860-era parlor.

Above bottom: The guest bedrooms, recently redecorated by the new owners, feature fine old four-posters, fireplaces, colonial-style quilts, and comfortable chairs.

But in a fascinating twist, she returned to Hillcrest for the birth of her first child because she believed that "if you're not born in Virginia, then you shouldn't be born at all." That child, the third generation to bear the name, is Frederica DiZerega Crabites Pecora who still lives near Middleburg. She grew up in New Orleans, but her summers were spent at Hillcrest with her grandmother. Happy days they were, riding horseback over to see her Uncle Augustus and her ten cousins at Sleepy Hollow and to visit Mercer House where her aunts Emily and Frances DiZerega were living.

It was about that time that racial problems erupted in Loudoun County. They had seldom surfaced until then, but by the 1930s, the Great Depression found poor, unskilled, uneducated people, both black and white, struggling to survive. And competing for low-wage jobs.

Then the Klan arrived. The field adjacent to Hillcrest was their meeting place and the training ground for local rednecks. Dressed in white sheets, klansmen began terrorizing local villages, burning crosses on hillsides and threatening ministers and citizens who protested their activities. Fortunately, wiser minds prevailed and life soon returned to normal, though it was not until 1962, when Pres. John F. Kennedy made Middleburg his second home, that schools and restaurants in the area became integrated.

After more than a century of DiZerega ownership, Hillcrest was finally sold in 1965 to Jean and Bill Costin' who whimsically changed its name to Briar Patch (which still doesn't sit too well with Frederica Pecora whose childhood memories speak of Hillcrest).

But the additions the Costins made to the home are delightful, regardless of its name. A new kitchen and breakfast area overlook a flagstone patio, gardens bloom with color, old trees offer shelter, and a sparkling pool invites a cooling dip on hot summer days, while views of both the Blue Ridge and Bull Run Mountains lend majesty to the scene.

This was more than just an historic home to the Costins. It became a center for the arts. A love of theatre encouraged Jean, who had once played in "Captain Jinks and the Horse Parade" with Diana Barrymore and Gregory Peck, and Bill Costin, a Broadway producer, to start the Middleburg Players, which has for over thirty years encouraged local talent, putting on shows ranging from *Carousel* to *The Best Little Whorehouse in Texas*. After Bill Costin's death, Jean married Jay Gold and continues her involvement

Jean Costin Gold was the gracious mistress of Briar Patch for over thirty years, during which time she brought her talent for theatre and laughter to Middleburg. Here she is (center) surrounded by the cast of Guys and Dolls *in 2002.*

with the Middleburg Players to this day. An illustration of her love for Middleburg is a short story written by Thornton "Doc" Saffer about his boyhood. He tells of a simpler time when kids spent summer days fishing in Wankopin Creek and evenings at the old Esso station singing to the tunes of a fiddler named Herman Poston; it's a place where everybody knew everybody, and the town wrapped its arms around you.

Jean took that story, called "It was Mostly Fun," and turned it into a standing-room-only, smash hit. Some of us like to believe that Middleburg is still that kind of town and a lady named Jean Gold makes that belief possible.

New owners now walk the old pine floors, sit before a glowing fire, and perhaps wonder who came before them at Briar Patch. Like many recent residents, Ellen Goldberg and her husband, Dan Haendel, both work in Washington, but fell in love with the serenity of the Piedmont. The goal of these two attorneys is to use the old home as a bed and breakfast for a few years until they retire to enjoy it, and the community, on a full-time basis.

Winter's white splendor and the crimson geraniums of summer continue to embrace the walls of

Briar Patch where history has made its mark and friends have received a warm welcome for almost two centuries.

Jean Costin Gold

Exning appears golden under an autumn sun.

EXNING

*D*escendant of noblemen, scion of the House of Peyton of Iselham, England, and landowner in Prince William County, Valentine Peyton was a man to be reckoned with.[1]

He was a gentleman at a time in history when the word connoted a classical education, culture, courage, talent, determination, and wealth. And wealth meant land. Valentine acquired a lot of land, including eight hundred acres on the south side of Goose Creek, which he purchased from Dr. Charles Green around 1740.

Valentine and his wife, Frances Harrison, had six children[2] who were to become powerful players in the history of Loudoun. As court justices and vestrymen,[3] they wielded tremendous influence in a growing area like the Piedmont. And like their father, they also amassed a good deal of land.

Henry Peyton owned 675 acres near Pot House; Craven Peyton, a Loudoun County court justice, owned the fine brick home and tavern near the Leesburg Courthouse. Valentine's only daughter, Eleanor, married William Powell, whose son Leven inherited five hundred acres of Peyton land around Goose Creek. And Francis Peyton, a member of the House of Burgesses, would carry the famed "Resolutions" that he, Leven Powell, and Thomson Mason had drafted to Williamsburg in 1775.[4]

Listen to what they said: "We will, with our lives and fortunes, support our suffering brethren of Boston…until our grievances shall be procured and our common libertyes be established."

Strong words from strong men. When it became obvious that war could not be avoided, Francis Peyton joined General Washington as a colonel in the Continental Army as did his brothers, Valentine and Henry,[5] while John, Harrison, and Robert served as captains. A valiant family lineage it was indeed.

But it is with Valentine Peyton, Sr., that our story of the property (which later became known as Exning) begins. Although he sold 214 of the original eight hundred acres to his son Robert and his wife, Ann Guffey, the balance of the property may have been the home of Valentine's son Francis and his wife, Frances Dade.[6]

Exning in the early 1900s on a winter day. Courtesy of Thomas Underwood Dudley IV.

There was only a small, stone patent house there at the time that Francis enlarged it into a manor home, for he was a wealthy man, owning twenty-five slaves and serving in the House of Burgesses in 1769, and later as a state senator in Richmond in 1789. Two sons were born to Francis Peyton. Francis Peyton, Jr., a medical graduate of the University of Edinburgh, Scotland, was shot and killed on the streets of Leesburg in 1808 by William Littlejohn. Townsend Dade Peyton, who as a young boy served as an ensign in the Revolution,[7] later freed his slaves and moved to Oxford, Ohio, in 1833.[8]

Meanwhile, Francis Peyton, Sr., died in 1806, followed by his wife, Frances Dade, in 1815. Whether their home and plantation stayed in the Peyton family following these events is unknown, though Charles Lee, an attorney of Leesburg, married Margaret Scott Peyton in 1809, and their son, Charles Lee, Jr., is shown as the owner of The Log Cabin at Exning in 1869.[9] One of the treasures of the old house is a hand-inscribed "calling card" found in the attic, which reads, "Compliments of Mrs. Robert E. Lee."

As fate would have it, Exning's connection to the Lee family continued with its purchase in 1878 by Bolling Walker Haxall of Richmond. The Haxalls were close friends of General Lee, and after Appomattox it was on his way to Barton Haxall's home that the general rode through the silent streets of Richmond. Of that day it was said, "even Union troops doffed their hats in his honor as he passed by, while the ladies of Richmond lay weeping behind closed shutters."[10]

But Bolling Haxall married not a belle from Richmond, but Miss Lavinia (Lena) Noland, daughter of Col. Burr Powell Noland of Chestnut Hill in Middleburg. Soon after, he purchased the old Peyton property, which he called Exning in honor of his family home near Cambridge, England. Thus an eighteenth-century plantation in Virginia was named for a sixth-century Saxon village in England.[11]

The Haxalls enlarged Exning. "We just kept adding more bedrooms as more children arrived," said Lena Haxall. Bay windows, Victorian-era moldings, a spacious dining room, an indoor kitchen, and a gracious veranda across the whole front elevation were also part of the expansion along with a huge dairy barn, granary, carriage house, and stable. Plus innumerable small out-

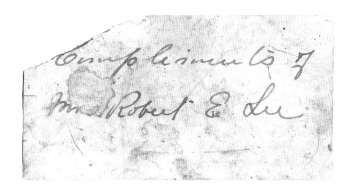

buildings that have survived to this day, though as we shall see, some have been converted for more contemporary usage.

Meanwhile, Thomas Underwood Dudley had arrived on the Middleburg scene as a wealthy young planter in the 1850s. In 1859 he married Fannie Cochran[12] and served as mayor of the town (1865-66) during that turbulent time when Confederate soldiers were returning home to burned barns and barren fields, and the hated Northern Reconstruction agents (carpetbaggers, as they were called) were confiscating land from local farmers.

Whether it was the carnage of war or the death of his twenty-six-year-old wife, Fannie,[13] soon after the war Thomas Dudley decided to enter the ministry. Upon graduating from the Theological Seminary of Virginia, he was appointed to Baltimore and then elevated to bishop of the diocese of Kentucky. After his second marriage to Virginia Rowland Fisher in Baltimore, his firstborn son, Thomas Underwood Dudley II, was born in 1870.[14]

In 1901, that son returned to Middleburg and married Bolling Haxall's daughter Anne. Members of the Middleburg Hunt, active in banking, owners of Rowland Farm (a home they built on the site of the Chinn family's old Mount Recovery[15]), and parents of several young children, the Dudleys were deeply in-volved in community affairs. But after Rowland Farm burned in 1919,[16] they moved to Anne's childhood home at Exning where they replaced the old roof with new tin and stuccoed the stone, brick, and frame exterior.

Tom Dudley is remembered to this day for his kindness to everyone. For example, Mr. Dudley observed a young hunchbacked black boy walking into Middle-

Above: A hand-inscribed calling card of Mrs. Robert E. Lee was discovered in the attic.

Below: This desk, which once belonged to Bolling W. Haxall, bears a tag asking that it be delivered to him at The Plains railroad station in Fauquier County, Virginia. It stands in the family room at Exning.

Above, right and left: Bolling W. Haxall and Lavina Noland Haxall at the wedding of their daughter Anne to Thomas Underwood Dudley II in 1901. Courtesy of Thomas Underwood Dudley IV.

burg one day. "That boy shouldn't be working in the fields; bring him up to the house," he said. And for the next forty years, Raymond Washington served proudly as butler, chauffeur, and all-around factotum to the Dudley family. He became part of the family, and so close was their friendship that Tom Dudley paid to send Raymond's son to college.

After President Roosevelt's "Bank Holiday" in 1933, Tom Dudley emerged as the new president of the Middleburg National Bank. A few years later, in 1938, Anne Dudley proposed the idea of a Middleburg Garden Club—not that the ladies were all that interested

Judge Thomas Underwood Dudley III served as president of the Middleburg National Bank in 1933 and as mayor of Middleburg in 1953 and 1954, almost a century after his grandfather, Thomas Dudley I, held the same position.

in petunias, but they were very concerned about local politics. Middleburg roads were awash in debris; chickens roamed at will along Washington Street (pigs had been outlawed just a few years earlier). Junk automobiles collected on empty lots, litter on roads and sidewalks. And the town fathers were doing nothing to correct the situation.

So Anne Dudley, Anne Carrington Montegue, Ethel Humphrey, Julia Whiting, Eugenia Fairfax, and a few other ladies of the newly formed Middleburg Garden Club confronted the town council with a "Clean Up Middleburg" campaign. "No money," said the council. "Well then, we'll do it ourselves," responded the lad-

ies. So they hired a street sweeper, started a regular trash collection service, and paid to have empty lots cleared and junk cars hauled away.

When World War II erupted, Thomas Dudley became head of the Selective Service Board for Loudoun County. To avoid any perception of favoritism about the draft, his son John Rowland Dudley[17] became the first to volunteer in the United States Army from Loudoun County.

At war's end, John and his bride, Mary Cary Walker, or Polly as she was known, settled into "the cottage" at Exning where their three sons grew up and Polly Dudley lived until recently.[18] John, a lawyer by profession, also served as a Loudoun County judge and mayor of Middleburg, 1953-54, almost a century after his grandfather had filled the same role.

John and Polly's eldest son—Thomas Underwood Dudley IV, though everyone calls him Tim—has fond memories of childhood at Exning when it was a working dairy farm. He milked the cows, played in the ruins of the old mill at the end of the lane,[19] rode horseback across Exning's four hundred acres, and moved cattle from one field to another, across Route 50 when there was so little traffic that a whole herd could cross without encountering a car!

Before heading off to boarding school at Episcopal High School in Alexandria, as have four generations of the family beginning with Tom Dudley II, class of 1886, Tim's grandmother, Anne Haxall Dudley, often told him stories about the family and the farm.

One tale excited the young boy's imagination, for it involved a tavern that once lay along the road just west of Exning where an old well-head still stands. The tavern is long gone, but when the well was drained in the 1930s (after one of their cows had fallen in) remains of both Confederate and Union soldiers were discovered in its depths. Their names are lost to history. Only their buttons and buckles survive.

After Anne Haxall Dudley died in 1969, Exning was sold and its four hundred plus acres were subdivided into large residential lots.[20] But the manor house had long suffered from neglect and delayed maintenance, and its once beautiful grounds, overgrown with weeds and gnarled trees, had become a jungle.

In 1976, the old house and ten acres was purchased by Lt. Comdr. Robert and Eileen Mickley, who had lived in Washington, D.C., while Bob Mickley was stationed at the Pentagon. They removed five (at least!) layers of old wallpaper, re-plastered walls, installed period lighting fixtures and moldings, restored the kitchen, modernized bathrooms, and turned the jungle into a lovely garden.

After Eileen's death, Bob Mickley sold the house and its memories to his daughter Pamela in 1992. An architect by profession, Pam Mickley grew up in this house, and her love for it, along with an incredible flair for interior design, has accomplished wonders at Exning.

Every room has a totally different flavor, and though the library is a study in black and white, other areas literally sing with color. The living room is full of bright floral chintzes, the stately dining room reflects shades of a sun-kissed tomato, the old butler's pantry has become a cozy breakfast room, while a contempo-

rary new kitchen with a huge semi-circular counter and seating area invites friends to watch the intricacies of Pamela's gourmet cooking.

Pam Mickley married William Albers in 1997, and they've since added a family room that dances with brilliant reds and touches of yellow. Sunshine splashes through French doors onto brightly cushioned chairs and toys that litter the floor.

The family room, you see, is a mecca for the Albers' little son, named Carter in honor of Pres. Jimmy Carter for whom Bill Albers worked as deputy assistant to the president for political affairs at the White House before opening his own political consulting firm in Washington.

The Albers' also restored the balconies on the rear

Above: Pamela Mickley Albers spent her childhood at Exning and is now its owner. As an architect and talented interior designer, she's brought color and verve to each room, as illustrated by these sun-kissed tomato walls in the dining room.

Opposite, left and right: By 1976, Exning's glory days seemed over. Fortunately, its new owners, Robert and Eileen Mickley, restored it to its former beauty, while preserving its architectural integrity. Photos courtesy of Pamela Albers.

elevation and created a charming patio of fieldstone squares and soft grasses surrounding the old well pump and sparkling pool. Wide lawns, buffered by ancient trees and new flower gardens, offer views of the Bull Run Mountains, which loom in the distance.

Exning has come a long way from its beginnings as a small stone patent house on a Peyton plantation. It has survived Revolution and Civil War and known fascinating old Southern families: Peytons, Harrisons, Lees, Haxalls, and Dudleys, who have all played large roles in Virginia history. It has known bad times, and good, though it has seldom seen the beauty and seren-

ity that surrounds it today.

But that is only part of the Exning experience, so join me now as we explore the rest of its story.

Above and opposite: The barren lawn of yesteryear is now enhanced by a beautiful pool that reflects the new additions to Exning.

Above: Tree-shaded lawns surround this unusual home, known as The Dairy Barn.

Opposite: The ancient silo is long gone, but its base now encloses a lovely patio.

THE DAIRY BARN

*I*t is rare when outbuildings from the eighteenth and nineteenth centuries survive and find themselves reincarnated into twenty-first century homes. All too often, these wonderful old buildings are abadoned, used for storage, or razed to make way for subdivisions—their ancient trees felled and their history destroyed.

But that didn't happen at Exning. Not only did an early eighteenth-century log cabin survive, but the manor house and adjacent cottage still stand, as do Bolling Haxall's 1880 additions. They are now lovely homes, hidden away on a quiet country road. One of these once served as a cattle barn, dairy, and creamery.

When Exning was sold and divided into parcels in 1975 by Bud Morency, a Middleburg realtor and contractor, he converted the hundred-foot-long, board-and-batten dairy barn into a home. Fortunately he respected its history, for although the interior was completely renovated, all of its original exterior architecture was preserved. It has been sold and resold a few times since then, but each owner has delighted in and never changed its character

A circle of stones at the front entrance, once the base of a silo, forms a delightful curved patio surrounded by old trees and masses of brilliant spring tulips. A blue door opens onto a slate foyer where an antique grandfather clock from Baltimore tolls the hour and alludes to other treasures waiting to be discovered.

The living room, which has acquired a fireplace, runs the width of the old barn and glows with fine old portraits, paintings, and oriental china, while sunlight reflects on pots

Above and right: A slate floor and dappled sunlight accentuate a magnificent antique grandfather clock in the foyer.

Opposite: A collection of China plates captures attention in the hallway where the polished pine ceiling (once the floor of the hayloft) leads to the master suite.

of lush fern and brilliant orchids. Along the long corridor leading to the bedroom wing, attention is captured by a showcase of rare and unusual china plates collected by the current owner from all over the world.

Original pine flooring from the attic, where hay was once stored, has been carefully sanded and polished and now serves as the ceiling along the hallway leading to a charming master suite. Hard to believe that cows were once herded in to be milked in this room, but today that wide entrance features French doors opening onto a private patio.

The history of The Dairy Barn continues outdoors where great, black, wrought-iron tongs that once hauled hay into the upper reaches still hang on the side of the old house. A century-old stone creamery, now a convenient potting shed, stands out back by the garden; a red-painted granary with its 1880 cornerstone stands on the hillside; and a well that once provided fresh water, now covered with a coat of glossy green ivy, lies near the enclosed porch.

Cherry trees, brilliant in early April, lead to an old

Above left: A cornerstone of the rugged barn built by Bolling Haxall bears the date 1880.

Above right: Wrought-iron tongs, once used to haul hay up to the attic, still hang on the side of The Dairy Barn.

stone wall where well-mulched garden beds lie sleeping, waiting for the warmth of spring. The most distinctive feature of The Dairy Barn, however, is a spring-fed stream, which once provided water for the entire Exning property. Today, it flows from the fields in back of the dairy barn, under the house, to the front lawn where clutches of daffodils bloom along its banks. Unusual? Indeed. And a delightful way to preserve an old landmark.

Left: Surely the most unusual feature of the home is the stream that flows underneath, cooling it in the summer.

Below: The old stone creamery behind The Dairy Barn now serves as a convenient potting shed.

Above: The Carriage House as it stands at Exning today.

Opposite: The 1880 Carriage House before its restoration.

THE CARRIAGE HOUSE

*I*t's impossible to imagine horses neighing in their stalls or carriages rolling through the doorway of this lovely home today. Yet during the nineteenth and early twentieth centuries, it was a ten-stall stable and carriage house for the Haxalls and Dudleys.

By 1975, while Exning lands were being subdivided, The Carriage House was purchased by Mr. and Mrs. Jack Malone. Long unused and deserted, delayed maintenance was terribly apparent, but the surrounding three acres were beautiful. Savoring its flavor, the Malones preserved much of the history of the Carriage House while turning it into a delightful home, designed by local architect Catherine Eekels.

Old wrought iron grillwork, which once divided horse stalls from the carriage area, was preserved to greet visitors at the front entrance and take them up the interior staircase to the original hay loft, which is now a guest suite.

The carriage area became a charming dining room, where sunlight reflects through French doors leading to a lit, airy solarium. And the old horse stalls? They were turned into a spacious living room enhanced by a twelve-foot bay window, which overlooks rolling meadows and century-old trees. Finely crafted book shelves line the entire rear living room wall, while the tack room was reincarnated into a small but modern kitchen. Fortunately, the huge, old wooden timbers that once supported the stable and hay loft were incorporated into every room so that The Carriage House's past has become part of its present.

When it came time for the Malone's

Above left: Century-old grillwork and wooden timbers were incorporated throughout the home to preserve its history.

Above right, top and bottom: The current dining room, replete with new French doors that lead to a delightful solarium, formerly held the Haxall and Dudley carriages.

Opposite top: Now a bright living room, this area was once home to ten horses.

Opposite bottom: The dormered hayloft is now a cozy guest suite, where twin beds made of walnut enhance the architectural strength of The Old Carriage House.

to leave Middleburg in 1986, a friend and "shooting buddy" of Thomas Underwood Dudley IV bought The Carriage House. Robert Rogers and his wife, Pat, lived in Great Falls, but Pat was (and still is) an avid member of the Middleburg Hunt who used to haul her horse out to the country every week. So she loved the idea of a second home near Middleburg.[1] The Rogers added a dressing room and closets to the master suite, trees and flowering shrubs, as well as gardens and an enclosed rear patio around the old frame building.

Chicagoans Mary and Arthur Osteen made The Carriage House their Virginia home a few years ago. A delightful couple they are, and what a romantic story they have to tell.

They both grew up in Durham, North Carolina, where Mary's father, Harvey Brinkley, was a doctor. Mary and Arthur went to high school together and were childhood sweethearts. He was tall and handsome; she was vivacious, petite, and charming. But Mary married someone else, Dr. Norman Allen, a faculty member at the University of North Carolina's College of Medicine.

Arthur moved to Chicago where he became an administrator for the American Medical Association and a lover of the arts. But he never married. Meanwhile, Mary and her husband and two sons, James and Thomas, moved to Columbus, Ohio. Many years later, Arthur and Mary met at an Ohio State convention. Then after her husband died, they met again at a high school reunion in Durham. And in one of those fairy tales that sometimes come true, the sweethearts of the fifties married in 1991. Upon Arthur's retirement, luck (and Mary's two nearby grandchildren) brought them to The Old Carriage House near Middleburg.

Although its ambiance is casual and inviting, elegant Victorian loveseats and chairs dot the Osteen's home today, along with a series of Japanese lithographs that change with the seasons. The most fascinating pieces, however, are twin, four-poster beds in the upstairs chamber. Remember that Mary Osteen's father had been a doctor? Well during the Depression years, patients were often unable to pay their medical bills.

It seems that one such patient had a massive walnut tree fall down in his yard during a storm. His

neighbor had a small lathe and he talked the neighbor into making two beautiful beds out of the walnut tree limbs to repay Dr. Brinkley for his care. Used by Mary all through her childhood, then by her children and grandchildren…now, some fifty years later, they stand proudly in the hayloft—the guest bedroom of The Old Carriage House at Exning.

The Log Cabin today.

THE LOG CABIN

*I*t is appropriate to end the story of Exning with The Log Cabin since it may well be the oldest home at Exning. When Valentine Peyton sold 214 acres to his son Robert and his wife, Ann Guffey, they built the log house with a gable roof, which would have been quite pretentious in the virtual wilderness of the 1700s. It had two downstairs rooms with thick white poplar ceiling beams and two large stone fireplaces. A corner staircase led to a large bedroom on the second landing and another in the dormer.

It is tempting to picture this young aristocrat, Robert Peyton, sitting beside one of the drawing room fireplaces, boots on the fender and glass in hand, planning and plotting strategies against the British. But that didn't happen. Although Robert served as a captain during the Revolution, he sold his home and 214 acres to Thomas Gibson in 1765.

Thomas was part of a prolific family, which came to Loudoun County in the 1730s and soon spread all over the Piedmont.[1] Though many of their descendants served the Confederacy,[2] there is no record of their Revolutionary activities. But the Gibsons did make a lasting mark on the history of the area. Abner Gibson was a Middleburg attorney in the early 1800s; Joseph Gibson owned a plantation called Blakely's Grove in 1830; Jordan Gibson was sheriff of Loudoun in the 1850s; Charles Gibson was a state senator; and Dr. James Gibson, who married Fredrica Crabites,[3] is credited with saving the life of then Vice Pres. Lyndon Johnson when he suffered a heart attack while visiting Middleburg in the 1960s.

Beginning back in the 1760s, though, Thomas, and then his son Levi, lived at the Log Cabin, between them staying for a total of fifty years.

An interesting piece of Americana arose during that time. Virginia was, of course, still an English colony in the 1760s, and stealing was a crime punishable by prison. Thousands of abandoned children, who stole food just to survive, were picked up off the streets of London and shipped to America as indentured servants. Poor children in Loudoun County fared no better.

Over 2,750 orphaned, illegitimate, and abandoned children, from five to fifteen years of age, were indentured as apprentices to local families beginning

Above: Hugh Smith, owner of The Log Cabin from 1820 to 1859, was a "Physician, Lawyer and Shopkeeper" according to the 1820 census. He and his wife, Elizabeth Jones, raised twelve children in The Log Cabin. Courtesy of the great-great-grandchildren of Hugh Smith: Patricia Smith Boatright, LeMaine Chilton Payne, and Benjamin R. Humphreys, Sr.

Opposite top: Another treasure at The Log Cabin is the original kitchen fireplace—a massive stone affair that provided venison stews and hot tasty soups to generations of Peytons, Gibsons, Smiths, and farm managers for the Haxalls and Dudleys.

in 1757.[4] The concept was good. Poor youngsters would be given a home; boys would be taught trades such as black-smithing, harness-making, or farm husbandry, and girls would learn weaving, cooking, and household duties. But the reality was much different for they were often treated as little more than slaves.

Thomas Gibson was a proponent of the indenture system and over the years "adopted" seven youngsters aged from seven to fifteen. One of them, a boy named Terence Currey, ran away from Tom Gibson in 1768, however, and upon being caught was hauled into Leesburg Court and ordered to serve "extra time" for his escape.[5]

Meanwhile, Tom Gibson and his sons, Levi and David, added another two-and-a-half-story addition to The Log Cabin and opened up the two first floor rooms to create a marvelous "great room" with stone fireplaces at either end. This is truly the jewel of the home, complimented by the basement kitchen with its brick floor, massive fireplace, including a 7' 6"-wide, 6' 2"-high and hand-hewn wooden mantle. It's a magnificent example of early construction with its great, black iron cooking crane, which still hangs within its deep recess, and one can almost smell the porridge and wild turkey stews that once bubbled over its low-burning flames.

Then in 1820, David sold the house and its land to young 27-year-old Hugh Smith, son of Capt. James Smith who served in the 7th Virginia during the Revolution, later moved to Middleburg, married Nancy Atwell, and built a large home called Hill Farm north of town. Sadly, James died in 1792, leaving two young children, and a third, Hugh, who was born after the death of his father. But his mother, Nancy Atwell Smith, soon married again to David Gibson, and the Gibson-Smith family lived together at Hill Farm until Nancy's death in 1831.

Meanwhile, Hugh Smith had become quite a prominent part of the Middleburg community. In the census of 1820, he listed his occupation as "Physician, Lawyer, and Shopkeeper." He also became a large landowner, high sheriff of Loudoun County, and a justice of the peace.[6]

That same year, 1820, Hugh purchased The Log Cabin at Exning where he and his bride, Elizabeth Jones, raised their twelve children and lived for the next forty years.

But remember that the Smith family came from Ireland? Well, Hugh Smith was an ardent Catholic, and the first Catholic service in Loudoun County was

held at his home in 1852.[7] And yet, in an unusual (for the time) spirit of ecumenism, Hugh and Elizabeth sold (for just five dollars) land for the Asbury Methodist Church on Jay Street.[8]

Perhaps feeling that his end was near,[9] Hugh sold The Log Cabin and its two hundred acres to his son-in-law, fellow Catholic, and long-time mayor of Middleburg, Col. Lorman Chancellor, in 1859.[10] But Chancellor owned the lovely old stone house on the southeast corner of Jay Street, so The Log Cabin property became a tenant farm and began a slow but steady three-decade decline. Charles Lee, an attorney in Leesburg, and his wife, Margaret Scott Peyton, acquired it, and they too used it as a tenant farm, but sold it to Bolling Haxall, Sr., in 1878. Finally, the original Peyton plantation came full circle bringing the whole estate back into one entity called Exning!

The Haxalls not only enhanced the manor house, but turned all the lands of Exning into a profitable dairy farm along with corn, wheat, chickens, pigs, and

Above bottom: By 1965, when Anne Haxall Dudley sold the property to Bard Sullenger, The Log Cabin had seen better days.

Above and opposite: The bay window and porch, which the Chapmans added to the house, overlook a gentle pond, rolling hills, and acres of open country.

cattle. Thus The Log Cabin became home to generations of farm managers who worked for the Haxalls and Dudleys. But after Thomas Dudley died in 1949, it became impossible for Anne Dudley to maintain all its buildings. For fifteen years she tried to hold the place together, but, like so many prominent Southern

families, the Dudleys were land rich but financially poor.

So in 1965, Anne sold The Log Cabin, which by then was a disaster, along with seven acres, to J. Bard Sullenger, a member of the Virginia Preservation Society. Sullenger began its restoration by paneling the great living room with barn wood from Old Welbourne,[11] but unfortunately, he was transferred to Kentucky just a year later.

So it fell to Scottie and Henry Otis Chapman to complete the restoration of The Old Log Cabin.

(Scottie's name is really Judith, but while at Vassar she acquired the nickname because of her red hair, which was certainly appropriate since her ancestors were indeed Scots).

The only cooking facilities at The Log Cabin when the Chapmans arrived were the ancient fireplace in the basement and a tiny kitchenette wedged into a corner of the living room, so a kitchen addition became their first priority. They found an old log cabin in West Virginia, had it hauled to the site, attached it to the existing house, and transformed it into a

charming dining room and modern country kitchen. A bay window, filled with flowers and plants, and a spacious porch now overlook beautiful gardens and rolling hills with a backdrop of the Bull Run Mountains.

"We were so welcomed when we arrived from Long Island in the 1960s. Middleburg was still a small town then," say the Chapmans. "Elizabeth Furness, the Oliver Iselins, the Clarks, and particularly Thea Randolph, just opened their arms to us. They were the 'Old Guard' but they really welcomed young people." One suspects that such a welcome was due to the charm of Scottie Chapman.

As The Old Log Cabin emerged into a large and gracious home filled with fine antiques and oil paintings garnered from their families, friends from all the Chapman's varied interests—Middleburg Players, golfing buddies, and of course, the tennis club crowd— soon found their way to its door.

Henry Chapman traveled the country on business, while Scottie became "Mom" to a whole generation of neighborhood youngsters and friends of the three Chapman children, Henry, Mary Stewart, and Catherine. All found laughter and a warm welcome in her kitchen, and many of those "kids" still visit her years later.

The polished pine floors and plaster walls of The Old Log Cabin have heard the voices of Revolution and Civil War. They've known the sighs of slaves and indentured children cooking millions of meals over a hot fire. They've watched exhausted tenant farmers cross its lintel at sundown and seen scarlet-coated members of the Hunt race across its fields. Now approaching its third century, its reincarnation has resulted in one of the most charming residences in Loudoun County.

A fascinating postcript to the story of Exning appeared in London newspapers in February 1907, captioned:

Peyton Heirs are Sought

Solicitors are seeking the descendants of Rodger Lacey Peyton of Birmingham, England, who emigrated to the United States…and are heirs to the vast Peyton estates in the northern part of England which are worth over £2,000,000.

Wouldn't it be interesting to know if the Peytons of Exning were among the lucky heirs of Rodger Lacey Peyton?

Opposite and below: The great room is the jewel of The Log Cabin. It offers two marvelous conversation areas where old fireplace mantles provide a wonderful background for the Chapman's paintings. The ceiling is supported by huge poplar beams dating from the 1750s, and the walls are partially paneled with wood from the barn at Old Welbourne. Fortunately, the north end still exhibits its early log and mortar construcion.

Although part of the farmhouse at Groveton dates from the eighteenth century, the main section was built by Francis Carter in the 1840s.

GROVETON FARM

*I*t was one of those incredible, late, Indian summer mornings when mist envelops fields as far as the eye can see and sunlight occasionally breaks through red, gold, and orange foliage in bursts of brilliant color. One of those cool, crisp days when one feels that God's in his heaven and all's well with the world. A perfect day, in fact, to watch the hundred or so members of the Middleburg Hunt gather at Groveton, as horses prance in front of a two-century-old barn and hounds impatiently howl to be off to the fray.

Across the narrow lane, called Lime Kiln Road (a lime kiln really did exist here a century ago), Jan Evans, the charming owner of Groveton, stands watching on the porch of the old farmhouse. As the horn blares the traditional call to ride, her eclectic assortment of guests, including ambassadors, diplomats, a prominent vocalist, a well-known psychic, and little grandchildren peering through cornstalks and pumpkins, gather round to wave off the foxhunters.

Inside the old house, parts of which date to 1790, on land granted to Robert "Councilor" Carter by Thomas, Lord Fairfax, a delicious country breakfast awaits in rooms inhabited by the Carters for one hundred and fifty years. Jonathan Carter, its original owner, and his wife, Elizabeth Rust, actually lived next door in what Jonathan grandly called his "mansion"—though even by standards of the time it was quite modest and, after being remodeled, has in recent years been used as a guesthouse by a handsome bachelor, Jan Hendrik van Leeuwen.

It was Jonathan's son Francis Carter and his wife, Margaret Pritchard, who incorporated Jonathan's outside kitchen and servant house into a large new addition in the then-popular Italianate style, which is the Groveton farmhouse of today. Upon his election to the Loudoun County Board of Supervisors, and then to the Board of Justices, Francis Carter's home became known as Carter Hall.[1]

It was on a fine October day in 1862 that Gen. J.E.B. Stuart (who said "If you think you can win, the battle is half-won" and "If in doubt, attack") led his Rebels over the Blue Ridge to stop General McClellan's Union forces from heading toward Richmond. They met at Mountville where a squadron of 1st

Hounds and masters of the Middleburg Hunt meet on the lawn at Groveton.

56

The groaning board in the dining room assures a hearty Hunt Country breakfast.

Above: Ben and Jan Evans with their daughters, Louise and Karla, and four-legged friends at Groveton in the 1970s.

Right, top and bottom: A portrait of the beautiful French author George Sand hangs in the living room at Groveton, while the blue crystal globe on the newel post once decorated the home of Guy de Maupassant.

Rhode Island cavalry, under the command of Capt. Lorenzo Gove, were resting along Lime Kiln Pike as their horses grazed on the meadows of Groveton. Now Mountville Road, at the time, it was little more than a cart track.

As the shrill, dreaded "Rebel Yell" suddenly pierced the morning air, Captain Gove tried to rally his men, but with the element of surprise, the Rebels had the upper hand and the Yankees could not make a stand. They scattered; Gove was shot and, at the direction of General Stuart, taken to nearby Creek Hill and tended by Dr. James Mount. He died soon after and was buried in the family cemetery at Creek Hill.[2]

Groveton was home to descendants of Jonathan Carter until 1932. Maybe it was tragedy that made the family sell the old place. Bob Humphrey, then a boy of about ten years who lived at Creek Hill, tells the story. "Mosby Carter rode out into the woods at Groveton and hung himself on a tree. Caused a lot of commotion and all us kids wanted to go see what

Left and above: This sideboard once owned by Pres. James Monroe bears his image on its shining brass handles.

was goin' on, but our moms wouldn't let us."

Almost forty years later, in 1970, Groveton Farm was purchased by Jan and Ben Evans of Washington, D.C., as a weekend retreat.[3] Ben Evans, an Indiana native and West Point graduate (as were six members of Jan Evans' family, including her father,[4] stepfather, two uncles, brother, and nephew). Ben's twenty-four-year career at the Central Intelligence Agency, under seven different directors and six presidents, included the role of executive secretary. Fortunately, he enjoyed many years in the Loudoun countryside before his untimely demise in 1987.

It was Jan King Evans, granddaughter of two fascinating families, who discovered Groveton and led the family to Loudoun. And what a heritage she holds. Her paternal grandmother, Lady Willmott Lewis, was known during the early 1900s as "the most beautiful

woman in Washington," a characteristic that obviously transcends generations, for Jan Evans is also a very beautiful woman.

Her maternal grandfather, Christian Heurich, came to the United States from Germany, established a successful brewery in the District, and built an impressive red stone, turreted castle on New Hampshire Avenue, which his descendants donated to the Historical Society of Washington a century later. Jan Evans grew up in that castle and developed a strong sense of historic preservation.

Groveton thus remains the simple country farmhouse beloved by the Carters in the 1800s. Its pine-floored center hall and spacious downstairs rooms boast no gilt or ornate furniture, though there are some surprises. A sideboard that once belonged to Pres. James Monroe mingles with pieces handmade

The original stone mansion house of Jonathan Carter dates back to 1790.

by Ben Evans' father in Indiana, while fine old landscapes and portraits in dusky gold frames cover the walls. Most fascinating is an original painting of a beautiful young woman who became a famed French author under the nom de plume George Sand.[5] Another interesting item is a blue crystal globe decorating the hallway newel post, which, though it seems somewhat incongruous in a country farmhouse, once belonged to another Gallic writer named Guy de Maupassant.

The country ambiance is enhanced by Jeffersonian windows with wavy hand-blown panes where a herd of Black Angus cattle can be seen grazing, while a

swimming pool, herb gardens, fragrant boxwood, and gnarly old trees stand tall along the country byway.

But the real treasures of Groveton lie in its outbuildings. There's the great stone barn built by the Carters in the 1700s, which was completely restored by the Evans, for which they received the Preservation Award of Loudoun County in 1986. Then there

Above top: This massive stone barn of the 1790s was restored by the Evans in the 1980s.

Above bottom: The early 1800s schoolhouse is believed to be the first in Loudoun County.

Today it's a delightful guest house, but originally, this building served as slave quarters.

are the slave quarters and the schoolhouse dating to the early 1800s, said to be the oldest in the area, once used by generations of Carters, Mounts, and other local youngsters. It too is now a delightful guest cottage.

Across the lane lie the original blacksmith shop, corn crib, and scale house where cattle headed for market were once weighed. All told, Groveton boasts thirteen historic old buildings, which make it one of the best preserved plantations in all of Loudoun County.

The concept of "noblesse oblige," once so prevalent among those born to wealth, is perhaps more rare today. But it is exemplified by Jan Evans who is not only the most gracious of ladies but gives unstintingly of her talents to charitable and cultural organizations all around the Washington area. Her affiliations run the gamut from the Historical Society and the Republican Party (the Evans and Bushes are old friends from CIA days) to the Washington Opera, the Red Cross, Cathedral School, YWCA, and the Abigail Adams Bank. One of her favorites is "The Oldest Inhabitants," where Jan was the first woman member in an "old boys'" club, accepted she says, "only because her grandfather was a founder and the ranks of their membership were dwindling." To those who know

her charm and abilities, that is a masterpiece of understatement.

As if all that social activism is not enough, Mrs. Evans also serves on the boards of Middleburg's Hill School (attended by her five grandchildren) and Oatlands Plantation.

So after all the Washington grand balls and political events, Groveton is a refuge where Jan Evans comes for fresh country air, the simplicity of an old farmhouse, and stars that can still be seen in a night sky. And with just a touch of nostalgia, she admits that Groveton reminds her of Belleview, her grandfather's farm in Maryland, which she so loved as a child.[6]

Over the years, Jan and Ben Evans acquired three more properties adjoining Groveton: Creek Hill, Gritton Mills, and Fairview, for a total of 1,150 acres around the historic little hamlet of Mountville. All three are now owned by the Evans' daughters, Karla MacMahon and Louise Turner.[7] So join me now as we walk along a winding country road to Creek Hill and Fairview.

Jan Evans on holiday in Nantucket with her family. On the left, Clifford and Louise Turner pose with their children Adela Griswold, Austin, and Benjamin. On the right sit Edward and Karla McMahon with Edward III and Alexandra.

The beautiful eastate of Creek Hill as it stands today.

CREEK HILL

*H*e was, as the saying goes, a character. His name was Ezekial Mount. Just a boy when he served in the Revolution, several years later, in 1796, he left Pennsylvania for Loudoun County, Virginia.

That same year, three major events occured in Ezekial's life: he married Sarah Prichard, sister of Margaret Prichard Carter of Groveton;[1] he acquired 370 acres of prime farmland, which was part of Francis Carter's estate; and he and Sarah had their first child, Stephen. Ezekial was obviously a man who moved quickly.

Five more children followed in quick succession,[2] but Ezekial spent his time wisely during those years. He built a home on the hillside for his family, along with a barn, stable, and blacksmith shop. The blacksmith shop, however, lay alongside a proposed new road called Snickersville Pike, and Ezekial didn't particularly like the idea of a new road. In fact, he didn't like it at all because wagons, riders, and herds of sheep and cattle being herded to market might disturb his horses.

Now in the early 1800s, orchards provided not only apples, but sweet cider and brandy, and were thus a mainstay of the local economy. So Ezekial consulted an attorney about his rights and discovered that no road could be put through an orchard, which at the time was described as just one or more apple trees.

So on an October morn, Ezekial had his slaves dig up an apple tree, plant it in the middle of the proposed road, pick its fruit, and cart it into Middleburg for sale! And thus Snickersville Pike was turned at a forty-five degree angle as it remains to this day. Meanwhile, Ezekial and Sarah's home had also been growing. The original keeping room and upstairs sleeping area kept pace both with their family and their prominence and soon included a fine living and dining room as well as additional bedrooms.

Now, an unprecedented religious fervor swept through America during the early 1800s. In Virginia, both the Anglican and Quaker faiths had been in a steady decline, and to people yearning for confidence in a new nation and a distant God, Baptist and Methodist beliefs spread like wildfire. Ezekial Mount

Above: This side view of the house shows the original stone structure built by Ezekial Mount in 1790.

Opposite: One of the numerous outbuildings that have survived two centuries.

became a Methodist and on a cold February day in 1808, welcomed famed Bishop Francis Asbury to his home. Asbury, who preached a million sermons and spread the gospel across an expanding west, wrote in his journal, "I preached to a full house today at Ezekial Mount's."[3]

That "full house" included Francis Carter and his family from Groveton. Francis's son John Carter later donated an acre of land as well as money and slave

labor to erect a Methodist chapel at the base of Creek Hill in memory of Francis Asbury. That fine old building still stands, though it has been well over a half century since its walls have heard a fiery sermon.[4]

Ezekial Mount died in 1834 leaving a sizeable estate to each of his six children. By then, the hamlet boasted several homes, a general store, a flour mill, two blacksmiths, a boot factory, and seventy-one residents, including slaves. Little could he imagine that the area would survive into the twenty-first century as Mountville, in his memory.

For over a century, Creek Hill remained in the hands of Ezekial's descendants, who followed not only his tradition of farming, but branched out into milling and merchandising. "Squire" Stephen Mount owned it until his demise in 1860. Then it was passed on to Dr. John Mount,[5] a beloved physician in Middleburg who tended to Union Col. Lorenzo Gove and buried him in the family graveyard.[6] Dr. Mount was photographed on the lawn of Creek Hill in 1897, just before his death, with his sons, James and John.

The year 1920 brought a new family to Creek Hill. Like the Mounts, their ancestors also came from Pennsylvania, arriving in Loudoun in 1764. They were John Humphrey and his sons, John, Thomas, and Abner, who served as an ensign in the Revolution from Loudoun County.[7] It was their descendant, Robert Lodge Humphrey, a noted race horse trainer, who became owner of Creek Hill in 1920.

The old house had seen many changes during that time. The separate kitchen had been joined to the main house and double-tiered verandas overlooked the rolling countryside. It was an idyllic scene where cattle roamed, horses grazed, and corn, oats, and wheat grew gold under summer sun.

That was until 1930: a bad year in Loudoun County. Not only had the stock market crashed, but a disastrous drought brought Loudoun farmers to their knees. Robert Lodge Humphrey lived at Creek Hill and tells the story of those times:

Our main water supply dried up but we had a spring-fed well from which we drew and hauled one bucket of water at a time. We had to haul it not only to flush the toilet [they were lucky and had indoor plumbing!] but for laundry and cooking and most important, to feed the cattle and horses. We couldn't keep the crops going however…they just dried up.

Everyone had to work in those days. At ten years old, I got a job as the janitor of the new Mountville school. I was up every morning at five o'clock to fire up the stove with coal or wood and clean the school rooms before everyone else arrived. Then once a month I had to oil the floors and for all that I earned two dollars a month.

A horse show was held in Mountville in 1930 to raise funds for that school and in one of those won-

Dr. Mount, Miss Jane Devaney, and sons John and James Mount at the old house in 1897. Courtesy of Robert Humphrey.

Above: A snow scene during the 1930s. Courtesy of Robert Humphrey.

Above: The Humphrey chidren—Jean, Robert, and Rufus— at Creek Hill. Courtesy of Robert Humphrey.

Left: Bob Humphrey when he was old enough to wear knickers and clean the school daily for two dollars a month. Courtesy of Robert Humphrey.

The grounds brilliant with spring color.

derful twists of fate, the old schoolhouse where he spent so many childhood hours has been the home of Bob Humphrey and his bride, Mary Warren, for over fifty years. After Bob returned from World War II, he bought it and enlarged it as a home for Mary and their children, Robin and Mary Elizabeth.

Interestingly, though Bob grew up as a Methodist and Mary as a Baptist, they were married at Emman-uel Episcopal Church in Middleburg, which Bob had embraced in his "courtin' days." And more than fifty years later, that's where you'll find them every Sunday morning.

In 1957, Creek Hill was sold to Lou and Jean Gibbs, who again enlarged the home with a long porch, stables, a guest house, and a lovely pool and garden. They also paneled the library with wood from the old toll booth, which once stood at the end of the drive, creating a warm intimate ambiance. In 1984, Ben and Jan Evans acquired Creek Hill and its 210 acres from the Gibbs' estate.

The Evans' daughter Karla and son-in-law Edward MacMahon, a prominent attorney, now call Creek Hill home. It's a magnificent property with old outbuildings: a spring house, meat house, corn crib, and pump house, as well as a marvelous old barn, all date back to the 1790s.

Wide dining room windows overlook the garden, while a small family room, part of the original house, bears a low door and antique lock. The living room of later vintage is beautifully decorated, and a great entertaining kitchen and screened porch complete the lower floor. Looking out over the rolling countryside, Creek Hill seems a quiet, restful place.

Suddenly, the peace is shattered as a brightly cocked rooster screeches across the garden on an early spring afternoon trying to escape the clutches of the MacMahon's younger children, Edward and Alexandra.[8]

Then a new puppy joyously squeals and leaps in and out of their arms as the quiet of a spring afternoon dissolves. Though Creek Hill is far grander than it was in Ezekial Mount's time, and the lifestyle of its owners far more sophisticated, it's not hard to imagine Ezekial's six children playing in the garden with roosters and puppies just as the MacMahon youngsters do today.

From the garden, a path leads down a gentle slope, past a sparkling pool and row of trees, to a bower where lie, almost hidden away by underbrush, two old gravestones. The names engraved upon them are those of Sarah and Ezekial Mount. Above them, tender green buds appear on the branches of an old apple tree. And somehow, in Mountville, where the road turns at a forty-five degree angle to protect a one-tree apple orchard, that seems an appropriate tribute to a man whose name and home have survived for two centuries.

Sheltered by an ancient apple tree at Creek Hill lie the graves of Ezekial Mount and his wife, Sarah.

Fairview in springtime.

FAIRVIEW
"A Dear Little House"

From all over Europe they came to this new world called America. Some came willingly and others on prison ships. English gentlemen, Scots Dissenters, French Huguenots, indentured children, Dutch adventurers, and Germans seeking religious freedom or economic opportunity.

Five members of the Fuhr or Foer family (which became Furr in America) were among them. Fuhr, in German, meant a carter or hauler, while Foer meant forest and, interestingly, Forrest occurs as a baptismal name in future generations.

The first Furrs to appear in Loudoun County around 1765 were Edwin, Abraham, Moses, Enoch, and Jeremiah. They were farmers, millers, and merchants who settled in Leesburg, Bloomfield, Aldie, Unison, and Middleburg. The hard work ethic so common to German settlers often led them to prosperity and intermarriages with landed families like the Berkeleys, Littletons, Leiths, and Fraziers.

But it is Moses Furr who intrigues us, and we hear his story through the voice of his grandson, Carl.[1]

My grandfather crossed the Delaware with Washington. His name was Moses Buckner Furr. He fought in two wars: the Revolution and the War of 1812. He got grants of land. After he came back to Leesburg and was made a magistrate, he married a Miss [Margaret] Tracy from Fauquier County. His father was Moses Furr, who came from England.[2]

By 1860, the slumbering shadow of Civil War, which would wreak such havoc throughout the South, hung darkly over Loudoun County and over the Furr family.

Some Furrs supported the Confederacy and sent six of their sons to join its ranks. Others, joined by kinship but divided by allegiance or commerce, signed an oath demanded by the Union of any Southerners who wished to continue farming or trading without constant harassment. That oath read as follows: "I solemnly swear that I will support the Constitution of the United States and its laws as the supreme law of the land…"[3]

Kemp Furr. Courtesy of Mrs. Joan Furr of Arlington, Virginia.

Moses Furr, the farmer of Bluemont, was a Southern supporter, and his son, Kemp Furr, served the Confederacy at both First and Second Manassas. "At the first battle, these people came with carriages and lunches, likker and good horses, and after they was offering any kind of money to get away from there. Was far from a picnic," said Kemp.

Captured by Union troops at Furr's Mill at Millville (which Federal troops burned to the ground along with all its wheat and corn), Kemp ended up in a Pennsylvania prison along with his cousin, Clinton Furr, and good friend, Howard Leith. It took them six weeks—walkin' awhile and workin' awhile—to get home at war's end.

"My father [Kemp] was a right smart man," said Carl. "He was supposed to be one of the strongest men in the whole country. He was also a quick man with his fists and in Bluemont managed to 'take out' all three of the Payne brothers who loved nothin' more than a fight." Bluemont, according to Kemp,

"was one of the roughest places around." Must have been much like Snickersville in those days according to this account:

> *Snickersville on Saturday Nights*
> *was loud with gunshots*
> *and liquor and lights*
> *and flashing knife blades*
> *and sudden fights*[4]

But Kemp "never smoked, never drinked, and when he died, the Carters told me if there was everybody like him they'd have to tear down the courthouse." He was also a very prolific man. His three wives—Mary Ann Chappell, Amanda Gochnauer, and Margaret Miley—are said to have borne him twenty-three children.[5] Three of his sons were named Kemp, but only the youngest survived.

Kemp was also a "right smart man" about land. He owned a lot of it, including what is referred to in the family as Grandfather's Mountain, now known as Mount Weather, or to locals as the underground White House.

The family lived, however, at a place bearing the marvelous name "Stony Lonesome," near Pot House, but when that burned, they moved to a two-hundred-acre farm in Mountville where they remained for some seventy years. It was a simple farmhouse, built of wood, where women boiled soap out of lye and grease over open kettles in the yard, killed and plucked chickens roamin' around their feet for dinner, and made fresh hot corn cakes every day for breakfast. Carl remembered when Jack Hibbs "used to butcher meat in a grass field nearby, cut it up and hauled it the next day. Sold for ten or twenty cents a pound in 1913."

All the Furrs were horse people, and Carl was one of the best. He left Loudoun as a young man to work for the DuPonts as their horse trainer in New Jersey (at the incredible salary in the 1930s of ten thousand dollars per year). It must have been quite an experience for a country boy to live at Belleview (William Dupont's estate) where he "had five women and one man to wait on me." He later moved to Fair Hill, the DuPont estate in Maryland.

Kemp owned a lot of farms around the Piedmont and left his wife, Margaret Mylie, well provided for. After her demise, the property was divided among the surviving children, and Carl apparently received the old family farmhouse, as well as the big stone house and Fairview.

Like most country folk, Carl was no easy mark. When the road through Mountville was about to be paved and Miss Charlotte Noland opposed it because she wanted her Foxcroft students to ride on dirt roads, he said, "Miss Charlotte, no pavin'… no huntin'!" And so the road was paved. Carl's brother Walter lived with him at the old homestead, but after a while, Carl leased the family farm and moved down the road to Fairview where he was joined by their two widowed sisters, Etta and Violet.

If Carl had a passion in life (neither he nor Walter ever married) it was horses. Never missed a race, a meet, or a hunt until his death in 1981,[6] and as for many horsemen, home was simply a place for Carl to hang his hat. So, although he had a live-in, all-around handyman and chauffeur, Carl's properties were old, dark, and needed a bit of work.[7]

That changed in 1981 after the acquisition of his two hundred acres by Ben and Jan Evans. All three Groveton Farm properties were beautifully restored by their son-in-law Clifford "Okey" Turner. At Fairview,

Left and above: Carl Furr competing in Pennsylvania, circa 1940, and in his later years. Courtesy of Jeanne DuPont of Austin, Pennsylvania, and Betty Furr of Middleburg.

Above: A trio of red buildings at the end of the lane at Fairview.

Opposite, top and bottom: Two tastefully decorated drawing rooms flank a wide center hall.

white pillars march proudly across the original two-room stone cottage, while additions, including bedrooms and a sunny new kitchen, have tripled its size.

A shiny black tin roof accentuates its brilliant white exterior, while red barns and outbuildings play counterpoint, starkly silhouetted against an azure sky. A tiny log cabin, now a playhouse, brims over with flowers. The fragrance of fresh daffodils greets a visitor at the open door and wide foyer leading to the original parts of the old house, where polished floors and shining mantles are enhanced by paintings, prints, and floral chintzes glowing with color.

All old homes have a "feel" to them, transcending bricks or stone and mortar, reflecting perhaps the people who live there. At Fairview the feeling is one of gentleness. A little hand reaches up to say, "Would you like to see my room?" Hand in hand, up the stairs

Above and right: A narrow staircase leads to the children's dormered hideaway.

we go to the dormered retreat of the three little daughters of Anthony and Jennifer Siriani, close friends of the Evans' and current residents of Fair-view. Alive with color, with little beds overflowing with stuffed animals of every description, the dormered attic has become a children's paradise.

Later, two dogs follow the little girls out the door, leaping among pots of flowers on the verandah with the gaiety of puppies, yet never letting the children out of their sight. Even the graveled road leading past a white rail fence and open fields, seems serene. As Mrs. Evans says, Fairview is indeed "a dear little house."

Above: Mercer House on a soft summer morning. Its charming Victorian-era verandah encircles the front and south side of the old house.

Opposite: Charles Fenton Mercer, circa 1830.

MERCER HOUSE

*H*e was a handsome young bachelor and Princeton graduate who, after securing his law degree and traveling around London and Paris, decided to settle on his inherited property, known as Mercer's Quarter, which had been granted to his grandfather John Mercer in 1731.[1] That was in 1804, and the gentleman's name was Charles Fenton Mercer.

After arranging for a small, two-story clapboard home to be built on a hillside overlooking old Belhaven Road (which by now was called the Ashby Gap Road), he began his practice of law in Leesburg. A brilliant barrister, he was so successful that by 1807, he was able to contract with William Moore for a large dual-powered mill along Hungar Run on the site of John Mercer's small corn mill, which dated back to 1748.

He also ordered a dwelling house for the miller,[2] several outbuildings, and a fine home on the hillside for himself. That home, and the mill, became the nucleus of a village that Mercer called Aldie in honor of the family's ancestral home in Scotland. Created of bricks handmade by his slaves on the site, his new home was joined with the earlier clapboard building and boasted six rooms, five fireplaces, a wide center hall with fine fanlights over the front and rear doors, and a sheltered portico across the entire front elevation.

A brick wall, seven feet high, marked off the estate along the main road with entrances to the property flanked by arched gateways and porters' lodges. A fine greenhouse, servants' quarters, stable, carriage house, dairy, meat house, laundry, fishpond, and shelters for cattle completed the many outbuildings. Surrounding the home were "gardens and pleasure grounds." It was a grand estate, fit for the family of a successful man.

Yet Charles Mercer never married. Noted for his moodiness, it was said that "he was only happy when he was in Paris as a young man,"[3] and some believe that he shared "a love whose name could not be spoken," in the religiously oriented period of the early 1800s. Yet he was beloved by his friends, many of whom named their children in his honor. He was also, as befitted the well-educated Virginia gentleman, an active participant in the events of his time.

In addition to his law practice, he served for seven years (beginning in 1810) as a delegate to the General Assembly in Richmond. At the same time, during the War of 1812, he became a military aide to the governor, rising to the rank of brigadier general. And in 1817, he was elected to the United States Congress as representative of Loudoun County—a post he held for twenty-two years! Oh yes, in 1829, he also served as a member of the Virginia Convention. Mercer was a man who thought seriously and cared deeply about the challenges that confronted his generation. And there were many.

An advocate of suffrage for all white men, not just landowners, he was also a proponent of a public school system in Virginia, a radical concept at a time when education was limited to the children of wealthy landowners. (This bill was eventually passed years after Mercer left the Virginia Legislature).

Mercer's most controversial crusade, however, was the movement to return—and colonize—freed blacks in Africa. Recognizing, as did many enlightened men of the time, that slavery was inherently wrong, and believing that it would be impossible for the two races to live together in harmony,[4] Mercer strongly supported the "Back to Africa Movement."[5] The Loudoun County chapter of this endeavor was started in 1817 by Ludwell Lee of Belmont and Rev. John Mines, pastor of the Leesburg Presbyterian Church.[6]

This massive effort had a strong religious component and resulted in the return of thousands of freed blacks and the founding in 1847 of Liberia, the first democracy in Africa. Its capital was called Monrovia in honor of Pres. James Monroe who also strongly supported this endeavor.[7]

But Mercer had other problems as well. By 1835, perhaps because of his demanding political roles, which allowed little time for his law practice, he found himself in a financially precarious position. So he sold the mill and all its buildings to Capt. John Moore.[8] Then five years after the financial and economic panic of 1837, which destroyed land values and stock prices all over America, this aristocratic Virginian left Aldie to take a job as a cashier for a bank in

Opposite: The entrance foyer at Mercer House is typical of the Georgian and Federal center-hall homes popular in the early nineteenth century. The gorgeous oak floors are original, though the fan-light doorway once led outside, allowing cool breezes to flow through the lower rooms.

Florida. His beautiful estate and 1,300 acres of land was leased to William K. Ish, Esq., and advertised for sale "on terms accommodating to the purchaser."[9]

The buyer, in 1843, was Augustus DiZerega[10] and his wife, Eliza Utendelle, who remained at Mercer House for only a few years before returning to Manhattan. But their son Alfred and his wife, Alice Almeda Gasquet, put down roots in Aldie, as did their sons and grandsons who purchased nearby plantations. Augustus bought Sleepy Hollow and Gasquet purchased Hillcrest (now Briar Patch).[11]

Civil War soon erupted and Aldie was alternately occupied and ravaged by troops from both North and South. The story is told that Union officers rode up to the entrance of Mercer House one day and upon being rebuffed by the DiZeregas, rode their horses right through the front door, across the polished floors, and out the back.

The village became a battlefield in June of 1863 when the woods around Little River provided cover for Rebels, and Mercer's mill offered haven to Yan-

kees, who, when pursued by Mosby's Rangers, jumped into its vats for cover. Again, in '64, Union General Grant ordered savage raids in and around Aldie to destroy the hiding places of Mosby's Rangers.

Alfred DiZerega's two daughters, Fannie and Emily[12], lived on at Mercer House all their lives, though they were either so independent (or incompatible) that Fannie lived in the main house while Emily moved into the old greenhouse and servants' quarter. After Fannie's death in 1935, the property was auctioned off for back taxes on the steps of the Leesburg Courthouse where the buyer was Emily Irvine DiZerega.[13] Thus Mercer House remained in the same family for well over a century—from 1843 to 1960.

It was then purchased by Bullis Schools, a highly regarded Maryland private school for boys. Bullis poured a fortune into renovating the property, yet never opened its doors to Virginia students. Aside from occasional tenants, Mercer House stood empty for almost seventeen years. Sumac, creeping vines, broken tree limbs, and weeds took over the grounds while time and tenants wreaked havoc on the house.

One of those tenants in the 1960s was a family named Pearson and what a tragedy that turned out to be. It seems that their young daughter Lydia was standing in front of the fireplace in her bedroom one evening when suddenly her gown caught fire. Trapped by windows that wouldn't open, she suffered burns over her entire body and died that terrible night.

But Lydia's spirit lingered on at Mercer House. Its next owner, Jim Burton, is a graduate of the first class of the Air Force Academy, and an Air Force colonel who served his country in war and peace for twenty-seven years. He's also a down-to-earth, no-nonsense type of guy who doesn't believe in ghosts.

Yet when the Burtons bought the property in 1986 and screens fell off all the windows after being securely fastened; a painting of a young girl over Lydia's former bedroom fireplace flew across the room; all the clocks in the house, both mechanical and electric, inexplicably stopped at the exact hour of Lydia's death; and guests reported eerie occurrences, Jim finally called the previous owners.

"Oh, didn't you know there was a ghost at Mercer House?" they responded. But after her room was repainted, the ugly, old green carpeting removed, and a new painting placed over the mantle, Lydia's spirit seems to have quieted down. As Lina Burton says, "The least we can do is keep her happy."

Jim Burton is no stranger to controversy, however. His 1993 book *The Pentagon Wars* tells the inside story of the infighting and sometimes tragic consequences of high-level, but poorly conceived, military decisions. Since 1986, he has served as the representative from Mercer District on the Loudoun County Board of Supervisors, at a time when conflict over zoning and rapid growth with all its attendant problems, consumes both the supervisors and residents of Loudoun County.

His days (and nights) are filled with phone calls from constituents, Board of Supervisors meetings, appearances at local political events, responses to letters and the media, reviews of reports from Richmond, plus discussions with local legislators. If he's lucky, he gets a rare Sunday off to spend with his children and grandchildren.

The role of citizen-legislator, as both Charles Fenton Mercer and Jim Burton would attest, is never easy. The challenges and time commitments are enormous. Jim Burton has a secret weapon, however, in

Above top: Lina Burton relaxes alongside one of the Jeffersonian windows that flank the front elevation.

Above bottom and opposite: Now a comfortable family room, this was the first cottage of Charles Fenton Mercer, built in 1809. Mercer enlarged the house by adding this living room (opposite), which still includes the massive mirror left by the diZeregas.

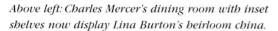
Above left: Charles Mercer's dining room with inset shelves now display Lina Burton's heirloom china.

Above right: This is the bedroom where young Lydia Pearson died. After its green carpet was removed, the walls repainted, and the painting over the fireplace replaced, her ghost no longer haunted the halls of Mercer House.

his charming wife, Lina, a soft-spoken native of Hills-boro, who worked for many years as a legal secretary in Washington.

Her books on office procedures are used in many college courses and she now works for publishers as an indexer, writer, and garden book troubleshooter. Her greatest attribute, though, lies in her love for Jim Burton. An ever-gracious hostess and supporter of all his endeavors, she creates a life at Mercer House that is both welcoming to guests and a peaceful refuge for their family.

Mercer House, now beginning its third century, still stands proudly on the hillside overlooking Aldie. The old mill has been restored as an historic site and the bridge over Little River carries hundreds of cars every day, rather than the few wagons of earlier times. But time has not changed the country village created by Charles Mercer, for it still boasts only a

few homes, little country churches, a few antique shops, a delightful "Little River Inn," and a general store.

Although only eleven of its original 1,300 acres now remain around the sixteen-room mansion, Jim Burton says, "We treasure this historic home and would never desecrate this property by subdividing it." In fact, the Burtons have applied to put the property into the Virginia Outdoors Foundation so that it will remain just as it is forever.

One hopes that would please its nineteenth-century owner: supporter of public education, proponent of an African Republic for freed slaves, lawyer, Virginia legislator, and United States congressman, Charles Fenton Mercer.

Above: Col. Jim and Lina Burton at the dedication of Middleburg's Jacqueline Kennedy Onassis Pavilion in October 1995.

The Miller's House.

THE MILLER'S HOUSE

There's a narrow stone bridge crossing Little River in the village of Aldie where the eye is drawn to the mill along the roadside. Masses of greenery and ancient trees hide, however, the treasure that lies beyond. 'Tis the Miller's House…though a mystery surrounds its date of birth. (Didn't know homes were born, did you?)

Well, it appears that one Simon Kenton, overseer for the old Ashby Gap Road, lived on this land in 1751.[1] Then around 1764, John Mercer, a Scotsman of Fredericksburg, officer of the Ohio Company, wealthy land investor, and said to be the most brilliant attorney of his time,[2] built a small corn mill along the banks of Hungar Run. Now since Mercer lived in Fredericksburg, he had to have had a miller on the site, so possibly he used the Kenton cottage or he built the original miller's house, which is part of the beautiful home of today.

His land, called Mercer's Quarter, was inherited by his son, James Mercer, a burgess of Stafford County, who turned it into a working farm with twelve slaves, a fodder house, cultivated fields and meadows, and an overseer. It was called Mercer's Quarter Plantation, leading to the conclusion that some building had to be on the premises.

And at this point in 1774, the past comes together in fascinating complexity. Just down river from Mercer's mill, a young man named Leven Powell (later the founder of the town of Middleburg) owned another mill, which Mercer believed lay on his property. So he hired a surveyor to resolve the conflict. That surveyor was none other than George Washington, a logical choice since Washington had surveyed all the surrounding land for Lord Fairfax years earlier. Washington decided in Powell's favor and just a few years later, Col. Leven Powell served with Gen. George Washington during the brutal winter at Valley Forge.

The year 1807 became a turning point in local history, however, when James Mercer's son, Charles Fenton Mercer, appeared on the scene. A Princeton graduate, Charles left Fredericksburg to practice law in Leesburg. But he did far more than practice law. Near or on his grandfather's small endeavor, he built the first dual-powered mill in Northern Virginia. Around it arose a tiny

Right: A bronze plaque designates The Miller's House with the National Register of Historic Places.

Below: This side view of the house shows the original stone cottage of the 1700s. The second story was a later addition.

village called Aldie, named for the Mercer ancestral home in Scotland.

This new mill ground not only wheat and corn, but sawed wood as well, so he also built "a store house, cooper, blacksmith and wheelwright shops, and a land plaster building." It soon became one of the most prosperous in the countryside, mentioned in the accounts of landowners from George Washington to George Carter of Oatlands. But nowhere is any mention of a miller's house being erected. Yet that would have been an absolute necessity, so again we return to the mystery: does the original stone cottage date back to Kenton's cottage of 1751; James Mercer's small enterprise in 1764; or did Charles Fenton Mercer build it there along with his new mill in 1810?[3]

Mercer's attention, however, was soon consumed by his law practice, his involvement in the "Back to Africa Movement" for freed slaves,[4] and his activities as a member of the U.S. Congress where he served for twenty-two years. By 1835, however, Charles Mercer was also deeply in debt.

So he sold his mill to Capt. John Moore, a most interesting man. He had served in both the Battle of New Orleans and the Seminole Campaigns before coming to Aldie. Per the custom of the time, he was paid for his war service, not in silver or gold, but with a land grant near Tallahassee, Florida, which had

Below and above: James Edwards Douglass, a descendent of Capt. John Moore, and his bride, Marion Skinner, were married in 1882. Their four children—Rosanna, Mary Virginia, Katherine, and John Moore Douglass—were all born in The Miller's House.

been "worked by his slaves" for several years. According to one account, he purchased the mill from Charles Mercer by trading that Florida property[5] in return for 541 acres of land around the mill at $26.50 per acre!

John Moore's marriage to Matilda Lacey[6] resulted in six children.[7] To accommodate such a family, plus their millers, laborers, and servants, an enlargement of the small cottage would have been imperative; so it must be assumed that Captain Moore was responsible for the second phase of The Miller's House, and probably the construction of the adjacent servants' cottage as well. He was, after all, not only the owner of the mill, but banker for much of the community, and as such, would have been a man of comparative wealth.

It was the marriage of his daughter Anna Maria to Jonathan Edwards Douglass in 1853[8] that brought the Moore and Douglass families together.

The Douglass' originated with Capt. William Douglass, a Laird of Ayrshire, Scotland, who arrived in Loudoun County in 1750. By 1761 he received a grant of nine hundred acres just outside of Leesburg (in the area now known as Lost Corner) where he erected a large home known as Garralland.

He was a good-natured soul and strong Methodist who kept a good table and hosted great festivities on St. Andrew's Day and again at New Year's, when "There was dancing and playing at cards, a very merry and agreeable company and the best dinner ever seen in America."[9] Perhaps because of his pleasant disposition, Douglass managed to retain his captaincy in the Loudoun militia during the Revolution...even though he shared Tory sentiments.[10]

The years following the marriage of Anna Maria Moore and Jonathan Douglass were turbulent, however, as the tiny hamlet of Aldie was occupied alternately by Confederate and Union troops, boys in blue and gray who fought bravely and died too young. It was said that the only reason the Aldie Mill escaped destruction by the Yankees was because Captain Moore was a Northern sympathizer.

But that turmoil was exacerbated by the death of Anna Maria in 1864, which left four young children aged from one to eight years: John Moore Douglass, Margaret, James Edwards, and Rosanna Lacy. But now another mystery arises. What happened to their father, Jonathan Douglass? Did he join the Confederacy, and, if so, was he the John Douglass of Loudoun County who was killed at the Battle of Wilderness in

Above: John Moore Douglass married Martha Strother and was the last of the Douglass family to live at The Miller's House. It was subsequently occupied by the Moores until the 1940s.

Below: The drawing room of the 1800s is quite elegant with its finely built-in bookcases and detailed mantle.

Left: This outbuilding was probably an early slave quarter for house servants, but was later enlarged into a guest house and now serves as an office for Gerry Keatinge.

Below: The original keeping room of the 1700s highlights a large fireplace in which the aroma of two hundred years of burning fires lends a distinctive and wonderful fragrance. The narrow staircase leads to the sleeping loft.

1864?

In any case, no further record of him remains, and all four of his children were living with Captain Moore in 1870. It must have been quite a household, for there were also two of the Moore's grown sons, Robert and Alexander, plus two millers, two black laborers, a black housekeeper and her three daughters, and another black servant![11]

Despite the sad end to the marriage of Anna Maria Moore and Jonathan Douglass, it resulted in six generations of Moore/Douglass ownership of the Aldie Mill.

James Edwards Douglass became the next owner. He and his bride, Marion Skinner, married in 1882, and their four children were all born at The Old Miller's House.[12] James Douglass was known as both a "real Christian gentleman" and a canny Scotsman who always made sure he got his full "toll" for grinding a neighbor's wheat or corn. He also managed to be "conveniently deaf" if someone were to ask for a loan.[13]

James's only son, John Moore Douglass, studied civil engineering and went off to work with the North-Western railroad around 1910 or so. But his father was getting old and someone had to run the mill. So John returned, joined the mill as a full partner with his father, and married Martha Strother, building her a beautiful big home on Snickersville Pike in 1918. Their three youngsters, John, Jr., James Edwards, and Martha Ann, were all born there. His father retired soon after and sold his share of the mill to his cousin John Douglass Moore, who moved into The Miller's House.

James E. Douglass (always called Ned) was a college graduate and a handsome young Air Force sergeant during World War II. He returned to the Aldie Mill and to a young woman, a teacher at the Aldie

school who would become his bride.

Her name was Sarah Love, whose parents, Morris and Ruth Love, and her brother, Jim, lived on a farm named Loveland in Hamilton, which had been settled by her great-grandfather.[14]

Sarah Love married James "Ned" Douglass in 1947, and they raised their sons, Ned, Jr., and Andrew Love, at the spacious farmhouse on Snickersville Pike where Ned had grown up. But he was to become the last miller of Aldie. After more than a century of family ownership, Aldie Mill ceased operating in 1971. They gave the mill and its ancillary buildings in 1981 to the Virginia Outdoors Foundation, which has completely restored the property and now uses it for tours, art shows, and local events.

Meanwhile, The Miller's House, which had been occupied by generations of Moores and Douglass', was sold by Mrs. John Douglass Moore in 1942, after the death of her husband. The buyers were the Delano sisters, relatives of Pres. Franklin Delano Roose-

Forty descendants of Capt. John Moore held a family reunion at their ancestral home in October 2002. Left to right: Harrison Williams, Tom Lloyd, Priscilla Williams, John Douglass Moore, Karen McCormick, Ann Ameigh, Chloe Staples, Elizabeth Staples, Hayes Forsten, Carter Conley, Elizabeth Forsten, Tyler Young, Richard Young, Pam Conley, Jack Forsten, Page Ochs, Frances Moore Israelson, Mark Barber, Connie de Bordenave, Jane Darling, Brian Smith, Maria de Bordenave, Bill Young, Andrea Williams, Cheryl Williams, Susie Moore, Sharon Williams, Win Williams, John Moore, and Sam Darling.

velt who is said to have visited them there. They began remodeling the old house in the 1940s, and in the 1950s sold it to Pres. Dwight D. Eisenhower's friend and historian, Col. Harold Potter. The Potters often entertained the Eisenhowers there, for both couples were avid bridge players. When the Richard Knops' became owners, they completed its renovation.

So over the years, as The Miller's House jes' kept on a' growin', a transformation occurred blending the tiny stone cottage of 1764 and the brick additions of 1809 with twentieth-century components. By creating a large entrance foyer, formal drawing and dining rooms, plus second-floor bedrooms, the dear old house leads from one unexpected place to another. Rippled windows overlook weathered barns, a meandering stream, ancient twisted trees, a guest cottage, which may once have been slave quarters, and an old spring house.

It's a charmer. But the most delightful spot is its genesis. The original keeping room dominated by a low, hand-sawed, beamed ceiling; narrow corner staircase; comfortable chairs; old cherry tables brimming with books; and a huge fireplace where a delicious pungent aroma, reminiscent of centuries of burning fires, invite good friends and interesting conversation.

It is here that Jerry and Betty Keatinge spend their days when they're not volunteering in local events or tutoring needy students in English and math in Leesburg every week. Their dedication resulted in being honored recently as "Volunteers of the Year" by Loudoun County.

The Piedmont seems to attract talented people and the Keatinges are no exception. Jerry's career as an engineering management consultant with Sperry Rand, took them to Mississippi where they restored a huge, old plantation home, a picture of which now decorates their dining room at Aldie. Then they were posted to Rotterdam in the Netherlands for several years, and finally, in 1980, they came to Washington, D.C.

It took months of searching before the Keatinges found their "home with a history," but it's been a love affair ever since. Their daughter Martha left The Miller's House as a bride, and their grandchildren, now college age, once played in its pool and chased through its woods.

To walk the wooden floors of this old house is to take a trip back in history. Early settlers, generations of millers, congressmen, and presidents have tread its boards, and though it's far different from the two-

Above top: Their hosts for the day were Mr. and Mrs. Gerry Keatinge, current owners of The Miller's House.

Above bottom: Connie and Tad de Bordenave organized the first family reunion.

room cottage of 1764, there is an authenticity here seldom found in old places, which have, with the best of intentions, been turned into mansions and lost their identity in the process.

That authenticity is reflected by the Keatinges, who find good books, good friends, good conversation… and a huge sense of contentment at The Old Miller's House in Aldie.[15]

Mosby Spring Farm. The small section on the left is the original part of the home.

MOSBY SPRING FARM

*M*aryland was torn in 1861. Its southern counties and eastern shore were dependent upon cheap slave labor, so Confederate sympathies ran strong. Lincoln could not allow Washington to be surrounded by Southern sympathizers, however, so he ordered Federal troops into Baltimore.[1] As the 1st Massachusetts regiment poured into that city, passions surged, riots erupted, and the first shots of the Civil War were fired.

An interesting sidelight of this Baltimore rebellion occurred when Frank Key Howard, a pro-Southern editor, was jailed during the riots. Ironically, Howard was the grandson of Francis Scott Key who wrote "The Star Spangled Banner," inspired by the defense of Fort McHenry during the War of 1812, which later became our National Anthem.[2]

But another song of defiance, called "Maryland! My Maryland!" emerged from the riots of 1861. Casting President Lincoln as a despot and sung to the tune of "O Tannenbaum," the lyrics incited revolution:

The despot's heel is on thy shore
His torch is at thy Temple door;
Avenge the patriotic gore
That flecked the streets of Baltimore.[3]

Many young men responded to that siren call and left secretly to join the Confederacy. Two young brothers, Charles Wiltshire and his seventeen-year-old brother James, were among them. Crossing the Potomac in the dark of night, they signed up with the 12th Virginia Infantry and later joined the 43rd Battalion…Mosby's Rangers.

During a skirmish near Charlestown (which became part of West Virginia in 1862), Charles was mortally wounded. But Jim, a blue-eyed, black-haired, fair-complexioned young man, fought on from Point of Rocks and Winchester, through Fairfax, Millwood, and Hamilton.[4] It was the famous "Greenback Raid," however, that would play a dramatic role in his future.

It seems that Col. John Mosby received a tip that a train carrying a huge

Above left: Col. John Singleton Mosby.

Above right: Dr. James Wiltshire served with Mosby's Rangers as a young man and later became a Baltimore physician. Courtesy of George Wiltshire.

Union payroll would be passing through Duffield Station, West Virginia, in October of 1864. Positioning his Rangers for an ambush, he stopped the train, captured the payroll (in priceless Federal dollars), and raced off, never halting until he and his men reached the safety of Old Ebenezer Church in Bluemont. And there, they divvied up the loot.[5]

Meanwhile—always riding by moonlight and striking with such wild fury where they were least expected that the region from the Bull Run to the Blue Ridge Mountains became known as "Mosby's Confederacy"—the Rangers rendezvoused at different places every night. One of those spots was a Revolutionary-era stone cottage just west of Middleburg.

Deserted and surrounded by old trees and brush, which offered cover and forage, and a flowing spring that provided fresh water for their horses, this cottage was an ideal hiding place. And as we shall see, it too would later play a role in the life of Jim Wiltshire.

Jim was just twenty-one years old when the war ended. He hoped to become a doctor, an expensive course of study even in the 1860s, and like most post-Civil War Southerners, he had no money. But remember the Greenback Raid? Well Jim had carried his share of the loot back to his family's summer home in Manapike, West Virginia, and telling only a trusted black servant of its whereabouts, he hid it in the trunk of an old tree.

Returning at war's end, he prayed that his treasure would still be there. It was! Thus the spoils of war enabled a young Confederate Rebel to achieve his dream, for it not only paid his way through a two-year course at Maryland Medical College (now Johns Hopkins), but allowed him to set up his own practice after graduation.

Dr. James Wiltshire went on to become a renowned physician and marry the lovely Frances Hill of Culpeper. Wintering in Baltimore and summering in Virginia, as did so many Maryland families, their son Turner grew up on tales of the Rangers' exploits and visited many of his father's Civil War haunts. One of them was the old stone cottage just west of Middleburg.

Another war erupted as Turner Wiltshire became a young man, and so he served as a major with the American Expeditionary Forces in Europe during World War I. Severely wounded (both his eardrums were blown out), he initially returned to Maryland. But his passion was horses, and what better place to be than Middleburg, which had by now become the heart of the Virginia Hunt Country? And what better home to own than the old stone cottage just west of town where his father once rode with Mosby?

It wasn't much of a place, but it had land. So he expanded the tiny cottage, adding a living room, kitchen, and a staircase to upstairs bedrooms. Amazingly, it is almost impossible to tell where the old part of the house ends and the newer part begins, for

Artist A.J. Volck's rendition of the Baltimore Riots of 1861 when Southern sympathizers attacked the 6th Massachusetts Infantry.

The stables, built by Turner Wiltshire in the 1920s, are considerably larger than the house.

Turner built it by hand, felling trees from the surrounding woods and hauling stones from the fields, just like the original settlers of the 1700s.

Then he turned his attention to the stables, which became a huge twelve-stall affair, considerably larger than the house, with adjacent sleeping quarters for grooms. He bred and trained steeplechase horses and rode with the Middleburg Hunt. But not until twelve years later did he finally decide to marry. His bride, Olive Kahlo, bore him two sons, James and George, both of whom attended Middleburg's Hill School and grew up as expert horsemen.

Middleburg has changed a bit in the intervening years, but it is still a place where family and roots and tradition mean something. So after years in Charlottesville as a vintner, George Wiltshire (who as a

child gave his home the name Mosby Spring) returned to the scenes of his childhood.

The old house with its log ceilings and stone walls now hosts some delightful surprises, for George Wiltshire is a collector of antiques and fine paintings. Like his father and grandfather, George is also a lover of horses, which once again nuzzle at fences hoping for an apple while waiting for the next spring race or autumn hunt.

And on a warm summer's day, his daughter, a lovely young girl named Annia, occasionally rides along a shady lane where almost one hundred and fifty years ago, Col. John Mosby and her great-grandfather, Lt. James Wiltshire, CSA, once rendezvoused.

And who knows? Perhaps in the dark of night the wind may still carry the strains of an old song set to

the tune of "O Tannenbaum," and the memories of the "Gray Ghost of the Confederacy" and a seventeen-year-old Rebel, may roam through the stone walls of Mosby Spring Farm.

This unusual door in the old stone section of Mosby Spring Farm is rare in the Piedmont. It still carries its original lock.

Above: Mount Beulah as it is today.

Opposite: An impressive pillared entry is accentuated by this circled flagstone patio, planter, and wide semi-circular steps.

MOUNT BEULAH

hen Henry Hudson sailed up a river in 1609 in a new continent known as America, he could never have envisioned the consequences.[1] Upon returning home to the Netherlands with tales of opportunity, fur trapping, and commerce in this new land, thousands of thrifty, ambitious, and religiously tolerant Dutchmen soon poured into a place they called Niew Amsterdam. The Dutch were far better merchants than warriors, however, for they surrendered their provincial town to the British without firing a shot in 1664. But their legacy and their names resound through American history: Stuyvesant, Knickerbocker, Rensselaer, Roosevelt, Minuit, and, of course, beloved Rip van Winkle.

Two descendants of those early Dutch adventurers of the 1600s entered the history of Loudoun County a century later, and as we shall see, their lives and families would intertwine. One was John Swaart whose family settled in Niew Amsterdam in the 1660s, then moved on to Pennsylvania, and finally to Loudoun County, Virginia. John built a home on a grant from Thomas, Sixth Lord Fairfax, which he called Valley View in 1770.[2]

It was James Swaart[3] who purchased 283 wooded acres from Joseph Jones in 1806, and thereby hangs another tale. Joseph Jones owned a good deal of property, yet he left no mark on the Piedmont except that a quarter-century later, he sold the rest of his land to his nephew, who just happened to be Pres. James Monroe. Monroe's magnificent 1830 estate, called Oak Hill,[4] stands not far from the home built either by Jones himself around 1790 or by James Swaart in the early 1800s.[5] And though few homes of the time could compare with Oak Hill, this one was handsome indeed.

Created entirely of brick, Federal in style, and facing east-west to capture warmth and sunlight, its two stories boasted stone chimneys at either end. A center hall, staircase, and lower rooms featured some of the most elaborate, hand-wrought wood carving in the Piedmont—raised six-panel doors, carved scroll brackets, a Tuscan column newel post, molded chair rails, and intricately carved mantles—while the drawing room mantle featured fluted pilasters on pedestals. Whether its creator was Joseph Jones or James Swaart, this was obviously the home of a man who appreciated fine things and could afford an impressive residence.

Religion played a huge role in the society of the 1800s. And so it seems fitting that the name Swaart chose for his hillside home had a religious connotation: Mount Beulah. The name, of course, originated with John Bunyan in his *The Pilgrim's Progress*, as "a place of Heavenly joy which lies beyond the Shadow of Death, where birds sing and flowers appear upon the earth every day."[6] But death did come to James Swart in 1834, and his property was divided among

his heirs. The "dower tract," including his home, was bequeathed to his wife, but had to be sold upon her death in 1867.

But now, we must return to the 1600s. Much had changed after the Dutch Colony of Niew Amsterdam became New York, for everyone was required to swear allegiance to King James II of England. One of

Above: John Franklin Gulick, circa 1886, when he purchased Mount Beulah.

Opposite top: Even before its restoration, the home (built most likely by Joseph Jones in the late 1700s) was lovely.

Opposite bottom: The foyer staircase illustrates the beauty of eighteenth-century craftsmanship.

those who did so was thirty-four-year-old Joachem Gulick who took the Oath of Allegiance to the king of England at the Kings County, New York, courthouse on 30 September 1687.[7]

He was, according to family lore, a shipbuilder in Holland who helped build the Dutch Reformed Church in New York. Like the Swaarts, by the late 1700s, his descendants also migrated to Loudoun County, Virginia, where they became prosperous farmers and merchants. One even served as a "gentleman officer" in Loudoun's Revolutionary 56th Battalion.[8]

James Gulick[9] made his contribution to Loudoun history by helping create the Loudoun Agricultural and Mechanical Institute on the grounds of Oak Hill in 1841—the oldest institution of its type in the entire United States.[10] The institute and its 421 acres were sold to James Gulick in 1846 for $4,821. And that same year, the two Dutch families of Niew

Amsterdam intertwined when James's son Lafayette W. Swaart married Hulda Gulick.

Civil War followed soon after and brought disaster to Southern landowners. James Gulick experienced terrible personal loss when his brother, nineteen-year-old George, and cousin John Milton Gulick were killed serving the Confederacy in 1864. Financial disaster followed. Despite the Dutch tradition of thrift and hard work, the Gulicks were in dire straits and their farms had to be sold for pennies on the dollar. Help arrived in 1883 with the bequest of a 610-acre farm known as Red Hill from John Franklin Gulick's cousin, John Franklin Allen.[11] By selling Red Hill, the future of the Gulicks was secured in a most interesting way.

In December of 1884, John S. Palmer advertised two hundred acres for sale, including "a home of seven rooms and five fireplaces with a beautiful view; an orchard of 300 choice Fruit trees, plus plums and grapes; eight fields for growing corn, raising cattle and pigs; and a beautiful yard of Oak and Shade Trees ...plus an ice house, pond and ten springs of fresh water." And for those who love trivia, mail delivery arrived twice daily! The name of that farm was Mount Beulah.

And in one of those rare and thus delightful turns of fate, in 1886 John Franklin Gulick and his wife, Flora Mae Saffer, bought the home owned by James Swaart in 1806.

Interestingly, though we tend to think that crime is a new occurrence around the Piedmont, in September of 1897, the Gulicks reported that "thieves broke into their meathouse and stole a lot of choice bacon, sixteen hams, eight middlings and a lot of shoulders."[12] A week later the *Loudoun Times-Mirror* reported that the thief was "a mulatto boy of this neighborhood who disposed of his booty in Alexandria and invested the proceeds in a stock of confectionary and returned to a colored church near here where a grand rally was being held, opened a booth and sold his stock presumably at a good profit."

John and Flora Mae Gulick had one son and four daughters who were all educated by a governess in one of the big upstairs bed chambers, which was turned into a schoolroom. Their daughter Jessica was

Above, bottom and top: Gulick's grandson, John Allen, perched on a tree stump at the old homestead in 1925, and Allen and his son, John F. Gulick, plowing the property in the 1980s. Photos courtesy of Mrs. Mildred Gulick.

married in the parlor of Mount Beulah to Charles Franklin Riticor[13] in 1913, and through his eyes we glimpse life in the early 1900s in Loudoun County.[14]

I started shoeing horses when I was twenty years old…very few could do it. I did all the blacksmith work too. We used to go to the Opera House in Leesburg on a Saturday night to see a movie. Silent pictures, they were, for ten cents and maybe a dinner at the Leesburg Hotel for fifty cents or to Beelers where you'd get a half-dozen fried oysters for a quarter. Used to pay six dollars a year then for telephone service…but we built our own line.

The Aldie church was Presbyterian…we took up a collection and ice cream socials to pay for it.

Then speaking of Oak Hill, the palatial estate owned by Sen. and Mrs. Henry Fairfax, where Frank Riticor owned the general store and post office, he

Above: Although the eighteenth-century stone kitchen could not be preserved, each of its notched beams has been retained and used in its restoration.

Left: Layers of paint were removed to reveal finely carved original mantles and edging on all the fireplaces.

said, "Mrs. Fairfax…they were very nice people. Owned a piece of woodland back on Nigger Mountain (now New Mountain) where they farmed wheat, corn, and hackney horses."[15]

Although Jessica and Frank Riticor never had any children, they adored the Gulick's son John Allen. "Uncle Frank" remained a beloved part of the family, even returning to live with them at Mount Beulah for three years before his death in 1977. John Allen became the next owner of Mount Beulah.[16]

John Allen Gulick and his bride, Myrtle Thompson, had just one child, John Allen, Jr., (always called Allen). Since Mount Beulah was a cattle farm, young Allen had chores to do before riding horseback down Tail Race Road to the two-room Aldie schoolhouse. That tiny school, incidentally, was greatly expanded to include a high school in 1915,[17] and still serves elementary children of the early twenty-first century.

Allen and his seventeen-year-old bride, Mildred Morris, moved into a cottage on the farm after their marriage. In his role as agent for Loudoun Soil Conservation, he designed many of the ponds that still dot the local landscape. After two sons arrived, Mildred returned to school, earned her teaching credentials and taught in Loudoun County schools for twenty-seven years! And one has to think that those youngsters were lucky indeed for Mildred Gulick has the kindliest of smiles and obviously adores children.

Her father, "Tipper" Morris, held the record for Show Ring Jumping at the Upperville Horse Show. So her two sons, Steve Allen and John Frank, also grew up on horseback. For fifty years Mildred and Allen Gulick lived, loved, and raised their children together at Mount Beulah, until May of 2002 when Allen died.

But two-century-old homes do not weather well without constant maintenance. So by the twenty-first century, though Mount Beulah was still a lovely property, it had seen better days. Then a young man who had played in its gardens, ridden horseback over its 215 acres, loved its architecture and its history, re-

Right and above: A whimsical note is etched in a stained glass barn scene inside the house, while the original old red barn at Mount Beulah still stands outside.

turned to the scenes of his childhood. After graduating from college and establishing a reputation as a fine builder, John Frank Gulick, the great-grandson of its 1886 owner, has now restored the home that was owned by his family for well over a century.[18] A perfectionist and workaholic by nature, John Gulick lives and breathes construction and historic preservation.

Every floorboard of the old house (which John believes was built by Joseph Jones and thus dates to the 1790s) has been taken up, numbered, restored, and replaced. Each fireplace and mantle, doorway, fanlight and lintel, every wall, chair rail, and molding, is true to its heritage. Unfortunately, the old stone kitchen, which had been the scene of millions of meals over the centuries, had to be demolished. And yet with the addition of two new wings—a glorious, glassed-in great room that was once a porch, plus a kitchen and baths—Mount Beulah blends the comforts of twenty-

first century living with the architecture of the past into one of the most elegant homes in the Piedmont.

Few can boast its expansive views over the Blue Ridge and surrounding countryside. Nor its long curving driveway and huge shimmering pond, outlined by board fences. Young trees have joined those of vintage years along with flowering shrubs and lawns. A weathered, old barn stands nearby, fields of clover and fescue grow tall in summer sun, and cattle low in the distance…for Mount Beulah is, once again, a working farm.

But it's also an incredibly beautiful, spacious, high-

ceilinged home for John Gulick, his lovely and talented wife, Stacy Rice, and their two young children, Thomas Riticor and Olivia, whose laughter now echoes through its halls just as the laughter of Dutch youngsters did two hundred years ago. Since most old plantations and historic homes in this "gentle valley" were built by Englishmen and German Quakers, there is a special significance to a property once owned by Dutchmen of the early 1800s and still owned by their descendents in the twenty-first century!

In the words of Bunyan, Mount Beulah is surely, once again, "a place of Heavenly joy where birds sing and flowers bloom."

Above, bottom and top: The rear elevation of Mount Beulah is almost as lovely as the front. Its sparkling pool overlooks a vast open horizon.

Above and opposite: A side view of Mount Defiance shows its original entry on the right, which led down to an Ordinary. The later front entry now stands just a few yards from the road.

MOUNT DEFIANCE

The Hatfields and McCoys may live on in song and story, but Middleburg had its Chinns and Powells. These two prominent, wealthy families played large roles in eighteenth-century Piedmont history—both vying for land and power. And both claimed ownership of several hundred acres of rich farmland west of town.

But at a time when boundaries were defined by an old oak tree, a pile of stones, a boulder, or meandering stream, it was difficult, if not impossible, to determine many decades later which lands were owned by whom. So the two families fought through almost forty years of litigation before the Leesburg Court, undoubtedly tired of the whole affair, awarded some of the disputed land to each family.

The Powell's portion included a large farm and farmhouse owned by Thomas Chinn just west of town where Middleburg Downs lies today. It is said by some that the Powells named their newly acquired farm Mount Defiance to celebrate their victory. But on the opposite side of the old Ashby Gap Road,

(now Route 50) an historic two-story stone house stood on a hillside, and that too was on Chinn property. Both homes lay claim as the original Mount Defiance though it is the stone house on the hill that has borne the name for well over a century.

Perhaps that only enhances its mystique, however, for although it dates back to the mid 1700s, the property spans both Loudoun and Fauquier Counties, and confusion resulting from this division resulted in many of its records being lost.[1] But its thick stone walls and basement kitchen (which was once used as a tavern), huge, rough-hewn ceiling beams, and

Above: The old slave quarter is now a charming guest house.

Right: This old door once led to a cock-fighting pit, which saw many a Saturday night fight at Mount Defiance.

great old fireplace testify to its antiquity. Its first floor originally boasted a keeping room and chamber, while a narrow staircase led to an upstairs sleeping loft.

A stone cottage with two doors, probably an original slave dwelling, stands nearby, while a reminder of nineteenth-century life also survives in the cockpit, which once provided Saturday night entertainment in earlier days. Until the 1950s, a lean-to shed for animals was attached to the tavern room, and a toll booth sat at the base of the long, winding driveway. The toll

The blacksmith shop, which played such a big role in the Battle of Middleburg in 1863, still stands.

booth dated from a time when Charles Chinn was responsible for maintaining this section of the old Ashby Gap Road. Chinn was thus entitled to exact a fee or toll from riders and wagons who used this section of road, which stands only a hundred feet or so from the front door of the house.

One of the oldest buildings at Mount Defiance is the blacksmith shop, which became a footnote to history during the Battle of Middleburg. It was a brutally hot July morning in 1863 when Union Gen. David Gregg, with cavalry and infantry troops from ten Northern divisions, swept through Middleburg on their way to Ashby's Gap.

Gen. J.E.B. Stuart aimed to stop the Yankees west of town at the rise known as Mount Defiance. He positioned the 9th and 13th Virginia Cavalry at the stone wall north of the road while troops of the 2d, 4th, and 5th North Carolina divisions, along with two cannons, were posted across the road at the blacksmith shop.

The battle began at ten in the morning as Union troops marched up the hill. Smoke enveloped both armies as "stones from the walls of the blacksmith shop flew in every direction when hit by enemy shells" and "Rebels hidden in the surrounding woods turned them into a slaughter house."[2] By early afternoon the battle was over. Vastly outnumbered, weary

Confederates slowly worked their way back to Upperville to regroup.

But who was living at Mount Defiance on that hot July day in 1863? Did a family huddle in terror as cannonballs whizzed by their windows? Ella Gibson Barton of Baltimore (of the large Gibson family around Loudoun and Fauquier) was the owner. Her husband, Bolling Barton, was a wealthy man, so like many Marylanders they would normally have summered in Middleburg.

But as the war raged on, Maryland may have seemed a lot safer than Virginia, so likely only their farm manager, his name lost to history, remained on the 366 acres of Mount Defiance. In any case, Ella died in 1872 and left the farm to her sister, Grace. But Grace predeceased Ella. And thus the old home was plunged into years of litigation.[3]

Gourley Hatcher[4] was the next owner of 120 Mount Defiance acres and the house, as shown in a deed from the heirs of Ella Gibson. Hatcher is also an old name around the Piedmont, which traces back to William Hatcher in 1775.[5] But whether this was a purchase or an inheritance is unclear, because Gourley may have been one of Ella Gibson's heirs.[6] In either case, Gourley, known as a wily trader who "never missed an opportunity to make a dollar," quickly sold the property to William R. Bishop. It was "Reg" Bishop who restored and enlarged the old stone house into the beautiful home of today by adding a spacious foyer, a sun-lit dining room with graceful French doors leading out to a garden patio, a butler's pantry, new kitchen, and a log cabin for a maid's room. An inspired idea was the removal of the wall between the two original first-floor rooms, thus creating a lovely, spacious living room. The old slave house became a guest house, and a huge stable for the Bishop's horses completed the transformation of a small home into a gracious estate.

"Reg" Bishop, related by birth and marriage to many old Piedmont families, including the Lakes of Atoka and the Haxall's of Exning, loved to ride and proudly walked off with honors at the April 1928 Middleburg Hunt Cup Race. That was, in a large sense, a turning point in the history of Middleburg, for it was attended by an incredible eight thousand spectators! A sleepy little Southern town had become a mecca for horse lovers and was fast becoming known as "The heart of the Virginia Hunt Country."

Humphrey is another old Loudoun County name, which appears in the annals of many historic homes

around the Piedmont.[7] And so it does here. In 1955, Dr. Rufus Humphrey and his wife, Gladys Johnson,[8] purchased Mount Defiance. Strangely, though both came from landed families,[9] neither gave a hoot about history. Old pictures of the house and the families who had lived there, as well as Civil War treasures culled from the run-in shed next to the tavern room, somehow just vanished. Even the historic toll booth at the end of the drive was destroyed.

But Rufus, who was born at Creek Hill, was a talented, fun-loving young guy with an infectious smile. He was president of his senior class at the old Aldie High School, and in their Graduation Testament he left his "good looks and happy smile to anyone who can use it as effectively as I can." Rufus went on to become a veterinarian and a beloved friend to horse owners around the Piedmont.

There's an old expression that "you can't fool a small town neighbor." So this tribute, written at his death in 1993 by James Young of Denton, master of hounds of the Orange County Hunt, speaks volumes about how many people around Middleburg felt about Rufus Humphrey.

I lost my hero today. Rufus Humphrey was my veterinarian. He epitomized the definition of horseman…he knew horses…took pride in and revered each and every one, and respected those who nurtured them. Soft spoken, every word he voiced spoke volumes to those who knew how to listen.

This was a man with no ego, no artifice. I paid my bills to Rufus each month. But how do I pay him for everything else he gave to me? Unbridled dedication. Unfettered friendship. Uncompromising expertise. And total trust. Rufus Humphrey set the standard for a horse-man's hero.[10]

The Humphreys' daughter Cathy and her husband, Richard Collette, now live at Mount Defiance and cherish its history. Cathy grew up in this old house. Its thick stone walls, its polished brick and pine floors, rippled, hand-blown windows, centuries-old heavy doors with their great black locks, and beautiful grounds hold many memories. The Collettes obviously love the place and have passed that affection along to their daughter Katie.

Only five acres now remain of its original 366, but with all its mystery and claim to history, Mount Defiance will always stand as one of Middleburg's finest landmarks.

Above top: The gracious living room created by the Bishops in the 1920s is enhanced today by the family antiques of Cathy Humphrey and her husband, Richard Collette.

Above bottom: The beloved veterinarian of Middleburg, Dr. Rufus Humphrey, and his wife, Gladys Johnson.

Opposite: Additions the Bishops added to the old stone house included a sun-lit dining room with graceful French doors that lead out to a garden patio.

Above and opposite: Mount Harmony from the entrance and the front view.

MOUNT HARMONY
(Woodwind)

Over 47,000 acres of prime Loudoun land was granted by Thomas VI, Lord Fairfax, to Robert "King" Carter (please say Cahtah) in the 1730s. "The Land Baron" he was called, and though he was said to be the wealthiest Virginian of his time, he was not necessarily the most beloved.

As the years went on, his vast land holdings were divided among his children and their heirs, and by the late 1700s, a portion became the legacy of his grandson Jonathan Carter, who lived at Groveton in Mountville.[1] Like many planters, Jonathan owned several farms. Corn, wheat or oats grew on some, while cattle and sheep grazed on others.

Each farm (often simply known as field one or two, etc.) held a small home for the use of a tenant farmer. One of those farms lies at the junction of Sam Fred Road and Snickersville Pike and later became known as Woodwind, while today it's known as Mount Harmony. Typical of most, it was built of stone and boasted one room on the first level with two tiny curving staircases—one leading to an upstairs bedroom, the other to a basement kitchen, each of which held a fireplace.

Jonathan's son Francis Carter inherited the farm in 1866 when the South was still reeling from the results of Civil War. The loss of its young men, of inexpensive (though certainly not free) labor, and the breakdown of an established way of life were devastating. Even well-to-do farmers were left with no way to plant or harvest crops, and much of the South was plunged into economic disaster.

And perhaps that's why Francis Carter sold the property in 1868 to a Leesburg lady called Betsy Breckenridge.[2] They were simple, but ambitious, hard-working people. Betsy's husband, Alexander, was a blacksmith in Leesburg; his father and brother, Samuel, were harness-makers, and like most

Above: The original kitchen in the basement served its families for over a century and remains a reminder of days when cooking meals was a full-time job.

Below and opposite: An old log cabin rests nearby, as does a brilliant white barn.

people of the time, in addition to plying a living, they also farmed their own land.

Accustomed to hard work and long days, Betsy Breckenridge, her son John, and his son, yet another Alexander, managed to hold on to their farm for seventy years. During the late 1800s, they expanded the small stone house with a frame addition: a new entrance with a narrow hallway leading to a living room downstairs and two smaller bedrooms on the upper level—though the only access to those bedrooms was the tiny staircase of 1790.

One member of their family achieved fame and fortune far beyond the limits of Loudoun however. Born in 1870 to the harness-maker of Leesburg, Hugh Breckenridge studied at the Pennsylvania Academy of Fine Arts and then in Paris. He returned to Philadelphia; exhibited in New York; established studios in Gloucester, Massachusettes, and Pennsylvania; won exhibitions all over the world for his landscapes; and at his death in 1937 was called an artist "whose influence on America's outstanding arts cannot be over-estimated." And his portrait of Justice John Marshall

still hangs in the Loudoun County Courthouse.

Hard times hit everyone in the 1930s, and so the Breckenridges leased the farm to Tom Crouch, a blind farmer who knew the land and said to his son, "git me a handful of dirt and I'll tell you when it's ready to work" or "hand me a fistful of hay and I'll tell you when it's time to mow." "Then one day, a trader came 'round and sold old Tom a horse…who was also blind. But Tom didn't know that so he hitched him up to the wagon and that blind horse led the blind man all around the farm for many a year."[3]

Alexander N. Breckenbridge sold the farm in 1938. The buyer was Margot Smith, the wealthy wife of Crompton Smith, who lived down the road at Featherbed Farm. Avid participants in the Middleburg Hunt scene for many years, the Smiths bought Woodwind and rebuilt the stable there for their prized horses, since most of the land at Featherbed Farm was devoted to dairy farming. They later conveyed it to yet another Smith, a lady named Elizabeth from Massachusetts, who had lived there as a tenant and finally purchased it in 1946.

Elizabeth was considered somewhat of "a character." She had two children and was also known as Betty Wilson after she married an Englishman, known to local kids as "a grumpy old man." Five years later, she gave the property to her daughter Elizabeth Smith Moray, who quickly sold it.

Newlyweds moved to Woodwind in 1951. The old basement kitchen with its great stone fireplace was still the only place to cook, for the outside "summer kitchen" had long since been abandoned. So the young newlyweds, Betty Fox and Cliff Miller, soon added a new kitchen, a downstairs powder room, and a lovely terrace and gardens. The pool, an early unfiltered version, had to be drained and manually refilled, however, so it was seldom used and later filled in. After their divorce,[4] Cliff Miller married again, and he and his new wife, Carol,[5] remained at Woodwind until 1962 when they sold the house and its fifteen acres to Philip Thomas for $29,500.[6]

By that time, Pres. John F. Kennedy had made Middleburg his second home and a bevy of politicians, statesmen, government officials, corporate execu-

tives, movie stars, and entrepreneurs followed. Property values skyrocketed, so by 1991 when Douglas Scott acquired Woodwind (whose name had by now become Mount Harmony), he subdivided it and sold the old house on just seven acres to Philip and Michelle Duke as a weekend retreat.

The Dukes completely updated the bank barn, enlarged the old summer kitchen into a lovely little guest house, and a few years later, they too sold the property.[7] And would you believe somewhere along the line, an elevator was installed in this little old house to transport its residents up to the master bedroom?

The new owners (the twelfth family to own it, not counting the tenants who have called it home over the centuries) are Jean Ann and Ralph Feneis. They might be called the "Fascinating Feneises," for their backgrounds and interests are as far ranging as their home is charming.

They were both living in Germany in the 1970s and 1980s. Jean Ann was director of recreation for the American armed forces under the aegis of the Department of Defense. Heidelburg, that delightful ancient city founded on a hillside overlooking the Neckar River in 1386, was her home base. Ralph was a young Army captain stationed near Nuremburg, but they never crossed paths until 1982 in Florida at the wedding of a mutual friend. Even then, their romance went slowly for they didn't marry until 1989 in Jean Ann's hometown of Evanston, Illinois, where she was then superintendent of recreation. Months away from each other followed as Ralph, not yet a full colonel, was posted to Bamburg, Germany, then to the Gulf War, the War College in Pennsylvania, followed by Naples, Holland, and finally Croatia.

"That's it! We're settling down," said Jean Ann. So they both took early retirement and in 1997 found a home along a quiet country road in the Virginia Hunt Country. It was Mount Harmony. Ralph became a consultant for Booz-Allen-Hamilton, handling logistical military operations, and yes, he still travels a lot.

But the Feneis' came to Loudoun at a time when its population was exploding beyond the county's ability to build schools, roads, and infrastructure to support massive growth. Farmers, many of whose families had lived on the land for generations, wanted to sell their property to developers at high prices, saying, "We can't make a living on a small farm anymore."

Sometimes it takes a newcomer to find solutions

Above, top and bottom: Antiques, like this hand-painted German armoire and bakers rack filled with copper pots and earthenware, fill every niche at Mount Harmony.

Opposite: The entryway features a rose toille paper accented by antique samplers and old prints.

Left and below: The dining room at Mount Harmony is an appealing area to share the company of friends, and its tiny staircase leads to the original upper sleeping chamber.

to a problem. But it isn't easy to come into a new community, become involved in local issues, and offer viable options to opposing factions, both of whom have legitimate concerns. Yet that's exactly what Jean Ann Feneis did.

It started with herbs and flowers from her garden, which she made into fragrant bars of soap in her kitchen and then wrapped in beautiful colored papers with silver seals and ribbons. She took them to the Farmer's Markets in Washington, and within one year she sold over a hundred thousand dollars worth of soap!

Today, the Feneis' provide jobs for sixteen people, show their products at eleven different markets every week, and delight as their fragrant soaps are offered to guests at upscale hotels such as the Ritz Carleton in both Washington and Boston. But more than that, they've shown that there are ways to preserve the beauty and open country of the Piedmont by exploring new ideas—that small farmers can become self-supporting and still stay close to the land.

Despite their business acumen, there's a gentleness, a reflective quality about Jean Ann and Ralph Feneis that is mirrored in their surroundings. A horse

Above: Beautifully wrapped soaps, fragrant with herbs from the gardens of Mount Harmony (handmade by Jean Ann Feneis and sold at Washington markets), prove that old farms, which once grew oats, corn, and wheat, can still be viable in the twenty-first century.

quietly nibbles sweet new grass along their fence, spring flowers (soon to become new soap fragrances?) pop up around a flagstone terrace garden as a soft morning sun drenches the land.

Inside the front door of their old house a soft, rose toile wallpaper backgrounds a tall armoire and old framed prints. Adjacent rooms offer bright chintzes, fine antiques, intriguing oil paintings, and comfortable furnishings that somehow meld with rough ceiling beams, old stone fireplaces, and tiny staircases into a charming home.

The Feneises' dining room, once the original keeping room of the house, often serves an elegant buffet under candlelight. Although wind no longer rages through the woods, there's always a warm welcome at the old stone house from a little Yorky called Annie who begs to be picked up and petted, at a two-century-old home aptly known as Mount Harmony.

Above: Each bedroom is attractive at Mount Harmony, but this one seemed especially welcoming.

Above and opposite: Noland Ferry House as it stands today. The original center section dates from the 1760s, while the wings were added later.

NOLAND FERRY HOUSE

"The House of My Heart's Desire"

The Old Carolina Road, once an Indian trail then the first highway in a new land called America, once ran all the way from New England to the Carolinas. Its path was broken, however, in places where rivers ran wide. The Potomac was such a place. Indians had long crossed the "Potomack" in bark canoes at a spot where rapid flowing waters were gentler, and white men soon followed their example.

One man built a ferry there to carry horses, sheep, building materials, wheat, provisions, spices, wagons, passengers, and everything needed to sustain life in a wilderness, between Frederick County, Maryland, and Loudoun County, Virginia. Philip Noland was his name.[1] The year was 1760, and Noland was a "gentleman" at a time in history when the term connoted education and culture. He not only built a ferry but also a magnificent home of pink brick, ballast from ships that arrived in the port of Alexandria from England and Ireland. Sitting astride the Old Carolina Road, it was described as "the finest example of Georgian architecture in Northern Virginia" and well suited its chatelaine, the lovely Elizabeth Awbrey whom he married in 1765.[2]

Of course, Philip's position as a wealthy plantation owner, captain in the Virginia militia, and member of the Loudoun County Board of Justices demanded a fine home. Was it spectacular for its time? Well, Gen. Anthony Wayne, that legendary, Revolutionary hero and renowned rake who "loved to pinch the ladies," stayed with the Nolands during the Revolution, calling it "the house of my heart's desire." Wayne described its location in "a grove of towering oak trees, its spectacular river views and beautiful winding staircase as graceful as any in Virginia."[3]

In early May of 1776, the Nolands also offered a warm welcome to one of the most brilliant Virginians of their time. A lone horseman and his servant, Bob Hemings,[4] tarried there while waiting for the ferry to carry them across the Potomac on their way to the second Continental Congress in Philadelphia. That horseman was chosen soon after to write a daring document called the "Declaration of Independence." His name was Thomas Jefferson.[5]

The mansion also saw the Nolands' sons, Thomas and Philip, Jr., march off to join General Washington during the Revolution. And it heard the cries of slaves chained in its cellars and the gutteral language of Hessian soldiers imprisoned nearby, who carved the fine crown moldings and mantles at Ferry House and were then shot while trying to escape.

It watched as Washington dined under its crystal chandelier upon his return from Harper's Ferry in 1783;[6] it saw graceful ladies in silken gowns and finely clad gentlemen in embroidered waistcoats and ruffled cuffs dance under the fourteen-foot ceilings of its grand ballroom or meander among its fragrant magnolia gardens during that time known as "The Golden Age" of the Piedmont.

Thomas Noland and his wife, Mary Eleanor Luckett, inherited the Ferry House, and, upon Thomas's

demise in 1811, it was bequeathed to their sons, Dale, Samuel, and Lloyd. But there was a proviso in Thomas's will: his wife, Mary Eleanor, and his daughter, Betsy, were to have use of the property, the house, stables, gardens, and farms for as long as they lived or Betsy remained single. And since Betsy never married, she remained on the plantation until 1832.

A decade later, the rise of railroads presaged the demise of ferries for commercial use, although, during the Civil War, Noland's Ferry carried many Marylanders into Virginia to join the Confederacy as the Battle of Ball's Bluff and skirmishes between North and South raged around it. And surely the old house must have chuckled as "The Gray Ghost of the Confederacy," Col. John Singleton Mosby, outwitted Union patrols who searched in vain for the gold he had supposedly hidden within its walls.

By the late 1860s, however, the once lovely old house was used as a post office and began a creeping descent into decay. Many of Philip Noland's descendants headed west into Arkansas, Indiana, and Kentucky after the Civil War.[7] Then the early 1900s brought a bridge across the Potomac, and the advent of automobiles signaled the doom of the ferry built by Philip Noland in 1760. It had simply outlived its usefulness, and the once lovely old home was soon abandoned.

Times may have changed, and many early families have vanished from the Middleburg scene, but some left an indelible mark on the history of the Piedmont. Philip Noland's descendents appear in the annals of almost every old plantation family from Col. Lloyd Noland of Glen Ora, Lena Noland Berkeley of Pembroke, Powell Noland of Burrland, Lavinia Noland Haxall of Exning, Ann Noland Dabney of Creek Hill, and the famed "First Lady of Middleburg," Charlotte Haxall Noland of Foxcroft.[8]

The Wayne Brookins' of Washington found the old deserted house hidden away on a country lane (the Old Carolina Road, now Route 15, had by now been moved further west) early in the twentieth century. It was in terrible shape.[9] Many of the old hand-blown windows and wooden shutters were missing. Every wall and ceiling had to be repaired, and all its heart-of-pine floors, staircases, fireplaces, and mantles needed restoration. They also added a new kitchen and bathrooms, and its colonial gardens, now just a jumble of weeds, were refurbished along with an old log cabin that was transformed into a studio for the Brookins' daughter. Years of effort restored the magnificent

Above: Several of the Noland family headed west during the early 1800s. This is a studio portrait.

Opposite: This room, with its Williamsburg green walls, was the original dining room where both Gen. George Washington and Thomas Jefferson enjoyed a toddy and fine repast as guests of the Nolands.

Above, top, bottom, and right: Emily Figuers exhibits three of her favorite dollhouses. Each is authentically furnished, and the Georgian mansion dollhouse (above right) is created entirely of tiny bricks.

seven-bedroom mansion to much of its former glory.

Then, in the mid-1930s, Noland Ferry House acquired another mistress, the wealthy Catherine Marshall Ignatius. She hired an architect who had done work for both Mount Vernon and Williamsburg to design two new bedroom wings for the Ferry House, along with curving entrance steps outlined with fine wrought-iron railings.

Now Catherine Igatious was "a perfect lady": a charming Southerner who should have been warmly embraced by the society of the time. And she was…at first. Unfortunately, her husband, who was said to be a "kept man," apparently went out of his way to be cuttingly rude to her guests, and so this lovely lady was turned down for membership in the Leesburg Garden Club! Seems silly today perhaps, but at the time, for a Southerner and owner of a beautiful home, to be rejected by society in a small town was devastating, and she moved away soon after.

The wrought-iron gates of Noland Ferry House swing open today as an early summer sun embraces the lady standing by its door. She is the gracious Emily Figuers,[10] who with her husband, Horace, a Naval

Academy graduate, has lived at and loved the old Ferry House for over a quarter century.

Dollhouses are Emily's passion, and they greet visitors in the entrance foyer where General Washington and Thomas Jefferson once strode through the door. These dollhouses sit on fireplaces and fill tables in the dining room, library, and morning rooms where softly painted silver-green, interior wooden shutters surround rippled windows.

Antiques are another passion. An American flag boasting thirty-six stars hangs in the foyer, a reminder of 1864 when Nevada became our thirty-sixth state. Mrs. Figuers gently points out low twin chairs designed for hoop-skirted ladies of the antebellum period. Chippendale chests, drums from Thailand that reverberate over two mountain ranges, and miniature furniture and antiques of every description, which would delight the hearts of Sotheby curators, fill every nook and cranny of Ferry House.

Horace Figuers, a former Marine captain who served in the Pacific during World War II, treasures a vast train collection that occupies much of the basement. He also holds court in the gardens of which, along with his grandchildren and Huguenot ancestry, he is justly proud. And what gardens they are! Huge old magnolias and English boxwood dot the grounds,

Above, top and bottom: This drawing room features many of the Figuers' antiques, including two velvet antebellum chairs designed for ladies wearing hoop skirts.

Left: The entrance hall leads to four chambers and showcases a 36-star flag from 1864 when Montana joined the Union.

Above and below: The rear of Noland Ferry House overlooks acres of old magnolias and a circular garden guarded by the little statue of a Confederate soldier.

flowers billow in unexpected places, and a little statue of a Confederate soldier, surrounded by masses of lush green vinca, stands guard in the courtyard. And, oh yes, still another dollhouse—well it's actually a full-sized, beautifully furnished playhouse—waits outside the garden wall for another generation of children.

The Figuers' love for this home, its land, and its history led them to set aside its remaining forty-eight acres for the Virginia Outdoors Foundation so that it will never be developed, and the halls and walls of Noland Ferry House will always be preserved. Those walls, say the Figuers', hold the spirits of those two Hessian soldiers, shot while trying to escape from Noland Ferry House during the Revolution, who occasionally scratch on a wall to make their presence known. In the drawing room, in an upstairs bath, or stomping up the staircase in measured tread at eight o'clock on a Sunday morning, they seem to say, "We too have been here…do not forget us."

An intriguing side note is that Noland Ferry House lies near a spot called "Lost Corner," so named because when the Old Carolina Road was diverted, the few homes in the area were forgotten by the post office and their mail was "lost."

But this magnificent home is as enchanting today as it must have been in the 1700s. Those who have seen sunlight drifting over its pink brick, climbed its curving, three-story spiral staircase, walked the pine board floors where Washington, Jefferson, and Gen. Anthony Wayne once strode—where young couples in silk and satin danced until morn in its ballroom, wandered through its gardens or gazed in awe through rippled windows as moonlight created a river of diamonds along the Potomac—would certainly agree that Noland Ferry House is indeed "the house of my heart's desire."

Above and left: An old log cabin, now enlarged into a guest house, stands nearby, along with an adorable playhouse, which awaits another generation of Noland Ferry children.

Glorious Old Welbourne as it appears today.

OLD WELBOURNE

*E*ven its name is delightful, invoking, as it does, both the patina of age and a gently flowing stream in old England. Its history actually began long before it acquired a name, however, as it was only a small part of the nineteen million acres inherited by Thomas, Sixth Lord Fairfax, in 1719.[1]

The illustrious Robert "King" Carter, who, as land agent for Lord Fairfax, acquired thousands of acres of the most desirable, arable land around the Piedmont, became its owner in the 1730s. "King" Carter's grandsons and their progeny inherited all that land and built many of the fine plantations that still dot the countryside of Loudoun and Fauquier Counties today. One of those properties followed a circuitous route, however, as it was bequeathed from Robert Carter's second wife, Elizabeth Landon Willis, through the female line to her great-granddaughter Elizabeth French Dulany of Maryland.

And so it is in Maryland that we begin the story of the Dulanys. Annapolis,[2] the little city at the mouth of the Severn, was, by the early 1700s, the social and political center of the British colony. It boasted tremendous wealth, a handsome state house and great mansions, well-crafted furniture, elegant carriages drawn by fine horses, ballrooms, race courses, sailing boats, and, it not only claimed to have "the first theatre…but the most beautiful and extravagant women in America!"[3]

The Dulanys played a large role in that society along with other established Maryland families: Tayloes, Youngs, Potts, Fitzhughs, deButts', Halls, Calverts, Carrs, and Addisons. It was Daniel Dulany, who had been cut out of his father's will with but a shilling, who established the Dulanys as a prominent part of Maryland society.[4]

Educated at Trinity College in Dublin, Daniel became a noted attorney in Baltimore. He married a wealthy young woman named Rebecca Smith[5] and built a magnificent brick mansion in 1728 on a twenty-thousand-acre estate along the banks of the Potomac, directly across from Alexandria, Virginia, where their nine children grew to adulthood. Their eldest son, Daniel Dulany II, an eminent barrister and general secretary of the Maryland colony, married Rebecca Bladen Tasker, daughter of Gov. Benjamin Tasker, and they too lived at Oxon Hill.

Above: The original log cabin built by John Peyton Dunlany for his bride, Mary Ann deButts, in 1810 on land given by his mother, Elizabeth French Dulany. Courtesy of Mrs. Janet Dulany Roszel Tayloe.

Below: Elizabeth French Dulany. Courtesy of Stephen Roszel.

But the following years found all the colonies buzzing over taxation without representation and the hated Stamp Tax. "The people here are Liberty mad …nothing but war is thought of," commented an observer. So irate had Marylanders become by 1775 that they burned the ship "Peggy Stewart" and its load of tea into Baltimore harbor! When the Continental Congress formally outlawed all drinking of tea in February of 1775 and established coffee as the official drink of the American colonies, merchants who sold or served the forbidden herb were tarred and feathered. Suddenly, to be in sympathy with the king of England was to be a hated enemy.

But the Dulanys of Maryland were supporters of the king.[7] After war was declared, their lands in Maryland were confiscated and their incomes vastly reduced as income from London investments and shipping ceased. The Virginia branch of the family, however, whose well educated sons had made good marriages to wealthy young women, were supporters of Revolution.

By far, the most important of those alliances was the wedding of Benjamin Tasker Dulany[8] to Elizabeth French, the beautiful, sixteen-year-old godchild of George Washington and ward of George Mason. She was called "the wealthiest and most desirable young lady in America."[9] Quite a coup for handsome Benjamin Dulany who married the lovely Elizabeth at Gunstan Hall on a cold Wednesday afternoon, 10 February 1773.

And it was the young Dulanys who gave Gen. George Washington a horse named "Blueskin," which he would ride from Virginia, through New York, New Jersey, Valley Forge, and finally to victory at Yorktown.

John Peyton Dulany was their seventh child, and like all twelve of their children, he was born at Elizabeth's family home, "Claremont" in Fairfax, Virginia. Upon his marriage to Mary Ann deButts in 1810 at Mount Welby in Maryland, his mother, Elizabeth French Dulany, gave him a tract of land, 503 acres of sweet fertile soil in Loudoun County on which he built a small log cabin.[10]

He called it Welbourne in honor of his bride's ancestral home in England. It was a simple home, "only two little rooms below and the same above," and far different from John Peyton's childhood home or the fine Maryland estate of Mount Welby where Mary Ann had grown up.

Yet when Mary Ann's parents, Dr. and Mrs. Samuel deButts, visited the young couple in 1813, Mrs. de-Butts painted a delightful portrait of the surrounding countryside and the people of the early Piedmont:

> [It is] a land rich with fine springs and two fine streams of water…plenty of wood and stone for building. The neighborhood chiefly consists of plain, industrious but independent people, chiefly Quakers. There are very few slaves…and the whole time I was there I never saw a poor person. Dr. deButts and I rambled frequently (on horseback) and introduced ourselves to several of the neighbors and were never suffered to depart without partaking of some good country fare such as excellent bread, butter, cheese, honey, apples, pastry, pumpkin puddings, etc…[11]

The early years of the nineteenth century were both exhilarating and challenging. A young America was trying to establish itself as a nation, pay off the debts of Revolution, and establish a federal government in an eleven-mile area known as the District of Columbia. Exploration of western lands drew thousands of settlers into Indian territory; Thomas Jefferson's Louisiana Purchase soon expanded its boundaries (and obligations) even further. Then, as James Madison sat in the White House—or as it was then called "The President's House"—Americans again found themselves at war with England.

Left: Dr. Samuel deButts and his wife, Mary Welby deButts, rode the Piedmont countryside while visiting their daughter at the log cabin, which was called Welbourne. Courtesy of Nathaniel Holmes Morison.

Above: The fiery Methodist minister, Stephen Samuel Roszel, married Julia Ann Dulany deButts in 1845 and moved into Old Welbourne. Three generations of Roszels would call it home. Courtesy of Janet Dulany Roszel Tayloe.

For those whose lifestyle was dependent upon English investments, the impact was traumatic. As Mrs. deButts wrote to her brother in London in 1813, "You can scarce imagine how much inconvenience we sustain by being so long separated from our income, but Dr. deButts has good credit or I know not how we should live."

Mrs. deButts goes on to say, however, that the young Dulanys were "perfectly content and happy in their snug cottage." And by 1833, by dint of hard work (never say that the ladies didn't do their share, for Mary Ann Dulany came down with a "violent fever after spending hours in a damp milk house"), they were able to purchase the far more grand home of Mrs. Joanna Lewis,[12] which lay not far away…right across the road from Mary Ann's brother, Richard deButts at Crednal. Again, they named their new home Welbourne Hall, so their log cabin and its lands soon became known as Old Welbourne.

And it is there, at Old Welbourne, where our story

Above: It was during this time that the old log cabin was abandoned, and a new home (also called Old Welbourne) was built. Of Victorian design, this is how the house looked in the early 1900s. Courtesy of Cricket Whitner.

continues…forty some years later when descendants of two old families intermarried.[13] In 1845, John Peyton Dulany's daughter, a young widow named Julia Ann Dulany deButts, wed that fiery Methodist minister, Stephen Samuel Roszel.[14] And on the land settled by her parents in 1810, they raised their seven children in a handsome, twelve-room, brick mansion with eight fireplaces, dependencies, barns, and stables, which is to this day still known as Old Welbourne.[15]

Samuel rode horseback preaching the gospel from Maryland, through Washington and the villages of Virginia, to the hill towns of West Virginia for forty-four years![16] Yet he and Julia Ann managed to beget seven children, including Stephen George Asbury Roszel who married Sarah Josephine deButts. (Don't you love how the old families kept intermingling?).

Well, Stephen George Roszel was a University of Virginia graduate and a lawyer. But he was deaf, which made listening to arguments in court a bit difficult. So he and Sarah returned to Old Welbourne where he became a farmer—a very successful farmer, in fact, raising fine cattle and good crops. Fifteen years later he decided to buy a place of his own, which he called Denton.[17]

But Old Welbourne stayed in the Dulany family. Col. Richard Dulany's youngest son, Dick, married Eva Randolph and inherited Old Welbourne, so their daughter Eva Dulany and her husband, Dr. Archibald Randolph,[18] moved in.

Now, the Randolphs are definitely "Old Virginia," harking back to William Randolph who served in the House of Burgesses in 1680 and amassed a fortune as a merchant/planter. His son Sir John (the only native Virginian to be knighted by the king) and grandson Peyton Randolph also served as burgesses, though Peyton was a strong patriot and later acted as president of both the first and second Continental Congresses.[19]

Randolph influence continued as Edmund Randolph served as an aide-de-camp to Gen. George Washington; John Randolph became a representative and senator to Congress, then U.S. minister to Russia; and George Wythe Randolph (a grandson of Thomas Jefferson) held the rank of brigadier general in the Confederacy.

Their descendant, Archibald Randolph, was quite a character. After retiring as a prominent urologist in Charlottesville and settling in at Old Welbourne, he became noted for his riding prowess. Especially on Election Day, when 'tis said that "he'd vote first at

Welbourne, then at Upperville and Atoka and finally at Rectortown!"[20]

Seventeen years later, their son Dulany Randolph and his wife, Sally, took over, at which point Old Welbourne became known as "the party place." Dancing, wild parties and escapades, hunt breakfasts with lots of toddies and even a guest who was shot in an upstairs bathroom livened up the old house…at least until Dulany and Sally divorced in the 1950s.

Then both the 440-acre estate and the house stood vacant and vandalized for several years. All the fine old brass locks, doorknobs, and chandeliers vanished; barns and outbuildings and the once lovely gardens were almost destroyed. Finally, after 150 years, the Randolphs' children sold Old Welbourne out of the Dulany family.[21] The buyer, Frederick E. Muhl, stayed there for only a short time, so it is the next owner who impacts our story. His name was Erskine Lott Bedford.

He was charming, debonair, and dashingly handsome. And it didn't hurt that his grandfather had founded the Esso Oil Corporation. Erskine's family originated in New York back in the 1600s and owned the farmland that, in the early 1900s, became a public housing development known as Bedford-Stuyvesant. By then, the family had moved to Maryland, however, where Erskine had grown up around horses.[22]

In 1961, he brought his fiancée, Lily Lambert Cross (whose grandfather, Gerard Barnes Lambert,[23] owned magnificent Carter Hall in Clarke County) to see Old Welbourne. It was a rambling old place. Snakes were crawling down the staircase, pony dung lay on the upstairs landing, and the house was a disaster. But Lily loved it.

The young newlyweds spent the next year in the groom's cottage at Old Welbourne while architect Washington Reed restored the old house, revamping its exterior into a far more impressive elevation with a curved entry and handsome pillars and preserving its marvelous floor-to-ceiling windows along the front portico. He also restored all eight fireplaces, its fine old floors, and sixteen-foot ceilings and finished the walls of the study with burnished barn-wood paneling. A century after its inception, Old Welbourne had again become a beautiful mansion.

Meanwhile, Erskine, a Cornell Agricultural School graduate, turned the property into a working farm. After discovering that cattle farming was not exactly a profitable venture, however, he returned to school and became a successful stock broker with Alex

Above: Dashingly handsome Erskine Bedford bought Old Welbourne for his bride, Lily Lambert Cross, in 1961. Within a year, they had restored and transformed the old home into one of the most impressive properties of the Piedmont.

Opposite: The entrance hall at Old Welbourne in its Christmas finery

Brown & Sons…and an avid sportsman. Never one to do things half-way, Erskine soon became co-trustee of Glenwood Park Race Course in Middleburg and, at the urging of Mrs. Theo Randolph, assumed a large role in the Piedmont Hunt, which had been started by the son of the first owner of Old Welbourne, Col. Richard Henry Dulany, back in the 1800s.

In the mid-1970s, Old Welbourne became a beehive of activity. Erskine and Lily divorced, and he married Nancy Gerry. With Nancy's two children from a previous marriage, a total of six heirs[24] now filled its halls. And an amazingly close relationship evolved among all of these children, who regard both Lily Lambert and Nancy Bedford as mothers and friends.

Erskine later became master of the Piedmont Hunt, a role he obviously cherished for he was called the "Best Field Master American Fox Hunting has ever seen." As a friend, Anna Dees commented, "no one knew the hunt country terrain like Erskine. He knew every creek, every tributary, every back country lane and every rock protruding from an embankment." Then on a terrible December day in 1998, tragedy struck. Erskine's horse suffered a heart attack.

Thrown to the ground, Erskine was rushed to Washington Hospital Center by helicopter with severe head injuries. He died just a few hours later with all of his children at his bedside. His funeral was one of the largest services ever held at Upperville's Trinity Church as hundreds of people thronged in from all over America and Europe to pay homage to a beloved friend.[25]

Erskine Bedford lives on at Old Welbourne, however, for his youngest daughter, Cricket,[26] and her husband, James Whitner, with their children, Harrison and Louise,[27] now call it home, and Erskine's pictures and trophies appear in every room. But he also left a sense of "noblesse oblige," for Cricket Whitner co-founded the Bedford Fund designed to promote land conservation around Loudoun County so that other properties like her family's 379 acre farm will survive into another century.[28]

Cricket Bedford Whitner was "born and raised" at Old Welbourne, and her strong sense of land, family, and home are reflected in these words:

This house provided a warm, safe haven for me as a child. My parents divorced when I was in elementary school so the house and farm were constants in my life which never wavered. The animals and land were such a magnificent

138

luxury...we had chickens, sheep, pigs, dogs, cats, a donkey and, of course, cattle and horses. This amazing place fostered such wonderful memories and experiences. I hope that Old Welbourne will continue to be a place for all of us, and our children, to come together so they can continue to share those memories.[29]

In a rare departure from Southern tradition, Erskine Bedford rests in the cemetery of Old Welbourne, the fourth "Master of the Piedmont Hunt" to be buried there. But he is the only non-descendant of John Peyton Dulany and Louisa Dulany deButts to be interred within its old stone walls! A final tribute to a friend named Bedford from his friends named Dulany.

And therein lies another story of Old Welbourne. Though only a chimney and crumbling roof beams covered with vines remain of John Peyton Dulany's log cabin today, hidden away behind a cornfield and sheltered by old trees, generations of his descendants, Dulanys, deButtses, Roszels, Halls, Whitings, and Tayloes rest in a cemetery shaded by old hemlock trees.

And they are remembered, as perhaps only Virgin-ians remember and honor their ancestors, in a most unusual way. Mrs. Janet Dulany Roszel Tayloe instituted a reunion, by invitation only, called "The Old Welbourne Graveyard Picnic" some twenty-five years ago. It has since become an occasional October tradition, bringing together members of the old families, infants to octogenarians, from all over the country, so that their history and their people will not be forgotten.[30]

But the little log cabin at Old Welbourne, built by John Peyton Dulany in 1810, was the genesis of several other historic homes, so join me now as we wander through Welbourne Plantation, The Old Church House, and Crednal.[31]

Above: Cricket Bedford and her husband, Jim Whitner, now own Old Welbourne and enjoy its history and its pleasures with their two little children, James Harrison V and Louise Lott Whitner.

Opposite top: The white walls of this gracious dining room provide a foil for fine paintings.

Opposite bottom: The library, added by the Bedfords, is paneled with pine from an old barn on the property.

Welbourne Plantation today.

WELBOURNE PLANTATION

*T*all stately pillars now march proudly across the façade of Welbourne …but this lovely home, which has seen so much of history and has been home to generations of the Dulany family, didn't start out that way. In fact, back in 1770, it was simply a small stone house in the center of a park surrounded by huge old trees. But I jump ahead of the story.

As noted in the story of Old Welbourne, the Dulanys had been prominent in the Maryland Tidewater area since Daniel Dulany arrived at Port Tobacco from Ireland in 1703, and they were large landowners in Fairfax as well. It was Daniel's great-grandson John Peyton Dulany and his bride, Mary Ann de-Butts, who settled in the Virginia Piedmont in 1811 upon receiving five hundred acres of prime farmland from his mother, Elizabeth French Dulany.[1] Their first home (Old Welbourne) was a simple log cabin, but by 1833, John Peyton Dulany had become a prosperous planter who owned nineteen horses (more than anyone else in the area) on which he paid eight cents tax for each every year. If one of them was a prized stud horse, he'd never have admitted it, for those were taxed at the incredible rate of ten dollars!

So in 1833 John Peyton and Mary Ann Dulany acquired the nearby home of James and Joanna Lewis who owned 581 acres near the mouth of Panther-skin Creek.[2] Bricks and mortar create more than a home, however; they establish an image, an outward manifestation of one's status in life—and both the Dulanys and deButts' had a proud heritage. So they enlarged their new home into a lovely Georgian structure with a great entrance foyer, spacious, high-ceilinged drawing rooms, a gable roof with five bays, and new chimneys. Later, two side wings, made of brick kilned on the plantation and plastered in the Italianate style of the time, were joined to the main house. One was a magnificent dining room with corner cupboards to hold fine, monogrammed china. The final touch, a long portico with pillars across the front elevation, turned Welbourne into one of the most impressive plantations of its time.

It was an ideal place for the Dulanys to raise their nine children, though sadly, only three would live to adulthood: Richard Henry, Julia, and Mary Ann.[3] A highly religious Methodist family who brought their family and servants to prayers every morning, the Dulanys sent Richard to Dickinson Methodist College in Pennsylvania where he proved far more interested in horses than in religion or academia, which led his father to write, "without an education, my dear Richard, you can never sustain a respectable standing in society."

But Richard did! Though he never graduated from Dickinson law school, at the age of twenty, Richard Henry Dulany founded the Piedmont Hunt, the oldest Hunt in America. Seven years later, he followed family tradition by marrying well. His bride (and cousin) was Rebecca Ann Dulany, daughter of Col. Henry Rozier Dulany and Frances Addison Carter. Rebecca was one of the wealthiest young women in the world at this time, having inherited a fortune estimated at nineteen million dollars (in 1995 terms) from her English aunt Rebecca, Lady Hunter.

They traveled well and widely, this wealthy young couple. From New Orleans and St. Louis, they returned to Welbourne for the birth of their first child, Mary Carter, then went on to a grand tour of Europe, visiting London, Rome, and Paris, where their second daughter, Frances (Fannie), was born in 1851. While in England, Richard shipped fine horses home to enhance his stables and cattle to improve his stock at Welbourne. Three more children soon graced their family: John Peyton, Henry Grafton, and Richard Hunter.

The young Dulanys epitomized the well-bred aristocrats of Virginia's Golden Age. They had great wealth, a fine family heritage, were well-traveled, and owned a beautiful home. But their joy was soon to end. The first tragedy was the death of Richard's mother, Mary Ann deButts, in 1855. Three years later, his beloved wife, Rebecca, died of tuberculosis leaving Richard with five young children, the eldest of whom was just seven years old. Richard was only thirty-eight …and he never remarried.

Without a doubt, John Peyton and his son Richard Dulany were now the wealthiest men in the Piedmont. Together they owned almost 1,700 acres of

prime land, plus bonds, securities, personal property and jewelry, forty-five horses, six carriages, 357 head of cattle, and ninety-eight slaves over the age of twelve. Their combined taxable wealth amounted to well over $300,000. And that was in 1859 dollars.[4]

But even great wealth could not forestall the events that followed. South Carolina seceded from the Union in December 1860, and despite their strong family connections in Maryland, the Dulanys of Welbourne were Virginians and would heed the Southern call. It came in April of 1861, after the fall of Fort Sumter.

Richard Henry Dulany rode off on a June morning in 1861 leaving his seventy-three-year-old father, John Peyton Dulany, in charge of a vast plantation, plus his five children ranging in age from four to eleven, assorted relatives, a tutor, nursemaid, servants, and over fifty slave families. The years ahead would not be easy for any of them. Colonel Dulany's daughter Mary told of times during the war when she and her sister Fannie had only one pair of shoes between them, so whichever one of them went out first got to wear the shoes.[5]

lantry, but with the fact that wound after wound was never used by you as a means of retiring from the conflict, but as soon as you could crawl from a sick bed you were in the saddle again. To me, you have become...an ideal man.

Meanwhile, Colonel Dulany raised and outfitted with uniforms and rifles his own cadre of soldiers, known as the Dulany Troop of the Laurel Brigade. Local boys, they were, who signed up at the little hamlet of Unison.[6] Though embroiled in battles throughout Virginia, and seriously wounded several times, he wrote home to his family almost every week, encouraging his children in their studies, directing his father regarding the animals and crops, commenting on various battles and skirmishes, and always asking for their prayers.

The courage of Col. Richard Henry Dulany of Welbourne was probably best summed up by Gen. William H. Payne, CSA, who wrote:

I do not exaggerate when I say that there is no man in the State of Virginia whose splendid generosity, loyal patriotism and gallantry as a soldier I have more respect for, than I have for you. You plunged instantly into the melee...staking fortune, home and everything upon the result ...and you fought to the finish.

I was always struck not only with your gal-

Meanwhile, war swirled around Welbourne. Colonel Mosby and his Rangers found food and shelter there, as did Gen. J.E.B. Stuart and many other Confederate officers. A sad day for the Dulanys, however, was 11 September 1863, when ten-year-old John Peyton Dulany died of diphtheria. The colonel was far away and could not even get home to bury his son.

In the mean time, Union troops raged across the fields of Welbourne, taking everything from scarce meat to precious horses, and, occasionally burning its barns and fences. As seventy-five-year-old John Peyton Dulany noted in 1863, "the Yankees encamped here covering almost the whole farm," and later, "The Yankees moved in some force on Middleburg yesterday. They carry desolation in their track."

It would be heresy not to at least mention the name of Maj. John Pelham at this point. "The Gallant Pelham," as he was known, was the epitome of the Confederate Cavalier. Twenty-three, devilishly handsome, and "as grand a flirt as ever lived," he was the heartthrob of many a Southern maiden, including the young Dulany daughters whom he visited at Welbourne. He was also "gloriously courageous," accord-

145

Above: The gallant Maj. John Pelham, "as grand a flirt that ever lived," won the hearts of the Dulany daughters. With one cannon, he held off ten thousand Union troops on a foggy December morning near Fredericksburg in 1862. He was killed soon after that at the Battle of Kelly's Ford, but his memory lives on at a home, built by Mary Dulany Neville, called Pelham. Courtesy of Nat Morison.

Below: Fannie Dulany Lemmon on the verandah at Welbourne in the early 1900s.

ing to Gen. Robert E. Lee, and just a month later, on a freezing December morning, he held off the entire Union army near Fredericksburg with just one cannon for nearly two hours. He was killed three months later at Kelly's Ford. But his memory lives on at Welbourne on a window he inscribed…and at a home built years later, across the lane from Welbourne, by Mary Dulany Neville who named it Pelham.[7]

On 1 January 1863, President Lincoln issued what he thought would toll the death knell of the Confederacy. The Emancipation Proclamation interestingly applied only to those slaves in Southern states (which Lincoln did not control) but did not apply to those in Union territory, which he did control. On a rare and dangerous visit home that year, Richard Dulany gathered fifty-four of his slaves on the green saying, "I have done all I can for you. If you wish to leave, you may have your papers. But if you leave, do not come back." Few of them left, and many remained at Welbourne as did their descendants for decades after Appomattox.[8]

Due to their loyalty, and the Dulanys' wealth, Welbourne survived the bitter reconstruction period and its fields soon boasted ripe crops of corn and golden wheat; thoroughbred horses and fattened cattle again roamed its hills and hollows, and Welbourne became the center of social and Hunt life in the Piedmont. Colonel Dulany's daughters were married at the plantation: Fanny to Southgate Lemmon, a Baltimore attorney and former Confederate officer, and Mary Dulany to an Irishman, Robert G. Neville, in 1876. Henry (Hal) Dulany never married, but the colonel's youngest son, Richard Hunter, wed Eva Randolph in 1877.

The Lemmons, who lived in Baltimore,[9] had eight daughters: Frances (Fannie), Isobel, Grace, Mary, Janet, Ethel, Elizabeth, and Neville,[10] all of whom spent their summers at Welbourne. And a merry place it was indeed. "Our idea of Heaven," said Neville of her years at the fine old mansion with its deep, covered verandas where children could run and play on rainy days. Terraced rose and flower gardens, big old pear trees, and fragrant mint grew down by the stream. And a bevy of cousins—Dulanys, deButtses, Carters, Tabbs, MacKenzies, Haxalls, Dudleys, and Randolphs—lived nearby. It truly was a version of heaven and a delight for the adults as well, for the parties and grand balls at Welbourne were always the social events of the season.[11] Regardless of how late they lasted, however, attendance at morning prayers in the front parlor was always a requirement at Welbourne.

When Fannie Lemmon inherited Welbourne upon Colonel Dulany's death in 1906, the family left Maryland, moved onto the old plantation, and for several years the good life continued. A new game called polo was played on a field laughingly called "Miz Lemmon's Bottom." But the cost of maintaining such a huge plantation (and seven daughters) began to take its toll, and Welbourne began a gradual decline into what is kindly called "faded elegance."

The Lemmons' daughter, yet another Fannie, and her husband, Nathaniel Holmes Morison, a Johns Hopkins graduate and cotton broker in New York, became the next owners of Welbourne. But time continued taking its toll on the beautiful old mansion. So in the 1930s Mrs. Morison began accepting summer guests, "with the right credentials, of course."

Their three children—Nathaniel Holmes, Jr. (always called Holmes), Southgate, and Frances—also enjoyed their childhood at the old plantation…and like their ancestors, they too all married well.[12]

Holmes Morison, Jr., a New York cotton broker, wed Sally Harris, the beautiful young daughter of Stoke,[13] and their three children, Nathaniel Holmes III, George, and Eleanor[14], divided each year between New York and Middleburg. Holidays at Welbourne became a highlight of every year, for Sally Morison, an elegant lady with a keen sense of humor, always had a huge party with a towering "Christmas Gift Tree," so that every guest could choose a remembrance. These "gifts" brought howls of laughter, since they were usually outrageous.

A good friend brought Sally a similar gift one day. It was one of those long, thin, stuffed animal things filled with beans or peas to prevent wind from blowing under the door. Sally promptly threw it around her neck like a boa and started dancing around the room. Just at that moment, who walked in but Sen. and Mrs. Birch Bayh! Without missing a beat, Sally

Fannie Dulany (on horseback) and her sister Mary (on the lawn) at Mount Vernon in 1867. Their cousin Septon Herbert (on right) was curator of Mount Vernon at the time. Courtesy of Janet Dulany Roszel Tayloe.

Above, top and bottom: The parlors, full of fine old furniture and artwork, tell of a different world when life was gentler and friends visited for weeks at a time.

Opposite: The great dining room at Welbourne showcases its beautiful blue-and-white Parisian china that bears the Morison crest.

Morison graciously welcomed them to Welbourne.

After the demise of his parents and grandmother, Nathaniel Morison (or Nat as he is known) and his brother and sister inherited the family estate. But it is Nat who lives there with his wife, Sherry Weymouth, and there their children, Rebecca, Ames, and Joshua, grew up.

Magnificent portraits of generations of Carters, de-Butts', Armisteads, Lemmons and Dulanys still grace the walls of Welbourne. Old oriental carpets cover its warm wood floors; antique furniture, tester beds, beautiful repousee silver, and paintings adorn every room. But the expense of maintaining such a property is horrendous…and constant. There's always a leaking roof, plumbing, or electrical wiring that needs repair; balusters, railings, and floors to be restored; walls and ceilings to be repainted or papered, cleaning to be done; gardens to be planted, lawns to be mowed, trees to be pruned; barns, fences, and stables to be maintained. So while guests find respite enjoying the spacious grounds and serenity of Welbourne, and young lovers marry under its magnificent magnolias, the Morisons live simply in a nearby cottage.

Nat, who obviously inherited his ancestor's love of equines, maintains over eighty horses on the property, while Sherry manages and plays gracious hostess at the old mansion.

The good times may have changed from the fancy

balls and hunts of yore…but they've never ended at Welbourne. Some forty years ago, Nat and his brother George Morison began playing "stickball" on the lawn with a broom handle and tennis ball on Sunday evenings with a few friends and relatives. Nat headed up the Mets team and George captained the Mokes. (Don't even ask where that name came from). The game grew, as neighbors and visitors and little kids stopped by and clamored to play. Pretty soon, thirty or more people started coming, and forty years later, they still show up every Sunday evening between Memorial Day and Labor Day to play or cheer on their team in front of the stately columns and deep verandahs of Welbourne.

But one of the most exciting events every year evolved because George and Nat's father, Holmes Morison, loved jazz. He loved it all, from N'Orleans to Chicago to Harlem, and counted many of the early musical "greats" as his friends. So every September a Jass[15] festival is held— alternately at Stoke or Welbourne—in his honor where top artists in the coun-

Above: The wide foyer of Welbourne Plantation is filled with portraits of ancestors and antiques illuminated by a wide fanlight over the front door.

Right: Old portraits may line the walls, but the Dulany heritage continues on into the twenty-first century at Welbourne, as attested by this portrait of Rebecca Dulany Morison Shaefer, daughter of Mr. and Mrs. Nathaniel Holmes Morison.

try perform to the delight of music and dance lovers. It too has become a Middleburg tradition and invitations are prized by those fortunate enough to be on the guest list.

Rarely has such an authentic historic property as Welbourne been preserved in its original form.

Placed on the National Historic Register and into the Virginia Outdoors Foundation so that its remaining 530 acres can never be subdivided, its other claim to fame lies in the fact that the Morisons are the eighth generation of the same family to live at Welbourne! They rank among the very few descendants of early

Left: Roger Rees, member of the Royal Shakespeare Company, portrayed Nat Morison in a screenplay, entitled "Goose Creek Story," in the summer of 2001. Mary McDonnell, a Broadway and film actress plays his wife.

Below: A rare photo of Nat Morison (who usually prefers very casual dress) with his son, Ames, reviewing old Carter family records with Mrs. Anna Dees of Crednal. Courtesy of Anna Dees.

settlers who, despite tremendous obstacles, have kept a beautiful old plantation alive to be enjoyed by future generations. And for that, they deserve an accolade from all who treasure the history of the Piedmont.

That accolade is now being given. A marvelous screenplay, written by Richard Squires, was filmed at Welbourne in 2001, telling the story of a man who tries to preserve an old family plantation against all the odds of nature, finances, family, termites, and time. Entitled "Goose Creek Story" it stars Roger Rees, a member of the Royal Shakespeare Company, and Mary McDonnell, a Broadway and film actress, best known for her starring role with Kevin Costner in *Dances with Wolves*.

So Welbourne, this beautiful old plantation, beloved by generations of Dulanys, deButts', Lemmons, and Morisons, and all those who have visited and married there, will continue to sing its song of the South and live on in the history and heart of Middleburg.

The Old Church House.

THE OLD CHURCH HOUSE

*I*t was remarkable for its time, this little church in the woods. The movement to bring Christianity to the black people of the South had long been encouraged by every religious denomination, from Anglicans to Baptists, Methodists, and Quakers. It had both religious and practical implications. Recognition of slave marriages made for happier servants; religion would instill concepts of honesty and loyalty; and the idea of Heaven would create a goal for happiness, which was perhaps not attainable in this life…but possible in the next.

Black people had long been trained as master craftsmen and excelled as fine carpenters, masons, tailors, cooks, metal workers and stone carvers. Thomas Jefferson himself praised the highly skilled slaves and freed men who built his three architectural masterpieces: Monticello, the University of Virginia, and the Virginia State Capitol. Recognizing the inherent problems of slavery, although unwilling to disrupt both the social and economic systems of the South, President Jefferson abolished international slave trade in America and encouraged the movement to "Christianize" black people.

As the movement spread, John Peyton Dulany of Welbourne and his son Richard built a charming little chapel in the woods for those who tilled their soil, cooked their meals, cared for their children, and were, in many ways, considered part of their family.

The blacks welcomed the chapel and soon created their own religious services based on the spirit world of Africa and the Christian world of America. And out of that dichotomy evolved a music that was being echoed in little chapels all over the Southland.[1] Its Gullah patois,[2] low and deep and hungering, expressed the hopes and dreams of an enslaved people.

They called it "The Blues," and though only an occasional fiddle, banjo, or drum accompanied their clapping hands and stomping feet, its strong, hypnotic, rhythmic cadence was to become the genesis of jazz, country, bluegrass, gospel, and rock and roll. In fact, as a noted musician said, "It is from the Blues that all American music derives its most distinctive characteristics."[3]

And again it was Jefferson who remarked that "blacks were far more gifted

Mrs. Southgate (Fannie) Dulany Lemmon restored the old church into a guest house in the 1920s.

than whites in music and movement," and there is, of course, a delicate irony that such a creative legacy resulted from such a nightmare as slavery.

Meanwhile, the drums of Civil War soon destroyed the peaceful beat of life at Welbourne. As both Union and Confederate troops poured through the Piedmont, the little slave church became a sometime haven for Mosby's Rangers, an occasional makeshift hospital for Union troops, and soon ended its brief existence as a place of worship. After the war, horses and hay filled its walls until it was finally abandoned, as were so many outbuildings on the old plantation.[4]

Although President Lincoln granted their emancipation,[5] and federal administrators set up shop in Middleburg to offer support for blacks during the Reconstruction Era, it soon became clear that "the cruelest promise of democracy is that anybody can be anything. All men may be created equal, but they become unequal in a heartbeat…"[6]

Fortunately for the former slaves of Welbourne, because of their close relationship with the Dulany family, their music continues well into the twenty-first cen-

tury in a charming French country chapel just down the road from Welbourne, which was designed and paid for by Colonel Dulany's daughters, Mary Neville and Fannie Lemmon.[7]

Fannie, Colonel Dulany's elder daughter, married Southgate Lemmon and later inherited Welbourne Plantation. Though they had no sons, the Lemmons did have seven daughters, six of whom married…but one did not. And around her revolves the next chapter in the life of the old church, which Fannie Lemmon had refurbished in the 1920s as a guest house at Welbourne, for that's where Beth Lemmon lived out her life.

Beth was quite a lady. At thirteen, she was already noted for her beauty and horsemanship. While attending Bryn Mawr, a private school in New Jersey,[8] she developed a love of theatre, music, and literature, which were to dominate and encircle her life. Her only beau was killed during the first World War, a loss from which Beth apparently never recovered. But incredibly, for a young woman from a small Southern town, she developed a wide circle of literary friends in New York.

One of them was Maxwell Perkins—"Dean of American Editors," chief of the elite Scribner's Publishing House, the most respected and influential book editor of his time who encouraged and promoted the careers of F. Scott Fitzgerald, Thomas Wolfe, Ring Lardner, Taylor Caldwell, Erskine Caldwell, and Ernest Hemingway!

And it was Max Perkins who, for twenty-five years, conducted an intriguing correspondence with the beautiful Elizabeth Lemmon of Welbourne. In 1922, Max wrote her:

> I always greatly liked the phrase
> dea incessu patuit
> (she revealed herself to be a goddess)
> but I never really knew its meaning until I
> saw you coming toward me
> the other night.[9]

Delicious? It must have been intoxicating to a young Southern girl to have so attracted the attention of the premier publisher in America. And yet, their long, loving relationship was apparently platonic.[10] Among the cache of letters from Max, discovered after her death in a bedroom closet, there is nothing to indicate a more intimate involvement.[11]

Many famous writers came to Welbourne in those days because of Beth Lemmon, including F. Scott Fitzgerald and Thomas Wolfe, but they never stayed at The Old Church House. That was her private preserve

where few were allowed to intrude, especially children who were sternly warned to "stay away from Aunt Beth's."

Beth Lemmon died in 1993, just shy of her hundred and first birthday, leaving her historic home to her great-nephew William Tayloe, whose family stands tall in early Virginia history. One ancestor, Rebecca Tayloe, married Francis Lightfoot Lee, who represented Virginia in both the first and second Continental Congresses, and many other Tayloes have served this nation well.[12]

Thousands of books still overflow the library shelves at The Old Church House. The dining room still holds a fine old table, beautiful china, and a bay window overlooking the stone walls that line much of Welbourne Road. Along that road, in June of 1863, Gen. J.E.B. Stuart's Confederates ambushed a Union cavalry detachment.

Now every old home has its mysteries. And the Old Church House is no exception. Buried in its dingy, dirt-floored basement, a loaded 1854 Navy Colt revolver, encrusted with rust and grime, and a cavalry sabre were discovered in the early 1930s. And one cannot help but wonder what happened to the young soldier (or slave?) who hid them there?

Today, The Church House is a two-storied, brick and stuccoed home, where on a summer's evening one can hear the laughter from a wedding party at Welbourne, the clip-clop of horses, and even an occasional carriage along the graveled country lane. But it will long be remembered for the music that once flowed through its walls and for a beautiful young woman named Beth Lemmon who lived an extraordinary life in a small Southern town called Middleburg.

Above left: The gravel road and abundance of trees lend an air of tranquility to the homes along Welbourne Road.

Above right: Elizabeth (Beth) Lemmon lived at Old Church House for most of her adult life. She died at the age of 101.

Below: This loaded 1854 Colt revolver was recently found hidden in the dirt basement of Old Church House.

Above, top and bottom: Crednal. The rear view (top) of Crednal shows the evolution of the mansion around the small stone patent house in the center.

CREDNAL

oth the history and architecture of Crednal lead down intriguing paths into a distant past. Just as people have faces and personalities, so do their homes. Few perhaps more than Crednal, which is comprised of four different architectural sections and whose name is an adaptation of Credenhill, the English family seat of Robert "King" Carter's second wife, Elizabeth Landon Willis Carter.[1]

As noted at Old Welbourne, Elizabeth Carter's great-granddaughter Elizabeth French Dulany inherited over two thousand acres of Piedmont land, and thus the story of Old Welbourne, Crednal, and Welbourne became inextricably intertwined. For in 1810, Elizabeth Dulany's son John Peyton Dulany received part of this acreage, which is now known as Old Welbourne, while Richard deButts purchased a thousand acres, valued at £1,500, called Crednal. Two years later, Richard deButts married Elizabeth Dulany's daughter Louisa.[2]

Only a tiny stone patent cottage dating back a half century or more[3] lay on the land at the time with but a keeping room and sleeping loft. But before his marriage to Louisa Dulany, Richard deButts built a huge basement kitchen with three-foot-thick stone walls and incorporated the old patent cottage into a large manor house. It had an entry hall through which breezes flowed from north to south, a fine drawing room; two tall brick chimneys, one of which bears the date 1810; and three second-story bedrooms. It was a fine home and most unusual because its staircase to the lower-level kitchen and upper bedrooms stands just to the left of the front door, a rare architectural feature in either Georgian or Federal architecture.

A daughter, Millicent, was born to the young deButts' in January of 1813, after which Louisa became very ill, so Richard took her back to his home, Mount Welby in Maryland, to recover.[4] A son, Samuel Welby, arrived in 1814, followed by another daughter in 1816 (named Richardetta for her father), and they grew up at Crednal amidst their nearby Carter and Dulany cousins.[5]

Despite economic problems caused by yet another war with England, Virginia was beginning its Golden Age when corn was growing tall, cattle grew fat, and prosperity flowed. The good life for children of prosperous planters

Above, right and left: Richardetta deButts married John Armistead Carter at Crednal in 1834. Courtesy of Richard J. Lundgren of Dover, Massachusetts.

Opposite, left and right: Col. Welby Carter, CSA, circa 1861, and his father, John Armistead Carter, in his later years. Courtesy of N.H. Morison

like Richard deButts was enhanced by private tutoring; picnics along the banks of Goose Creek; horseback and carriage rides; apple, pine cone, and nut picking excursions; sleigh rides; dances; and the festivities of Christmas.

There was also a good deal of visiting back and forth between families in Maryland and Virginia. On one of those visits, Richard deButts suddenly died—whether by hunting accident or illness is unknown—and was buried at his parents' home, Mount Welby. Louisa soon married again to Edward Hall, by whom she had four more children.[6]

The Halls also have tales to tell. Son of an ancient Norman/English family, Henry Hall, a Cambridge grad-uate, arrived in Anne Arundel County, Maryland, as the first rector of St. James Anglican Church in 1698. The family acquired a good deal of land, but in the early 1800s the widow of Richard Hall, left with three young children, was deprived of her dower rights to her husband's estate by his own brothers! That lady was Martha Hall, mother of Edward who married Louisa Dulany deButts of Crednal.[7]

By 1834, another member of the Tidewater aristocracy entered the life of Crednal. He was a son of Landon Carter and Mary Burwell Armistead.[8] But John Armistead Carter (always known as Armistead), though educated at Andover and in law at the University of Virginia, was a younger son and thus could not inherit his family estate at Sabine Hall. But he married well, to the lovely Richardetta deButts in the drawing room of Crednal on a cold February day in 1834. Armistead had purchased Crednal and its property from Edward Hall, so Carters once again became masters of land they had owned a century earlier.

Five years later, tragedy touched their lives when two of their three children died within a month, in 1839. Five-year-old Edgar and one-year-old Mary Winn were both laid to rest in the tiny Crednal cemetery, probably victims of the dreaded killers of the time, tuberculosis and small pox, which often wiped out entire families. Miraculously, one child survived. His name was Richard Welby Carter, and we shall hear more of him later.

Meanwhile, Richardetta died in 1847 at just thirty-one. Armistead never remarried, and, despite owning thirty-two slaves,[9] he soon discovered that his overseers were reaping more profit from the land than he was. So he gave up farming, which considerably reduced his fortune, and entered politics. For thirty-five years, this superb public speaker represented Loudoun County in the Virginia Legislature.

Both religious and political conflict came to a head in the late 1850s, and Armistead found himself deeply embroiled in both. Religious turmoil arose when this devout Methodist, who helped to build the little chapel in Unison,[10] headed a committee of the Southern Methodist Church, which decided to break with Northern Methodists because of their opposition to slavery.

The political crucible peaked in 1861 at the convention in Richmond to decide whether Virginia should secede from the Union. Though Middleburg voted 112 to zero for secession, many Loudoun landowners, including Sen. Armistead Carter opposed it.[11] Not a popular move for someone whose relatives at Welbourne, and a dozen other plantations around the Piedmont, donned Confederate gray, as did Armistead's only surviving child, Richard Welby Carter.

Welby, as he was always known, was just ten years old when his mother died and since his father spent much of his time in Richmond, he was sent away to Hallowell School in Alexandria and then to Virginia Military Institute. Like his Welbourne cousin, Richard Henry Dulany, Welby wasn't enthusiastic about education, although they both shared a love for horses. Though Welby had a less-than-distinguished career at VMI, upon returning home to Crednal at sixteen, he bred a stable of thoroughbreds that would later make Crednal famous. He also became the first secretary of the Upperville Colt and Horse Show, and in 1858, won its coveted Silver Cup.

As his father agonized over political and religious issues, Welby raised a company of militia and rode with them to Harper's Ferry during John Brown's raid in 1859. When Civil War erupted in 1861, he reactivated his troop, outfitted them with uniforms and guns, and was rewarded with the rank of major (later colonel) in the 1st Virginia Cavalry. Six foot, two inches in height, with hazel eyes and a portly build, he cut a striking figure and rode off with all the optimism and gallantry of the Southern aristocrat. Along with his

Sophia deButts Carter with her six daughters. From left: Mary, Juliet, Mrs. Carter, Nina, Fanny, Rebecca, and Sophie. Courtesy of N.H. Morison.

Carter, deButts, Turner, Ashby, and Dulany cousins, he was initiated into the tragedies of war at Point of Rocks and First Manassas. Four years of horror followed.

But Welby's service to the Confederacy was soon marred. Though he was commended in 1861 by J.E.B. Stuart as a gallant officer, served nobly in many battles, and suffered capture and imprisonment, he was accused of cowardice for leaving the scene of battle at Tom's Brook. A court martial followed and found him guilty. He was relieved of his command in 1864.

But the verdict was appealed on the basis of bias on the part of his accuser, Gen. Thomas Rosser, and with an appeal to Pres. Jefferson Davis pending, Welby continued to serve the Confederacy. Again he was captured in February of 1865, this time by the 8th Illinois Cavalry, at Glen Welby, the home of his fiancée, Sophia deButts Carter. A former slave had turned him in and, according to Union General Geary, "were it not for his strong family connections in Virginia, he would have been shot!"[12]

These events devastated Welby's father, Armistead Carter, who lived out the war alone at Crednal. By now ill and almost blind, this old man rode on horseback alone to Richmond where he secured Gen. Jubal

Early's support to restore the honor of his only son.[13]

Six hundred thousand men in blue and gray lost their lives during the Civil War. Welby was one of the lucky ones who survived. Released from prison after Appomattox, he returned home to Crednal and Sophia deButts.

Sophia was quite a catch: well educated, fluent in both Latin and French, she was also a fine pianist and singer. Three suitors vied for Sophia's affections and therein lies a love story that could only have occurred in the midst of a devastating war.

One of her suitors was the Reverend Samuel Skinker[14] who, upon being rejected by Sophia, killed himself at Glen Welby. Another was Capt. James Keith Boswell, CSA, who penned this description of Sophia in his diary: "She combines the perfection of female beauty, an exquisite voice, a bright and cultured mind, and belongs to a family which has no superior in Virginia." His diary goes on: "I have loved you for years; I have never loved another and never can."[15] Convinced that he had to distinguish himself in battle to win her hand, Boswell was killed soon after at the Battle of the Wilderness.

The third suitor was Welby Carter. The old deButts

Above and left: Crednal as it appeared in the late 1800s and mid 1900s.

family Bible tells the story: "At Glen Welby, Fauquier County, Virginia, July 3, 1866. Rich'd Welby Carter and Sophy deButts Carter were united in marriage by the Reverend I.D. Blackwell." [16]

It was certainly a fruitful relationship, for six daughters and two sons were born to Welby and Sophia during the ensuing years.[17] Crednal, however, was going steadily downhill.

Like most plantation owners after the war, neither Armistead nor Welby had enough money left to maintain the horses, crops, and cattle that had once been the mainstay of Crednal.

But Welby continued to play the wealthy plantation owner, living the good life, enjoying a ready glass, and raising thoroughbred horses, which commanded high prices. Yet "despite the fact that his family was often in dire financial straits, he often re-

turned home after a good sale with no more in his pockets than he started with."[18] The money was gone, the slaves were gone…only pride remained.

Pride is a big word. It survived in the South because of women like Sophie deButts Carter. Welby died before both his father and his wife,[19] so it was Sophie who somehow found ways to educate their eight children (the youngest of whom was only one year old), dress them well, and instill that sense of family, culture, and belonging, which they carried on to future generations.[20] All six of Sophie Carter's daughters were married at their Crednal home where her famous eggnog recipe was served and may delight others today:

Egg-Nog Receipt
Qt. cream, whipped until a froth through; sweeten.
8 eggs, beat yolks with a tumbler of sugar. Add whites well beaten to yolks of eggs. Add tumbler and a half of whiskey. Pour in cream …beat mixture well all the time.

Then in a postscript Sophie says: "A little good brandy improves nearly everything!"[21]

It was early in the 1920s that an automobile sales-

This rare staircase arrangement leads both upstairs and downstairs to the original kitchen.

man drove out to some of the Middleburg plantations hoping to make a sale. Pulling up to the front door of Crednal, he was greeted by Sophie Carter who admired the vehicle and asked what kind it was. "A Lincoln" was the response. "Well, if you hope to sell a car around here you'd better change its name," said Sophie. Somewhat chastened, the salesman drove across the road to Welbourne where he encountered Sophie's mother, Fannie Dulany Lemmon. Again, he was asked what kind of car it was, and again the response was a crisp "You'll never sell a car around here with a name like Lincoln." Reputedly, the dejected salesman returned to Washington reporting that "there sure are some mighty strange ladies out there in Middleburg."[22]

Sophie did her best, but little was left for her children. Almost everything of value, including much of the land, the fine furniture and beautiful old silver had to be sold. A fragmented paper written by Nina Carter Tabb tells of five surviving children dividing the few pieces that remained after Sophie's death:[23]

> Nina: a dozen broken forks, a silver Cruet set, two stuffing spoons, glass salt cellars, a cracked bowl, and glass dish.
> Armistead: Carving set, china beer mug, two tablespoons, soup and breakfast plates, and a glass covered dish.

It was a far cry from the great farms, fine silver services, china, elegant furniture, and riches that were heired to the progeny of Robert "King" Carter a century earlier.

Although Sophie's daughter, Fannie Marshall, lived for several years at Crednal, after her death in 1945, it was virtually abandoned. Even family members refused to stay there as word spread that the old house was haunted. Children, especially boys who lived along Welbourne Road, dared each other to climb through its windows, race up and down its staircases, and tell spooky stories about the ghosts who walked its halls.

Finally in the late 1950s, after more than a century and a half of ownership by the intertwined deButts, Halls, Dulanys, and Carters, Crednal was purchased by Gen. Halley Maddox. The general retained local contractors John Talbott and Bud Morency to restore the old place. And it was then that another fascinating tidbit of its history occurred.

It seems that at the same time Crednal was being

Above: The spacious entry hall at Crednal today offers a lovely spot to relax with a good book.

Left: The illustrious Dolley Madison once owned these granite steps, which now lead to the entrance of Crednal.

restored, a home in Washington was being renovated, and many of its architectural accoutrements were offered for sale, including its front entry steps. They're simple actually, made of granite with curved wrought-iron railings—nothing spectacular about them, except their history. That home once belonged to the lovely Dolley Madison, wife of our fourth President …and it is her steps that now grace the entrance to Crednal.

General Maddox sold the property upon being transferred to Texas a few years later. Then in 1975, Anna and Stanley Dees became its new owners.[24] As noted earlier, Crednal has emerged in four distinct parts. It began as a small stone patent house that

Richard deButts developed into a two-story brick manor. Armistead Carter added on the west wing and the Dees completed the home with the final addition, which, however, is far from new.

In fact it dates back to circa 1830, and it was once home to Dr. John May Burton. The Dees found the old Burton house in Greene County and had it carefully taken apart and reconstructed as the east wing of Crednal. Today, Dr. Burton's portrait welcomes visitors in the hallway of his old home, while his mortar and pestle hold a place of honor over the fireplace.

Crednal's charm continues with a large pond shimmering in the distance; a pool surrounded by sheltering trees lies nearby; a large log cabin, now a tenant

Above, right and left, and below: The formal dining room at Crednal is filled with fine antiques, while a sunlit passage leads to the new dining room wing.

Above: The keeping room of old, with its bold fireplace and rough timbers, is a delightful retreat on a cold afternoon.

house, sits on a hillside; a smaller log cabin has been reconstructed as a farm manager's home; and a silvery old wooden barn has been brought in to replace the one that once held the fine horses of Armistead and Welby Carter.

And far behind the house and the stable, the old cemetery, which began in the early 1800s, lies hidden in a grove of trees surrounded by a rock wall. A handsome headstone is dedicated to Col. Richard Welby Carter, CSA, where on a brilliant afternoon, over a hundred and fifty years after the "War Between the States," a tiny Confederate flag waves in an autumn breeze.[25]

But perhaps it is the lady who lies beside him, Sophie deButts Carter, who is the real heroine of Crednal.[26]

Above: The old family cemetery in the woods behind Crednal comprises seventeen graves, dating back to 1839 when little Mary Winn Carter died at just one year old.

Above: Poor House Farm now beautifully restored as a bed-and-breakfast.

Opposite, right and left: Poor House Farm as it looked in the 1980s. The chimney still bears the initials of its builder, William Burson, and the date 1814.

POOR HOUSE FARM

"Ole Boo' is gone. So is crippled Jon Tabb who walked on his knees. Mr. Cummins, Uncle Henry, Aunt Lucy and all the others...not even their names remain on stones in the old graveyard to tell of their existence."[1]

But for over a century, from 1822 to 1946, hundreds of "po' folk" from all over Loudoun County, both black and white, lived out their existence at Poor House Farm.

The Anglican Church had always cared for indigents, but after its disestablishment as the official church of Virginia following the Revolution, it became the duty of the counties to assume that responsibility. It wasn't until 1822, however, that Loudoun County bought a 229-acre farm on an obscure backcountry road to serve as an almshouse.[2] It was a Georgian brick colonial, built in 1814 by William Burson,[3] and would be home to both former slaves and impoverished aristocrats for over a century.[4]

One of those aristocrats was none other than Benjamin Carter, son of George Carter, founder of Oatlands Plantation, and Elizabeth Grayson Lewis. Poor Benjamin. After a rather desultory showing in the Civil War, where he managed to shoot himself in the foot twice, and an unfortunate marriage to

Above: Benjamin Carter, shown here as a child, with his brother George, came from one of the wealthiest and most influential families in Virginia. He ended his life, however, at the almshouse along with his former slaves. Courtesy of Oatlands Plantation.

Susan Fitzhugh, Benjamin managed to squander his quite sizeable inheritance. A nasty lawsuit against his only brother, George Carter, Jr., alienated his entire family so he ended his life living on the bounty of the county…along with his former slaves.

Finances were always a problem at Poor House, but the Civil War years were particularly rough. In 1864, Gen. Philip Sheridan and his army of the Potomac Cavalry Corps raged through the Piedmont, burning homes, stables, and crops, including those at Poor House Farm. During the Reconstruction period, money to support the indigent became even scarcer. It took over fifty years for Loudoun County, and indeed most of Virginia, to recover from that tragic time.

Now Poor House Farm was designed to be self-supporting, and all its twenty-five to thirty "residents" were supposed to work. Well, some were really old and couldn't, some were young and wouldn't, and still others showed up with the first snowfall and left with the spring thaw. The rest fished in the creek, worked in the vegetable garden, tended chickens, chopped logs for fires, helped in the cookhouse, and

Above and opposite: An attractive sitting room, with its great fireplace, random-width floor, and cozy corner dining area, offers a nice retreat for weekend or long-time visitors.

168

plowed the fields.

But despite the lack of funds and the disparity in social background, a sense of community slowly began to evolve among the residents. Though they didn't share living quarters (a new dormitory had been built for whites while blacks used the old slave quarter) they all shared the outdoor privies, which sat on wooden platforms built over a lick of Dog Branch.[5]

And they'd also get together on the old wraparound verandah at the "Main House," share an old tale, and watch the little ones, born in the "birthing room" next to the kitchen, take their first steps. As they grew up, the mostly black youngsters were "bound out" to local farmers until they were eighteen, when they'd be given the then-princely sum of $100, plus a horse and bridle, and sent on their way.

The end of World War II brought a degree of prosperity to Loudoun County, and the number of indigents had diminished. So in 1946, the Poor House supervisors decided to sell all its 420 acres to H.H. Kelley of Bluemont for just thirty thousand dollars.[6] Turns out that the Kelleys farmed the land and sold off much of it, but never lived on the property. So the

once fine, old Georgian home, which had seen little in the way of either preservation or restoration for well over a century, slipped even further into decay.

John Talbot, a local realtor and building contractor, made an attempt to restore the old place in the early 1980s. He recognized its potential, but it wasn't until a young couple with a dream arrived on the scene that crumbling walls, which had seen so much of history, began the long journey toward reincarnation.

It began on a cold February day in 1987 when Fred Mace, a former naval officer and executive with TRW, brought his wife out to Poor House Lane. Fred Mace saw opportunity. Dorothy Mace saw broken fences and shutters, fields rampant with weeds, outbuildings on the verge of self-destruction…and refused to get out of the car! A second trip in April elicited the same response, as walls riddled with mold and the lack of a kitchen and bathrooms became apparent. "You're out of your mind…this place is a disaster," she said.

But then came September and still another visit when Dottie saw ripples in century-old windows, fine Federal architecture hidden under layers of dirt,

incredibly beautiful views over the countryside, and the seduction of an historic old house started to touch her heart. She also began to see the potential for a marvelous bed and breakfast tucked away on a country lane in the heart of the Piedmont.

Only photographs can attest to the wonders that have transpired at Poor House Farm since it was purchased by that young couple with a dream. Months of sanding uncovered old random-width floors with square-head nails under two centuries of grime. Months of scraping revealed seven fireplaces with marvelous old mantles, hand-carved dentil moldings, chair railings, and balusters. Then a new kitchen, plumbing, heating and air conditioning, and bathrooms for all five bedrooms in the main house were added, while still retaining the architectural integrity of the early 1800s.

Above: This space once served as the birthing room at Poor House Farm, but has since been turned into a bountiful kitchen, filled with antiques and meals specially prepared by gourmet hostess, Dottie Mace.

Opposite top: Years of hard work transformed the living room of the old almshouse into a charming and welcoming place.

Opposite bottom: Comfortable furnishings, good books, and old prints invite relaxation in the library at Poor House Farm.

Right and above: Old dependencies, once the cook house and slave quarter of the early 1800s, have now become guest cottages that overlook this tree-encircled pond.

Charming? Absolutely. It's a treasure of old Loudoun. The ancient kitchen where "Aunt Lucy"—who never appeared without her stocking cap and bore "eight chilluns' without worrying 'bout marryin'"—once held sway is now a delightful guesthouse as is the Overseer's Cottage. The old slave quarter has also been rejuvenated into another guesthouse. Every inch of this beautiful place sings with color and charm. Plump couches and marvelous old tester beds promise luxurious comfort; fine antiques, lovely old prints, and paintings delight the eye; and rockin' chairs on the verandah overlook fragrant gardens where only the chirping of cardinals and crickets mock the quiet of a country home.

There must lie within anyone whom life has led to distant places a longing to put down roots, to be part of a community. After twenty-two military and corporate moves, Fred and Dottie Mace found those roots and that sense of community at a derelict old property north of Middleburg.

Dottie Mace's eyes sparkle as she speaks of its history, of William Burson who built a beautiful home in a wilderness; of Mosby and his Rangers who sought refuge here; of the poor people who worked its fields and sang songs as an evening sun went down; and of all the people, farmers, tenants, slaves, and slave-owners who have been embraced by its walls for almost two centuries.

Some of them lie nearby in the old cemetery. And though all inmates who died at Poor House Farm were buried in similar six-dollar pine boxes, white quartz headstones stand apart from the black, unmarked stones in a quiet corner, memorializing the separation of races even unto death.

The beauty created by the Maces is confirmed by the guests who return here year after year, entranced by the charm of its innkeeper, its gracious accommodations, the quiet of the countryside, and the intriguing history of Poor House Farm.

Pot House as it appears today after three hundred years.

POT HOUSE

$\mathcal{L}$ike ghosts of the past, a thousand stories swirl around the building and little country crossroads known as Pot House. They begin back around 1768 when James Leith (known locally as Jamie the Scot) purchased some 620 acres of land along Goose Creek. It was most likely this canny Scotsman who built the Pot House, then sold part of it in the 1770s to a wealthy gentleman named John Kyle. Kyle built a beautiful Georgian mansion called Locust Hill (now Foxcroft School) on that land for his bride, the tragic Jane Ball, whose spirit would haunt the grounds of the old mansion for almost two centuries.[1]

The bricks for Locust Hill were made at Pot House where potters, their names long lost to history, created strong building materials out of straw and rich Virginia clay. The kilns of Pot House also produced earthenware for farmers' tables as well as the kitchens of the wealthy.

Leith then sold Pot House to another wealthy gentleman, a "dandy" named Joseph Lane,[2] who after building his own Georgian mansion, called Farmer's Delight (also with bricks from Pot House), advertised the business for sale in the Alexandria Gazette in May of 1790. It was a "two story building 60 feet in length, 20 feet in breadth…and has a room laid off under the same roof with fireplace for the accommodation of a family." A fascinating insight into eighteenth–century life emerges here, for a good potter was an essential component of a growing area like the Virginia Piedmont. And yet, the potter and his whole family were expected to live in "one room with a fireplace."

There were no takers for Pot House at the time so it was not until 1834 that Joseph Lane finally sold the property to William Benton, builder of Oak Hill, the spectacular home of Pres. James Monroe. By that time, a cluster of little buildings had sprouted around the

Above top: Pot House as it looked prior to restoration in 1985. The second story had disappeared. Courtesy of Clifford "Okey" Turner.

Above bottom: An illustration of Pot House in 1905 by Clifford "Okey" Turner. Drawn from memory of an old photograph, it shows two floors, dormers, and pillared front porch.

pottery. There was a blacksmith, a wheelwright, and a small home, which today is known as Pot House.

Benton built his own home, which he called New Lisbon (now Huntland), directly across the road from Pot House. He was quite a man, this William Benton. Not only did he become the confidante and close friend of President Monroe,[3] but at a time when it was against Virginia law to educate slaves, he taught his to read and write. And he also continued making bricks by hand, which were used at both Emmanuel Episcopal and Methodist churches in Middleburg in the 1840s.

A religious resurgence swept through the South during the 1800s and the fields behind William Benton's home and Pot House soon became the site of annual, summertime Methodist camp meetings where farm families would congregate for week-long religious revivals. The traveling preacher may have sent a "hell fire and brimstone" message, but for almost fifty years (1872 to 1930) those campground meetings offered farmers a welcome change from farm chores, along with an opportunity to see old friends and

Above and left: Complete renovation of the old house by Okey Turner resulted in a spacious foyer and a dramatic staircase leading to the upper floor.

catch up on local news. It also gave young people from isolated farms a chance to meet and fall in love, for many a romance began here under the watchful eyes of parents and preacher.

When William Benton died in 1890, history came full circle as both his home and the Pot House property were purchased by the Leith family, whose ancestor, Jamie the Scot, had owned it during the 1700s. They were a happy bunch, the Leiths, who enjoyed the good life, the fun, the songs, the exuberance of Saturday night cockfights, and the delight of a good brew. Many of them served the Confederacy and returned home to barren fields. But somehow, by the 1890s, they owned five great plantations around Pot House, including Farmer's Delight, Turkey Roost, Locust Hill, and Huntland.[4]

The little hamlet around Pot House soon became known as Leithton and boasted all of sixty-five residents. But as the Industrial Revolution combined with railroad transportation to bring goods from far-off places to local merchants, Pot House began a steady decline as a viable business. For awhile it served as a post office where the Leith brothers would sit around, chew tobacco, and tell Civil War stories. Then it became a school and later a general store. It was acquired by Miss Charlotte Noland in the 1950s and used as faculty housing and a caretaker's house for her famed Foxcroft School.

Jump ahead now to 1985 when a local contractor named Clifford "Okey" Turner and his wife, Louise Evans,[5] purchased the Pot House property. Both the little house and the original pottery had been rav-

Above, top and bottom: The original pot house and kiln (which held "a room with a fireplace" for the potter and his family in the late 1700s) is now a marvelous studio for artist and owner, Karen Casey.

aged by time and innumerable tenants. But Okey Turner saw its potential. He restored the walls of the old house, joined small wings together to create a bright new kitchen and sun-drenched patio room, which overlooks a quiet, walled garden. A spacious central entrance foyer framed by arched openings leads to charming living and dining rooms and a staircase to upper-story bedrooms.

Ten years later a talented young artist named Karen Casey acquired Pot House. Its brilliant white walls and contemporary decor serve as a marvelous background for her joyously colored impressionist and modernistic paintings. And what of the old building, 60 feet long, where potters once fired bricks for mansions and earthenware dishes for kitchens? Well, Ms. Casey transformed that into an art studio, which is filled with glorious light on even a dismal day.

Only a few remnants of the original Pot House remain today: its mellow brick walls and the old kiln still stand, as does the ancient fireplace and living room ceiling. Yet there's a mystique to a landmark that has seen so much of history. It saw potters and slaves create bricks and earthenware culled from

clay; it watched as the young men of Loudoun marched off to fight a Revolution and shuddered as bullets pierced its walls during the Civil War when the gallant 7th Virginia Cavalry was driven off by Union cannon fire. And it probably snickered (if walls can snicker) as the finest whisky in Virginia was brewed in Pot House stills during Prohibition and whisked off to the homes of local gentry.

Time seems to have forgotten the quiet little country crossroads called Pot House. No McMansions surround it nor does business or industry intrude upon its tranquility. It stands as a gentle reminder of another time, over two centuries ago, when whole families lived and loved, were born and died, in a simple dwelling like "a room with a fireplace."

Above, top and bottom: Gorgeous open countryside surrounds Pot House and its adjacent guest house.

Above and opposite: Rose Hill (front and side views) as it is now.

ROSE HILL

*1*820 was a great year. In Britain, Walter Scott published his famed *Ivan-hoe*, the ancient statue of Venus De Milo was discovered on the Greek island of Melos, Washington Irving was at the height of his career, the Missouri Compromise allowed both Maine and Missouri to enter the Union,[1] and Virginia was at the apex of its Golden Age.

Three of the Commonwealth's sons had already been elected as presidents of the new Republic,[2] and Virginia's agricultural economy was booming. There were occasional rumblings about slavery, but in the lush landscape of the Piedmont, mills were busy and schools and churches were being built. Hamlets were expanding into towns with blacksmiths, harness makers, carriage builders, shoe makers, general stores, and inns to serve an ever-growing population.

It was in the midst of this prosperity that Amos Denham built a home on 316 acres purchased from John Carter for $2,504. Located along the Ashby Gap Road (now John Mosby Highway) between Middleburg and Upperville, it was constructed of brick in the Federal style so popular after the Revolution.

Boasting two-and-a-half stories with five bays and a gabled roof, it had four chimneys, hand-carved mantles on its eight fireplaces, a central staircase decorated with hand-carved scrolling, and a wealth of finely crafted woodwork in its large, high-ceilinged rooms. It was a mansion indeed.

But who was this Amos Denham? Well, he and his second wife, Amy, came to the Piedmont from central Maryland and built this splendid home as an inn, or ordinary as it was then called, and also as a home for their eight children.[3] They farmed their acreage with the help of slaves for whom they built a one-and-a-half story brick building that still stands near the house. After Amos died in 1833, Amy kept the inn going for twenty years.[4] But after she joined Amos and two of their children in the tiny cemetery in the orchard, the house and land had to be sold.

Enter the Glascock family.[5] Long-time stalwarts of the Piedmont, this family dates back to Peter Glascock, who served in the Continenetal Army under George Washington, received a Fauquier land grant in 1784, and is credited with founding the hamlet now known as Paris. Like the richly woven threads of a tapestry, the Glascocks are intertwined with almost every other old Piedmont family so that names like Rust, Fletcher, Francis, Lake, Tavenner, Frazier, Butcher, Chamblin, Lee, DiZerega, and Peyton appear through the generations.[6]

The Glascocks' "home base" was Rockburn Farm, a pre-Revolutionary home[7] owned by Aquilla Glascock and his wife, Susanna Lake, and noted in local history as being where Col. John Singleton Mosby was hidden after being shot by Union soldiers at the Lake house. It was Aquilla's son, Thomas Glascock, who purchased the Denham house on seventy-two acres in 1853. The price was $4,700.

Thomas enhanced Rose Hill almost immediately with a new, nine-room quarter for his twenty-four slaves[8] (said to have been one of the most commodious in the Piedmont) and a huge stone granary that was, on occasion, used for slave auctions.[9] An octagonal wooden icehouse and charming stone bridge over Plum Run Creek were also added along with a two-story verandah across its front elevation. To grace those verandahs, Tom Glascock ordered a beautiful railing in an intricate grapevine design from New Orleans! It was, and perhaps still is, the only such example of hand-wrought iron craftsmanship in the county.

Thomas's wife, Emily Ann Fletcher, presented him with a son, Bedford,[10] and a daughter, Tacie, who were witnesses to a lot of history as Civil War engulfed the Southland. Rose Hill unwillingly played host to Union Colonel Vincent and his 83rd Pennsylvania troops. Its barns were burned and its provisions stolen by roving foragers, as were those of all Piedmont plantations. But

Above: Stones marking the graves of Amos and Amy Denham, builders of Rose Hill.

Right: Thomas Glascock purchased Rose Hill in 1853 for $4,700 and owned over six thousand acres before his death in 1884. Photo courtesy of Thomas Glascock, Esquire.

Rose Hill also welcomed Confederate Gen. J.E.B. Stuart and Col. John Mosby, the "Gray Ghost of the Confederacy," who often found shelter within its walls.

Unlike many plantation owners who were financially destroyed after the war, Thomas Glascock had the funds to hire both black and white workers to rebuild his farms, which soon prospered with a wide variety of crops, growing wheat, oats, and corn, as well as grazing cattle. He also sold land at vastly reduced prices to his former slaves to help them adjust to this newfound freedom. Tom Glascock exemplified the spirit of reconciliation of the 1880s "where the passions and prejudices of Civil War nearly faded out of politics and passed into a common history where motives were weighed without malice and valor praised without distinction of uniform."[11]

In spite of this generosity, by his death in 1884, Thomas Glasscock owned over six thousand acres around the Piedmont, which was divided among his grandchildren. It was Tom's beloved six-year-old

The stone barn at Rose Hill was the site of slave auctions prior to the Civil War.

Above left: Thomas Glascock's granddaughter, Tacie Fletcher, inherited Rose Hill, married George Slater, and appears here with two of her sons, Thomas Glascock Slater and George Robert Slater.

Above right: George Slater at Rose Hill with his three sons, Thomas, Bedford, and George. It is unclear as to why they were wearing military uniforms, although the photograph dates to the World War I period.

granddaughter, Tacie Fletcher (who upon the death of her mother had been brought up by her grandparents) who inherited Rose Hill.[12] Unusual at a time when many girls married at a young age, Tacie took her own sweet time to wed, but finally chose her cousin, George H. Slater, in 1905.

George came from another old Piedmont family whose local roots go back to 1729, when his ancestor, also named George Slater, received land patents near Noland's Ferry and Tuscarora,[13] while his sons owned Mount Bleak at what is now Sky Meadows Park.[14]

Tacie and George Slater added a new kitchen, a long, stately dining room wing, and also united the old slave quarter, built by her grandfather, to the main house. Their sons—Thomas, Bedford,[15] and George[16]—grew up as privileged children of the time, attending Episcopal Academy in Alexandria and riding with the Piedmont Hunt, which often started from the doors of Rose Hill.

"Aunt Moriah," their generously endowed black cook was a big part of their childhood. Seems this lady had more than her share of "temperament" and didn't get along all that well with the other servants. So when the Slaters revamped the old servants' quarters, they put in a separate door to Aunt Moriah's room so she'd have her privacy…and the others would have some peace.

When Tom Slater and his bride, Hylton Rucker, inherited Rose Hill, the Ashby Gap Turnpike passed close to the front of the house. This had never been a problem during horse and buggy days, but as automobile and truck traffic increased, so did noise and dirt from the old graveled road. In 1952, when the state decided to widen and improve Route 50, the Slaters knew even more traffic, noise, and dirt would be heading toward their front door. Fortunately, Tom Slater, an avid horseman, realtor, and mortgage banker, had friends in Richmond who were persuaded to move the road a few hundred feet to the south, allowing a tree-shaded drive and beautiful, rock-walled, terraced park area to enhance the beauty of Rose Hill.

Tom and Hylton Rucker Slater's two sons, yet another Thomas and Robert, also grew up at Rose Hill, and it is Tom, Jr., the great-great-grandson of Thomas Glas-

Below and above: Rose Hill in the 1930s, when Ashby Gap Turnpike passed in front of its door, and Tom Slater jumped its fences. Photos courtesy of Tom Slater, Esquire.

185

Above and right: The foyer at Rose Hill welcomes friends of the Glascocks and Slaters into a warm library, which is original to the house.

cock, who, with his wife and children, owns Rose Hill's 325 acres today. After attending the little Upperville elementary school, he rode twenty-five miles a day by bus to Loudoun County High School and later graduated from VMI only because he won a football scholarship. (His father didn't believe in spending a dollar if it wasn't necessary). After attending the University of Virginia law school, he joined and is now a senior partner at Virginia's largest law firm, Hunton and Williams. It's quite a firm. It had fifty-three attorneys when Tom joined in 1969, and now numbers 750 attorneys with offices all over the world.

A lovely dining room was added by Tacie Fletcher in the early 1900s.

Tom Slater is a lanky guy who strides the grounds of Rose Hill like a sixteen-year-old. He's also a gracious, charming, unpretentious man who travels the world on business and returns to Upperville to bale hay, ride horseback along Goose Creek, and touch base with his roots. Richmond has been his primary home for thirty years, but Rose Hill bears his bloodline and his history.

Sadly, both Tom's mother and his wife, Katherine Holden, died of cancer several years ago, but in 1996 he married Scott (Scottie) Newell, a joyous lady who now graces both homes and actively participates in the Garden Club of Virginia. Tom's three children, Thomas Glascock (fourth in the family to graduate from VMI), Tacie (don't you love the way Southerners carry on old family names?), and Andrew Fletcher, spent their summers and holidays at Rose Hill. Andrew and Tacie live in Richmond while Tom III and his wife Beth reside in Lexington. A seventh generation has begun at Rose Hill with a dear little girl named Julia Katherine Slater.

In 1994 the fine old home built by Amos Denham in 1820 was placed on the National Historic Register. Corn, grain, and hay still grow lush on its fields; Black Angus cattle double in size from one hundred to two hundred head by calving season, and fine horses still graze in its meadows. The stucco has recently been removed from its exterior walls revealing the soft rose color of handmade bricks, which gave Rose Hill its name so many years ago. Beautifully maintained for almost two centuries, this home is an historic gem whose inside is enhanced by old pine floors, fireplaces in every room, hand-wrought mantles, and intricate stair carvings. And, of course, antique furniture of every description (Southerners never throw anything away) is beautifully accentuated with pictures, floral chintzes, and splashes of brilliant color.

Even its outbuildings have been well preserved. The stone bank barn with its huge strong beams, once Tom Slater's real estate office, is still used by his son Robert who lives right across the road at Plum Run Farm. The original smokehouse, the old slave quarter and granary, and an unusual hexagonal ice house still remain. As do the stone markers of Amos and Amy Denham who lie near the only surviving apple tree in an orchard of the early 1800s.

Most of all, Rose Hill is a symbol of the people of the Old South—of families who built its communities, fought its wars, survived their aftermaths, and, through good times and bad, preserved its history… and their own heritage.

187

Above: Shelburne today. A close look determines where the stone of the early eighteenth-century house meets in the center with the later addition.

Opposite: A stone marker is the only reminder of the "Mountain Chapple" built by Anglicans in 1763.

SHELBURNE

$\mathcal{L}$ike silken threads slowly emerging from a cocoon, intertwining and weaving their strands into a richly colored tapestry, the residents of a stone house called Shelburne, and their descendants, have embraced arguably more families and homes and certainly more of the religious movement of the eighteenth and nineteenth centuries around the Piedmont than almost any other.

It began with a man called Stephen Roszel[1] who left New Jersey to settle in the Piedmont in 1762.[2] He soon married Sarah Chilton, daughter of a prominent and wealthy local family,[3] and it was she who initiated the Roszel dynamic. Sarah dreamed that unless she named all of her sons Stephen, misfortune would befall them. So there was Stephen George, Stephen Chilton,[4] Stephen Watters, and Stephen Wesley—a tradition in naming that has continued in the Roszel family through two and a half centuries and eight generations!

Now Virginia at this time was, of course, a British colony, and though other religions were tolerated, all residents were required to tithe and support the Anglican Church of England. Each area of a colony was divided into parishes, and in 1764, Loudoun County became part of Shelburne Parish. A tiny log cabin called the Mountain Chapple had been erected a few years earlier as an Anglican place of worship for the growing population around Goose Creek and Beaver Dam[5] along the old Shenandoah Hunting Path. And in 1763, Francis Peyton and Leven Powell petitioned the Leesburg Court for the right to "build a road from their plantations near Aldie to the Mountain Chapple." It was called "The Mountain Road," or "The Great Road." Today it's known as Snickersville Pike. It was only a wagonload wide and deeply rutted, but at least it was passable…at least in good weather.

This old stone outbuilding still stands in back of the home.

In 1767, Stephen Roszel purchased two hundred acres along Beaver Dam and the old Shenandoah Hunting Path from Joshua Duncan. He built a fine two-story stone home on his land, as well as an outside stone kitchen with upstairs servants' quarters and, of course, the usual barns and outbuildings demanded of every farm.[6]

Recognizing an opportunity, he also opened an ordinary in his home to service travelers along the Great Road, as well as churchgoers on a Sunday morning. And since the Mountain Chapple stood on Stephen's land and was part of Shelburne Parish, the name Shelburne soon attached itself to Stephen Roszel's home.

By 1773, the Anglican congregation had grown, and the vestry of Shelburne Parish had bigger plans for the Mountain Chapple. First they purchased the two acres surrounding the little chapel from the Roszels for twenty pounds. Then they ordered that the log cabin be replaced by "a church of either brick or stone, 50' long and 40' wide with walls a full 2' thick." And so it was done. In 1774, a fine new stone church opened under the aegis of its first rector, Dr. David Griffith. It even included its own glebe, a piece of farmland allotted to the minister for the support of his family.[7]

The vestry of Shelburne Parish comprised some of the most powerful people in the Piedmont: Thomson Mason, Francis Peyton, Thomas Lewis, Leven Powell, and Thomas Owsley—"Gentlemen all." Little could they envision how quickly their world would change. Just two years later, on a hot August day in 1776, Sheriff Philip Noland stood on the steps of the Leesburg Courthouse and read the "Declaration of Independence" to a hushed crowd.

Mobilization began immediately as over two thousand farmers, wheelwrights, carpenters, saddlers, merchants, and gentlemen from Loudoun County—an incredible number from such a rural area—volunteered to fight with George Washington's Continental Army. Colonels Francis Peyton and Leven Powell would spend the bloody winter of 1777-78 with Washington at Valley Forge.

Others, such as Stephen Roszel of Shelburne, served in the militia providing food and supplies to their beleaguered compatriots just as minutemen did in Massachusetts. An interesting sidelight to this story occurs in 1781 when Benjamin Franklin was in Paris negotiating the peace treaty between America and England, and his British counterpart was none other than Lord William Shelburne,[9] one of the wealthiest men in England. So rich was the Earl of Shelburne, that just prior to the Revolution, he paid £97,000 to purchase a piece of land in Gloucestershire at a time when the total average wealth of an American Southerner was just £93.

The incredible spirit of freedom engendered by the Revolution and expressed in the Constitution of the new nation called the United States, extended beyond political independence, however. That document called for "a separation of church and state," and thus the Anglican Church, so long supported by forced tithing, began a downward spiral by 1776. The new code of laws enacted by the Continental Congress made no provision for tithing and "few parsons were willing to expound the Gospel to people without being paid for it."[10] By war's end in 1783, of more than two hundred Anglican churches and chapels in Virginia, only a few survived as active places of worship. The little stone church on the Mountain Road was not among them.

Any void, whether political or religious, is soon filled. In the Piedmont, preachers of the Baptist and Methodist faiths swept through its valleys and hills like avenging angels, pulling people yearning for belief into their folds. One of those preachers was Bishop Francis Asbury, an English evangelist from Oxford who rode through Virginia and the emerging western territories spreading the gospel of Methodism.

One of his converts was Stephen Roszel, who brought along his entire family. By 1791, the stone church built less than twenty years earlier by the Anglicans was taken over by the Methodists and renamed Roszell Chapel.[11] Stephen died a year later, but his sons had grown and married well.

It is through his first son, Stephen George, that we continue the story of the Roszel family and Shelburne. He married Mary Owen and, after her death, Mary Calvert of the Maryland Calvert family. Following the example of his mother, eight of his nine sons were named Stephen.[12]

It is impossible in the twenty-first century to vividly portray the role of religion in the nineteenth cen-

Above, top and bottom: Stephen George Roszel and his wife, Mary Calvert of Maryland. He was called the "foremost Methodist Minister of his time" and named eight of his nine sons Stephen. Courtesy of Janet Dulany Roszel Tayloe.

tury, when every action and every thought was dominated by the Word of God, as illuminated by men like Stephen George Roszel. These were years of hard-scrabble existence for many farmers. Sickness took their children early. A drive to town for provisions on Saturday afternoons and Sunday "fire and brimstone" services were their only diversions from the back-breaking, unending drudgery of farming. Religion was like a dangling carrot, promising a better world in the hereafter.

So for almost a century, summer religious revivals and camp town meetings were annually the religious and social events in many small towns around Middleburg. Stephen George Roszel soon became the foremost Methodist minister of his time, a "circuit rider" who went from hamlet to village to town on horseback preaching the Word of God, as had his mentor Francis Asbury.

A haunting note occurs in Asbury's diary from February of 1808. He writes, "Today I visited the widow Roszel and her afflicted children." Was this a reference to Stephen George's son, George Washington (the only son not named Stephen), who was mentally unbalanced? Or was it the death of Stephen George's wife, Mary Owen, or of his eight-year-old son, Steven Chilton, who drowned in Goose Creek? These three tragedies were sure to impact "the widow Roszell," who cared for her grandchildren while Stephen traveled from Williamsburg and Orange to Baltimore and Philadelphia, and was often away for weeks or months at a time.

Certainly Stephen George Roszel left a strong legacy during his fifty years of ministry. He was "the firm and unwavering friend of Methodism; the unflinching supporter of her doctrines and institutions. In the dark and troublous times, he was ever-ready, among the first to peril his all in her defense…shunning no labor, shrinking from no responsibility, opposing every innovation which he deemed subversive of her prosperity."[13] Interestingly, just twenty years later, the Southern Methodist Church would separate from their Northern brethren over the issue of slavery. Yet Stephen George Roszel, who had advertised a reward for the capture of his runaway slave, Dick, in 1818,[14] freed all his slaves in his will of 1841.

His fiery son, Stephen Samuel Roszel, following in his father's footsteps, also became a circuit preacher who was, according to one journalist, noted for his "style, erudition, eloquence…and withering sarcasm."[15] Yet these two men, father and son, merged the threads of religion and society into the plantation tapestry of the Piedmont.

The first Stephen Roszel brought the Chiltons into the family. Stephen Calvert married Martha Triplett. Stephen George married Mary Calvert of Maryland and their son Stephen Samuel married Julia Dulany deButts; their son, Stephen George Asbury Roszel, married Sarah Josephine deButts. Stephen Samuel wed Rosa Dulany Hall, while Richard Julian Roszel wed Janet Southgate Lemmon, and their daughter Janet married William Tayloe. Through those alliances, the Roszels became intertwined with the Frenches, Carters, Randolphs, Whitings, Gunnells, Gibsons, and essentially every prominent family around the Piedmont!

Meanwhile, Phoebe Roszel inherited Shelburne from her father, Stephen Wesley, and life continued on its country pace, ruled as always by the seasons. Corn and wheat were planted and harvested, cattle grazed in the field, horses roamed its meadows, and though Phoebe never married, the family always came together to worship at Roszell Chapel and to share Sunday dinner. Phoebe left Shelburne to her nephew, Dr. Robert Roszell Stephen Hough, who was both a physician and a minister. Thus it was the Houghs who experienced one of the most daring escapades to occur during the Civil War.

It happened on Snickersville Pike right near their Shelburne home on an early November afternoon in 1862. Nine hundred men of the 91st Pennsylvania Infantry were marching slowly toward Warrenton. Their commander, Col. Edgar Gregory, and his staff rode at the end of the column. Four horsemen, simple privates, all local boys in the 35th Virginia Cavalry, hid in the trees lining the road watching the long column with mounting excitement.

As the last wagons passed by, they burst from the trees with the fierce Rebel Yell and guns blazing. Taken by surprise, utter confusion ensued among the Union troops, and not knowing how many Rebels were involved, they broke ranks and fled. The four horsemen promptly ordered the last three wagons to turn around and head for the Blue Ridge where the gleeful Rebels discovered they had not only captured badly needed supplies, but the muster rolls, pay records, and regimental diary of the 91st Pennsylvania![16]

Twenty-five years later, the old Roszell Chapel was torn down and rebuilt, stone by stone, just a mile away in the village of Philomont. Its first service was held in 1891, and it is still a house of worship today.

The old Roszel Chapel, which played such an important part in local religious history, was moved in 1891 to the nearby village of Philomont where Methodist services are still conducted today.

Above: This photograph, taken several years ago after the Rodger Andersons turned the home into a fantasy land, shows the original fireplace from the early 1700s. Courtesy of Roger Rozsell.

Meanwhile, Shelburne, the old Roszel homeplace of 1767, had been expanded over the years with a great north wing, which sheltered several generations of Roszels, including Sarah and her husband, John Donohoe; Sally Roszel and her spouse, Rev. John Cunningham Dice;[17] and Dr. Hough and his family.

In 1906, though, Shelburne was sold out of the family. Rodger G. Anderson and his wife, Moselle, acquired it, and having no interest in antiquity, turned the interior of the old house into a "fantasy land." Cherubs rested on fluffy clouds on a bathroom ceiling, a Chinese figurine and carved snake watched over a Buddha in the kitchen, and Egyptian posters covered the walls. Now wouldn't those strait-laced, stern Methodists have just loved that decor?

Fortunately, the Andersons' fantasies didn't extend to changing the architectural integrity of Shelburne. Except for the addition of a curving, pillared verandah, the old stone house still looks much like the farmhouse of the 1700s. It's easy to picture the adamant preachers of yore wearily riding up the gravel drive on horseback, sinking into an easy chair by the parlor fire, leading the family in prayer under a flickering gas lamp in the dining room, or trudging sadly up the incline to the old cemetery where so many of their family rested.

In 1893, Dr. Robert Stephen Roszel Hough wrote, "It may be our glory that while we never had much money, yet members of our line have had a good endowment of brains and thus have made their mark in the world."[18] A modest statement that, for the Roszels had both brains and financial acumen and have

Left and above: The old cemetery at Shelburne, surrounded by a rock wall sadly in need of repair, holds generations of Roszel descendants. Stephen Roszel VI and his cousin Roger Roszell met there on an early autumn afternoon.

owned many fine manors and plantations around the Piedmont, from Shelburne and Old Welbourne, to Glen Welby, Crednal, Seldom Seen,[19] and Denton.

It is Denton that holds a special place in the heart of the sixth Stephen S. Roszel,[20] who was born and spent his childhood there. A remarkable man, Stephen was a pilot with the RAF and U.S. Army Air Force during World War II, spent years in the oil fields of Saudi Arabia, and once, during the Cold War years, was even recruited for a special mission by the CIA. Now in his early eighties, he still teaches at the University of Virginia and pilots his own plane. No, he's not a Methodist (having returned to the Anglican faith of his ancestors), but he travels to China and Tibet every year, financing a medical mission that brings surgical and pharmaceutical assistance to those in need.

A courtly gentleman, Stephen is a lover of the Piedmont. As he and his accomplished cousin, Roger Roszell,[21] walked up the gentle slope to the old cemetery at Shelburne on a warm September day not long ago, centuries seemed to coalesce. Both are dedicated, as were their ancestors, to the betterment of humanity. Some might call it the fulfillment of a legacy. With all the other Roszel and Roszell branches and two more generations of Stephens following in their footsteps, the family will undoubtedly continue to play a large role in the richly colored tapestry of the Piedmont.

But now, let's say farewell to Shelburne and wander down a dusty road south of Middleburg to another antebellum home known as Denton.

Below and above, left and right: Denton is still reminiscent of a traditional Southern plantation home. This side view illustrates the elegance of its design. The original home built by James Adams, prior to the 1840s, later became servants' quarters for the Tines family in the early 1900s.

DENTON

*I*n 1846 America declared war on Mexico, electric lights emblazoned the Paris opera for the first time, the Potato Famine brought devastation to Ireland, the Smithsonian Institute was founded, and Charles Dickens was drawing literary attention in London. None of those events impacted the rural community around Middleburg, however.

During that year, a man named James Adams gave his two daughters, Mary Ann and Elizabeth, and their heirs equal interest in four hundred acres of land in a woodland south of town. It was called Mountain Home Farm, and a house existed on the property—a small, picturesque, two-story brick house that still stands today. James Adams lived there along with his two daughters and Mary Ann's husband, James N. Hathaway.[1]

In 1853, Elizabeth sold her interest in Mountain Home Farm to her sister and James Hathaway for four thousand dollars.[2] But when Mary Ann died, James married Elizabeth! Four children resulted from these unions,[3] and we shall hear more of them later.

Meanwhile, Elizabeth and James embarked on the construction of a big, new home. It took longer to build than expected, however, because Civil War erupted and the most experienced brick layers and artisans had gone off to fight the Yankees. But finally it was completed, this large, two-story, Italian Renaissance-style home, built of brick, but plastered and scored to resemble an Italian villa, with a wide, pillared entry.

A romantic story arose during this time. It seems that Maj. John Singleton Mosby, the legendary "Gray Ghost of the Confederacy," was a friend of the Hathaways. Now Mosby had been away from his home and his wife, Pauline, since 1861. So the Hathaways invited Pauline to visit them in June of 1863, when Mosby had arranged to be in the area.

Unfortunately, word of the rendezvous reached spies, and as the young couple slept, a Union patrol surrounded the house and stormed through the front door. Hearing the commotion below, Mosby, who stood just five feet seven inches and weighed only 128 pounds, swung out of an upper bedroom window onto the limb of a giant walnut tree, hiding within its branches for hours as Yankee soldiers searched the house and the grounds. They found his boots…his plumed hat…and his cape. But they never found John Mosby.[4]

James Hathaway outlived both his wives and lived on at the farm until his death in 1893, when he left the homestead and 126 acres to his daughter, Mollie V. Hathaway Fant. But remember that James Adams had given the land equally to his daughters and their heirs? Well, that clause resulted in a divisive lawsuit among descendents of the two sisters that was finally resolved after several years of deliberation.[5]

In 1907, Stephen George Asbury Roszel[6] and his wife, Sarah Josephine deButts, bought Mountain Home Farm, or Western View as it was called by that time, and renamed it Denton for their family home in England. It had orchards, a smoke house where hams and sides of beef were hung after autumn slaughtering, dairy and wash houses, barns, corn cribs, and, of course, stables. It was a bucolic country environment for their four youngsters.[7]

Their eldest son, Stephen Samuel (known as Sam), loved that new game that had captured the imagination of America in the early 1900s. It was called baseball, and Sam was one of its stars. Picked up as a pitcher by the Baltimore Orioles, he was later traded to Omaha. And it was in Omaha in early 1907 that he received this message from his father: "Gentlemen don't accept pay for playing sports. Come home and tend the farm!"

Sam didn't know that his father was dying. But he returned home, buried his father at the old family cemetery at Old Welbourne, and married his cousin, Rosa Dulany Hall.[8] Sam also bought out his three siblings' interests in the estate and purchased the adjacent two hundred acres from Charles Hathaway.

Sam was a gentleman farmer and avid sportsman with the Rappahanock and Cobbler Hunts. He was active in local affairs and sired four children at Denton: Stephen VI, Sally Gunnell, James Page, and Norman Fitzwilliam. They too remember childhood at

Denton as it looked in the early twentieth century. Sam Roszel sits near the porch steps while his horse stands nearby. Courtesy of Stephen Roszel VI.

Left and above: Sam Roszel and Rosa Dulany Hall Roszel in later years, after they moved back to Middleburg. Courtesy of Stephen Roszel VI.

Denton as a wonderful, carefree life.

Stephen Roszel VI remembers when he and his sister Sally rode horseback on surrounding country roads alone when he was just four years old! He recalls fondly the Tines family who lived in the brick house nearby. Their people had once been slaves but remained devoted to the Roszel family for generations.[9] Mr. Tines was the herdsman and head groom, "Mammy" Tines helped care for the house and children, and the Tines youngsters, Lester and Annabelle, helped out on the farm.

Stephen remembers the 1920s when an ice pond was built at Denton with mules hauling a huge dirt scoop with handles on either side. Later, when the pond froze hard, the ice was hand-cut into squares with crosscut saws, loaded onto horse-drawn wagons, and carefully placed between thick layers of straw in the depths of the ice house. It lasted all summer and was a great place to cool sweet, fresh watermelon.

The new Hill School, which opened in 1926, was an introduction to academic knowledge for the Roszel youngsters. They were joined by the Hulberts, Iselins, Bettina Belmont, Janet Dulany Roszel, and a few other children from well-to-do families. Then, the Hill School consisted of just two rooms in a building later known as the Iron Jockey—far different from the beautiful campus of today. Still, the tuition was an incredible $350 per year, equating to over six thousand dollars in current terms.

Rosa Dulany Hall Roszel was a lady, born and bred. A lover of art, music, literature, and the theatre, she'd bundle her children onto the train in The Plains to attend plays and concerts, musicals and art exhibitions in Washington, Philadelphia, and New York. One of the most exciting events occurred when the

James and Sally Harrison Young are the current residents of Denton, which has been in their family for over seventy years. They are pictured here on their way to the Hunt with their sons, Stirling Harrison Young and James "Rob" Robson Young. Photographed by Marshall Hawkins, 1982.

whole family piled into their Locomobile touring car and drove to Alexandria to see Charles Lindberg and *The Spirit of St. Louis* on a naval cruiser on the Potomac in 1937.

Earlier, in 1919, Congress had passed the infamous Prohibition laws banning the sale of all alcoholic beverages.[10] In the Piedmont, however, illegal stills thrived in hidden mountain areas near Hume and Linden, known as the "Free State," where even Federal agents feared to tread. But Sam had been roaming those hills all his life, and many a time he'd casually ride home on horseback with a keg or two of delicious, home-brewed whiskey or apple brandy.

Sam and Rosa's years at Denton were numbered,

however. World War I had culled many young farm workers out of the fields, and expenses soon became greater than profits. As the Depression of 1929 set in and stock prices plummeted, Sam sold their land and home and headed to Wilmington, Delaware, where he worked for DuPont for the next seven years.[11]

Robert and Sybil Young moved to Denton in 1937. Part of the New York foxhunting crowd who poured into the Piedmont during the 1930s, Robert Young served as field master of the Orange County Hunt, a role taken over by Sybil Young during the early 1940s when the men were off at war. They were active in the movement to preserve the rural environment around Middleburg, including the beautiful old maple trees that lined Washington Street until 1939, and also strongly opposed the plan to widen Route 50.[12]

Their son, James[13] (Jimmy to his friends), and his wife, Sally Fendall Harrison,[14] who is related to most of the first families of Virginia, made Denton their home in 1980. Though the acres of Denton may be rich with cattle, it is thoroughbred horses that dominate the lives of the Youngs and their sons, Stirling and Rob. In fact, Jimmy Young has been field master of the Orange County Hunt for twenty years. Interestingly, the Youngs became close friends of the late Sally Roszel, a famed horsewoman around the Piedmont, who had been born at Denton.

If any further proof of Jimmy Young's love for horses was needed, one may note that this man—who once taught English, was a high-school principal, an educational consultant, and holds a doctorate in education from William and Mary—gives no evidence of his scholarly successes in his home. His degrees hang in the tack room!

And what has become of the fine house built by James Hathaway in the nineteenth century? Well, it hasn't really changed all that much. The plaster that once covered and scored its exterior walls was painstakingly scraped off and its bricks carefully re-pointed decades ago by the Roszels. A dumbwaiter and basement kitchen were added by the Robert Youngs. Of course, it acquired indoor plumbing and bathrooms, and the huge old Delta heating system of the 1920s was replaced with a far more modern model.

But its spacious, high-ceilinged rooms, strong walls, and glistening white steps, guarded by magnificent old trees, remind us of those who built homes in a wilderness, of a famed Rebel Raider who raced to meet his love there and of the Union troops who followed, of horse-drawn carriages that rolled up to its door greeted by ladies in hoop skirts, of a former slave family who repaid kindness with allegiance, and of Northerners who preserved its history.

The thousand-and-one repairs demanded by any home that has survived for 160 years are a constant challenge that is well met at Denton by Sally and Jimmy Young. They realize a home is more than just walls of brick and plaster, and although open spaces and places where horses race over hills and valleys may be its focus, its heartbeat lies in its history, and in the memories surrounding a lovely old home named Denton.

Above: Stoke is undoubtedly one of the most romantic homes in the Piedmont.

Opposite: The rear doors open onto a lovely green park with views over the surrounding countryside.

Photographs by Jim Poston.

STOKE

*M*any tales wait to be told about the courage of women during that tragic time known as the Civil War. One of these is the story of Mary Berkeley Cox, affectionately known as Molly.

Molly was a descendant of both William Berkeley, governor of the Virginia colony in 1642, and Norborne Berkeley, Baron de Botetourt, also governor in the 1700s. Her maternal grandparents, Maj. William Noland[1] of Noland Ferry House, and his wife, Catherine Callendar, settled a large plantation called Pembroke (now Berkeley House) in the hamlet of Aldie.

These two families came together in 1821 when William Noland's daughter, Frances, married Col. Lewis Berkeley. The young couple had five children: Molly, William, Edmund, Norborne, and Charles Fenton.[2] William, the eldest son, inherited Pembroke, and the other sons inherited equally large estates around the Piedmont.

Molly married Richard Cox, scion of an old Loudoun County family who was then mayor of Georgetown. The young couple and their four children lived on a grand plantation in Washington Heights called Berleith, but as Civil War erupted, they fled back to Aldie.

They traveled first to Stoke, which lies on a hillside overlooking the Aldie countryside, a home that had been built in 1791 by Mathew Rust[3] for his bride, Martha Triplett.[4] The Rusts conveyed the house and its five hundred acres to Lewis Berkeley in 1793; his son Norborne inherited it, was married there in 1849, and by 1861, when our story begins, it was the home of Molly's youngest brother, Charles Berkeley.[5]

War is always tragic, and so it was for Molly Berkeley Cox. We begin the story of Stoke with a letter written many years after the Civil War had ended, by Molly to grandsons she had never met, telling them about a world that had vanished—a world they would never know—and one that she would never forget. She told them about their family; their Georgetown home called Berleith; her "children's pet dog, Carlos"; of their five good servants; Aunt Violet, who was the best of cooks; of Harriet, the most faithful of nurses; and of Mary, Ellen, and Mason, "our stately carriage driver who all did so much to make us enjoy life."

Then, recalling the events of 1861, she tells of their flight to her childhood home at Aldie, their arrival at Stoke, and her experiences during the Civil War.[6] This is Molly's story.

Stoke 1898

My dear little grandsons,

As there are so many miles between us, I think I must try to tell you about the War, why we had to leave our dear old Berleith, and take our stand on Dixie land with all true Southerners. We crossed the Potomac, caught sight of the Confederate flag, cried "Hurrah" and then your Grandpa left us at Stoke…

My brother, William was living at Pembroke, our old home at Aldie and [after all four Berkeley brothers and Molly's husband, Richard Cox, enlisted with the Confederate Army[7]], he begged me to move there to be with his wife, Cynthia, and Norborne's wife, Lavinia.[8] We spent an anxious summer sewing flags, uniforms for our soldiers, sending supplies to the sick and nursing the wounded brought to us from Manassas. We spent Christmas at Aldie, cut off from town and the country store [by snow and Federal troops who were already prowling the countryside] hard put to get up anything for Christmas.

On the first of March [1862] our army fell back from Manassas and as we did not wish to be left behind our lines, we must go south. I left with my four children and Harriet [the children's nurse] and Mason driving the carriage. The roads were almost impassable. We hoped to go as far as Warrenton but only got to Evergreen[9] where your Uncle Edmund was sick with pneumonia. We started out early the next morn-

ing but did not reach Warrenton [a distance from Aldie of 18 miles] until 6 P.M.

Cold, hungry and tired, we stayed at the Warren Green Hotel where after a miserable supper, found it so cold because the wood had all burned out. The proprietor had a shutter split up the next morning so we had a little heat before we left on the last train [to Richmond].

From this point on, Molly and her children moved from place to place, often on a moment's notice, as battles raged around them. Traveling over dark roads at night with only a lantern to guide them over rustic wooden bridges that posed great risk to a loaded carriage or wagon, they stayed with cousins, in boarding houses, wayside inns, and at the Episcopal rectory in Hanover, Virginia.

At one point Molly says, "The only gleam of happiness that came to me outside of the weekly visits of your grandfather, was the birth of another child [Richard Cox, Jr.]. The only other pleasant memory was a visit from Mrs. Robert E. Lee who was able to walk into the house unassisted, though soon after was crippled by arthritis."

And then sadness, as Molly lost a little daughter. "This was a very wet winter and little Ellen went into a decline and was buried before we left the rectory." At the same time, she worried about her brothers who were all engaged at the Battle of Gettysburg: "It was sometimes days before we had any reliable news and the suspense was hard to bear. Three of my brothers were wounded in Pickett's charge and all were captured and interned in prison camps."[10]

By now we had to make shifts to get along …my dresses were cut over for Bessie [Molly's daughter Elizabeth] and white napkins furnished gowns for [Richard] my first war baby. The Rectory began to be too small for us so we moved to a rambling old house named Redclyffe with cheap furniture on the Pamunkey River.

One night a courier came from my husband to move me and my children back to the old rectory in Hanover thinking we'd soon be taken by Yankees at Redclyffe. At daylight we began packing trunks onto the most indifferent wagon and team of mules you'll ever see. We heard firing…the roads were narrow…and we had to

Stoke as it stood after the Civil War when Richard and Molly Berkeley Cox made their home here.

turn aside to let 20,000 troops pass by.[11] We had to cross a ford and our buggy got stuck and would not budge. Then a soldier rode up to say they expected firing there in fifteen minutes. I didn't dare show I was alarmed...but I saw tears rolling down Alice's dusky cheeks. We finally reached the rectory late that night. I was so tired.

General Lee and my brothers were encamped nearby expecting to be attacked at any minute. Campfires encircled the house. Early the next morning we were told we must leave immediately for we were between [armies]. We were soon on the road. No breakfast even for the children for there was no corn meal, milk or water. We rode [in wagons] further west into Goochland County...but it was difficult to find shelter.

Finally we reached an attractive old house, white with green shutters. My room held a wooden bed with only one sheet, which smelled of fish. The children's pallets were made of blankets so thin you could have darted straws through them. But they were so tired they could have slept on the floor. Twelve days we spent here...but our children took whooping cough. And that August, I had another baby, Custis, who had no flannel to keep him comfortable when winter came...

The only great event of this winter was the marriage of our children's faithful nurse [Harriet] and we tried to make it festive. With goose eggs at $25 [Confederate] a dozen and butter $25 a pound, the cake was costly. But the wedding was performed...and the bride wore the children's present...a pair of hoop earrings set with aquamarines.

Then came the end...our army was forced to surrender.

Above, top and bottom: The detailed moldings and woodwork in the library are found throughout Stoke. Rose draperies lend warmth to a busy corner where George Morison can often be found working at his grandfather's desk.

Incredibly, despite wounds, illness, capture, and imprisonment, all four Berkeley brothers survived the battles and hardship of war.[12] As did Molly's husband, Col. Richard Cox. But it was a different world to which they returned. The Coxes did not go back to their beautiful estate of Berleith, for that was "now in the occupancy of the negroes. The trees around it have been cut down and negroe huts have been built in the yard."[13]

So the Coxes and their five children returned to Stoke where another son, Thomas, was born in 1866 and died just a few years later. Compared to Berleith it was probably a rustic affair with but four rooms down, four sleeping rooms above, and a kitchen in the basement. But many Southerners returned to charred fields and silent chimneys…so although she would never forget Berleith or the experiences of war, hopefully Molly found some comfort at Stoke.

In 1907, the Coxes' children sold Stoke to Col. Floyd W. Harris, a gentleman of means, taste, and a great story. "I'm a real Virginian," he always said. Floyd, you see, was born in the area west of the Blue Ridge just before it became West Virginia in 1862. Graduation from West Point took him to Indian frontier duty in the territory of Washington and then to Belgium as a military attaché. His next assignment, during the Spanish-American War of 1898, was to the Philippines where he served under Gen. Arthur McArthur. And then, Floyd Harris was posted as an attaché to the royal court of Austria.

Vienna was then the social epicenter of Europe: a magical, dazzling place where the music of Strauss echoed through Shoenbrunn Castle's gilt-paneled halls, the famed Lippenzanners performed their marvelous feats, and Sacher's offered rich caffè and tortes to the nobility and their guests. Colonel Harris was one of them. He rode and hunted with Emperor Franz Joseph, enjoyed royal hospitality, and became a close friend of the royal family. This exciting, intoxicating world was a feast few Americans had ever imagined.

Upon retiring from the military in 1907, Colonel Harris and his wife, Eleanor Truax (whom Floyd had met during his time in the Washington Territory), returned to Virginia and began looking for a home. They found there an old house sorely in need of renovation, hidden away on a hillside overlooking Aldie. It was Stoke.

During the following years, the Harrises turned the old place into a stunning Italianate chateau. They added two two-story additions, each boasting a hipped,

Above, left and right: Eleanor Truax Harris and a charming painting of her daughter Eleanor.

tiled roof and French doors, rich wood detailing, classical balusters with fluted trim, wide, pillared verandahs, and a ballroom (which was also a trophy room filled with animals from Colonel Harris's African safaris).

The gardens were Eleanor's domain. An avid horticulturalist, she imported daffodils and narcissus (virtually unknown in Virginia in the early 1900s) from England and Holland and was delighted when a daffodil was named "Stoke" in her honor in Cornwall, England. But Eleanor also spread English and American boxwood throughout the Piedmont by giving slips to all her friends, as well as to the Middleburg Community Center and Oak Hill.[14]

Five children joined the Harris household,[15] including a daughter, Sarah (Sally), who married the son of one of Middleburg's oldest families. Nathaniel Holmes Morison of Welbourne, or Holmes as he was known, was a New York cotton broker, so the family divided their time between New York, Stoke, and Welbourne. When Sally Morison died, Stoke was left to all five of her children, but none could afford to support it, so it sat vacant for over a decade.

It was the Harrises' grandson George Holmes Mor-

Above: This portrait of Col. Richard Henry Dulany, CSA, great-grandfather of George Morison, hangs in a place of honor in the dining room.

Above and left: Col. Floyd W. Harris decorated the paneled ballroom of Stoke with exotic animals from his African safaris.

ison, who upon graduating from the University of Virginia, came home to Stoke to begin its restoration. And only he can tell this part of the story.

I've loved this place since childhood when I spent part of my summers here…and I adored my grandfather [Col. Floyd Harris]. He was very affectionate, a great raconteur, and I loved being with him. When he died, well into his nineties, one branch of the family insisted that everything in the house be sold. I was only twelve at the time and had all of $100 saved up. And they let me, "the little boy," buy all the animal heads in the Trophy Room for my $100. I never took them from Stoke…they remained there for the whole time it stood empty.

It was a love of the place, a love of old things, a love of family, and memories of my grandfather…which drew me back here.

Eventually, George Morison, who later became president and CEO of Patient First Corporation, acquired the interests of the other heirs, and Stoke soon became his raison d'être.[16]

A good decision? Perhaps. An easy life? No. The late twentieth century was far different from the Golden Age of the Piedmont. And perhaps only in the South, where family and heritage and sense of place mean so much, would accomplished men like George Morison of Stoke and his brother, Nat Morison of Welbourne, spend their lives supporting the homes of their ancestors.

Every old plantation has a touch of romance, but Stoke has more than most. It began back in 1791 with a young man, a lieutenant in the Revolution, Mathew Rust, who built a home there for his bride, Martha Triplett. The Rusts sold the property a few years later to the Berkeleys[17] and moved east to Arcola. Then Charles Berkeley was married within its

208

It was from these foyer steps that a Union soldier wheeled around to shoot Col. John Mosby

walls before he went off to fight in the Civil War.

So the walls and halls of Stoke speak of both tragedy and romance. Today Stoke is a paean to the Confederacy. Portraits of Robert E. Lee, Stonewall Jackson, John Singleton Mosby, and Col. Richard Henry Dulany, the great-great-grandfather of George Morison, peer down from every wall. Stoke, you see, sits on one of the highest points in the valley between Bull Run and the Blue Ridge and was thus an ideal observation post for Colonel Mosby's Rangers.

One day, a Union soldier burst through the front door, flew up the staircase, then wheeled around on the landing to shoot a Rebel he thought was Mosby. But the bullet missed its mark and hit the casing of the drawing room door, where its imprint remains to this day.

The romance continues, for Stoke has long been haunted by at least three spirits. You don't believe in ghosts? Well, George Morison swears that one of them kindly repaired two antique candlesticks in the dining room just a few years ago!

Music also owns a haunting quality, and the music of Stoke is jazz. Holmes Morison adored Jelly Roll Morton, King Oliver, and all of New Orleans's glorious music. So a memorial jazz service was held in his memory in 1974 at Upperville's Trinity Church. The traditional, solemn rolling of drums was followed by the funeral dirge, and then finally the triumphal blaring of trumpets signaled the ascent of a loved one into heaven. It was on that day that the Goose Creek Jass and Ragtime Society[18] was born. And for the last thirty years it has sponsored an annual festival hosted alternately at Welbourne and Stoke by Holmes's sons, Nathaniel and George Morison.[19]

Over two centuries have come and gone since Mathew Rust built his home on the hills over Aldie. And it has been 150 years since Molly Cox sought sanctuary there. So, yes, Stoke bears a faded elegance today. But its wide entry hall, high-ceilinged drawing rooms, pillared archways, and gardens tell of a world

Opposite bottom, above, and opposite top: The magnificent grounds of Stoke include a shaded colonnade, a quiet spot for contemplation, and an enchanting peony garden.

most of us have never known. They invite contemplation, the reading of a good book, or perhaps simply the enjoyment of a great park and vast fields where horses roam, forests stand tall in the distance, and bright spring wildflowers emblazon a mile-long winding drive that leads to the magnificence and romance that is Stoke.

Now some will say that the Civil War is over…so let it be. But Southern culture, a belief in the right of citizens to determine their own destiny, the memories of a young woman named Molly Berkeley Cox, and a man's love for his heritage live on in an incredibly beautiful corner of the Piedmont called Stoke.

Above: A gravel drive, brimming with flower beds, leads to Trappe Spring.

Opposite: The front elevation of today is far different from the tiny stone cottage of the mid 1700s.

212

TRAPPE SPRING

*L*egend has it that back in 1743, a small Huguenot settlement was nestled at the foot of the Blue Ridge along a dusty lane called Trappe Road. That legend also claims that a young Huguenot couple, Mathew Boucher and his wife, lived there in a one-room stone cottage while tending the land, called the Manor of Leeds, for its owner, Thomas, Lord Fairfax. While working in the fields one day, rampaging Indians roared over the Blue Ridge and brutally slaughtered the young farm couple; though incredibly, their five-year-old son, Peter, survived! It's said that his mother's ghost still haunts the old stone cottage searching for her son and that the killing gave rise to the name "Trap Road."[1]

But fifty years later, in 1793, Rawleigh Colston, a wealthy Welshman of Jefferson County, Virginia, joined his brothers-in-law, James and John Marshall, in the purchase of the Manor of Leeds. This was a fascinating relationship, for John Marshall, who as a young officer served with George Washington's Continental Army, went on to become the chief justice of the Supreme Court. And though an acknowledged conservative, he believed, as did President Washington, in a strong federal government as opposed to Thomas Jefferson's stance on states' rights—an opinion that brought Marshall into conflict with many of his fellow Virginians.[2]

Rawleigh Colston's share of the Manor of Leeds encompassed almost forty thousand acres of prime land in Loudoun and Fauquier Counties.[3] And therein lies a far more romantic tale of how Trappe Road got its name.

It was Rawleigh Colston's grandson, also named Rawleigh,[4] who came to live on the Leeds property. Like many young Virginia aristocrats of his era, he spent time abroad, and while in France, fell madly in love with a beautiful Parisian actress. They married and soon returned to Loudoun County where Rawleigh built a home for his bride. By joining together two existing stone buildings with a center hall, and adding second-floor bedrooms, finely mantled fireplaces, and handcrafted chair railings, he created a manor home that he called Snowden. Some said it resembled Mount Vernon.

Well, it may have been grand by Virginia standards, but to a Parisian actress accustomed to fine town homes—with marble floors and gilded ceilings, ornamented furniture and silken tapestries—plus glorious candlelight services at Notre Dame, the excitement of French theatre and fine dining and parties and balls, the isolation of life in a wilderness was a disaster! Writing to her friends she called Snowden "La Trappe," and two centuries later, the name remains.[5]

Rawleigh and his bride returned to Paris for the birth of their first child, Rawleigh Edward Colston, in 1825 and never returned to Virginia.

Snowden then became home to Rawleigh's brother, Thomas Marshall Colston, a graduate of Yale, and his wife, Elizabeth Fisher. A little headstone for their eight-month-old son, George Fisher Colston, dated 1837, still rests in the garden.

In 1845, Snowden was sold to a nearby farmer named William Littleton, which is another old name around the Piedmont dating back to 1766. William's sons served in the Revolution and the Confederacy and intermarried with the best local families.[6] His

Snowden Manor was a fine Virginia home in the 1800s, but a "trappe" for Rawleigh Colston's beautiful French bride who missed the excitement of Paris.

granddaughter Sarah Elizabeth married Townsend Frazier, who acquired over two thousand acres of prime land in Fauquier County, where he developed the largest cattle industry in Northern Virginia and gained the title "Cattle King of the Piedmont." Although Townsend and Elizabeth built a grand new manor home called Newstead Farm, their daughter Catherine Frazier lived on at Trappe Springs until 1941. Thus the property remained in the Frazier family for well over a century.

The next owners, Gen. Samuel Cummings and his family, only stayed at Trappe Spring for twenty years. By this time, however, the old Snowden manor house was so dilapidated that the Cummings moved into the nearby stone cottage that had once been home to the Huguenot farm couple of 1743. By the time Julie Moran Greenough[7] arrived on the scene in the 1970s, the Snowden house had been sold off to an adjacent farm, and so Mrs. Greenough also moved into the stone cottage, which required a small fortune to restore. Along with the restoration, she added a delightful, sun-filled solarium, large living room and kitchen to the original parlor, and dining room.

In 1980, it was Louise Ziluca who found Trappe

Above top: This large living room was added in the 1970s by Julie Greenough.

Above bottom: The headstone of eight-month-old George Fisher Colston who died in 1837 rests in the garden at Trappe Spring.

Spring in the quiet of the Piedmont countryside. Like many accomplished couples who migrated to the Piedmont in the late twentieth century, Paul and Louise Ziluca had seen much of the world, its beauty and its dangers. Louise, a Radcliffe graduate with a degree in anthropology, and Paul, a Harvard alumnus and colonel in the United States Air Force, moved fourteen times from Japan, Korea, and Vietnam to Germany and Greece.

During the early 1970s, Paul became assistant deputy chief of logistics for the U.S. Air Force in Europe, with twenty thousand American Air Force personnel under his supervision. This was a stressful role, to be sure, but nothing compared to his next assignment.

In 1976, at the height of the Cold War, the Communists were doing everything in their power to destabilize U.S.-Greek relations. Paul Ziluca was sent to Greece as commander of Hellikon Air Base, a key

U.S. logistics and intelligence post on the outskirts of Athens. Dangerous? The Soviets, using a Bulgarian front group, called the "17th of December," had already assassinated CIA Station Chief Jack Welch and bombed sixty American officers' cars, as well as the commissary and NCO Club! Paul Ziluca was their next target. Eight civilian guards accompanied him everywhere, from home and office, to restaurants in the Plaka (the old Athenian marketplace), to theatre at the Acropolis, even on holidays to the Greek Islands. After three years in Athens, Paul decided it was time to retire.

Surrounded by sixteen acres of beautiful trees, an old red barn, and fine stable, Trappe Spring became both a refuge and the beginning of a new life for the whole family. Paul's love of horses expanded with membership in three Hunts (Piedmont, Middleburg, and Rappahannock), and the walls of the stable are covered with ribbons won on Trappe Spring horses

This tiny room, with its low-beamed ceiling, is the original part of the home.

216

Right and above, left and right: Memorabilia of Guiseppe Garibaldi, Italy's most-beloved hero, fills Trappe Spring. Among them is a heavily carved wooden chest that once belonged to Garibaldi, his portrait on the dining room wall, and a photograph of King Umberto of Italy, great-grandson of King Victor Emmanuel, and Paul Ziluca, great-grandson of Garibaldi.

by his daughter Isobel, granddaughter Josephine, and, yes, a few by Paul himself.

One of the first things the Zilucas did was purchase the old Snowden manor house and thus reunity the original properties.[8] But the two-and-a-half-century stone cottage (the oldest building on the land) is the real jewel at Trappe Spring, for it is a veritable treasure trove of history. Paul Ziluca, you see, is the great-grandson of Italy's most beloved hero, the Patriot of Genoa, Giuseppe Garibaldi.

Garibaldi's personality and love for his country and the common man brought upon him the formidable wrath of the Catholic Church and the Austrian and French Empires. But with the support of King Victor Emmanuel, Garibaldi brought about the reunification of Italy in 1861!

In 1863, Garibaldi, this "Man of the People of Italy," wrote to Pres. Abraham Lincoln saying, "Posterity will call you the Great Emancipator…a more enviable title than any crown…and greater than any mundane treasure." And it is as "The Great Emancipator" that Lincoln is known to this day.

It's strange to enter a country house, on a dusty, rutted road in Virginia, and find unusual treasures such as Garibaldi's portrait on a dining room wall, his bronze bust on a deep window ledge, and his memorabilia everywhere. But also proudly displayed on a shelf is a photograph of Garibaldi's and King Victor

Emmanuel's great-grandsons, King Umberto II of Italy and Col. Paul Ziluca of the United States Air Force.

The Zilucas, though, are also busy with current issues. Louise serves on the Virginia Commission for the Arts and Paul on the State Republican Central Committee and Virginia Outdoors Foundation. When not working or riding, they relax with their children and grandchildren around the sparkling pool and huge cabana they've added nearby, and delight in the beautiful gardens that seem to spill over with brilliant color at every turn.

The serenity of their little piece of the Piedmont is

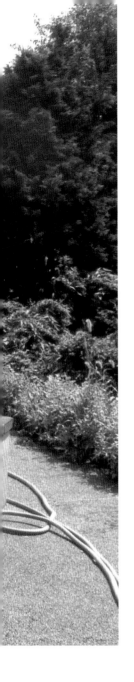

interrupted occasionally, however, by the appearance of a ghostly young woman who has been heard by many residents of Trappe Spring.[9] But whether she is the young Huguenot farm woman of the 1740s, who was murdered by Indians and is still searching for her child, or the lovely young French actress who felt "trapped" at Trappe Spring, we will probably never know.

Above top: The great cabana, built by the Zilucas, retains whimsical remembrances from their travels.

Opposite: Sheltering trees and gardens surround a sparkling pool.

Above bottom: An old buggy with red wheels welcomes visitors to Trappe Spring.

Vine Hill, the fine Federal home of 1804, still stands proudly on a hillside overlooking Middleburg.

VINE HILL

*I*t was the height of Virginia's Golden Age. She was a beautiful Southern belle named Jane Noland.[1] He was Charles Love, whose ancestors
dated back to 1744 in Prince William and Fauquier Counties.[2] And
they were in love.

Charles ordered a beautiful brick home to be built by Richard Cochran for
his bride in 1804. It sat on a hillside just west of town, where unending Southern views overlooked rolling meadows and green hills. Federal in style and
built of handmade bricks that had been hauled all the way from Fredericksburg, it boasted high-ceilinged rooms, eight beautifully carved fireplace mantles, a curving staircase of solid walnut sweeping gracefully off the entrance
foyer up three stories, and a basement kitchen with huge, indestructible poplar ceiling beams.

In the early 1800s, large plantations surrounded Middleburg, but the village
itself had only one other "great home" like the Loves' mansion.[3] A dozen small
homes, artisan shops, and an "ordinary," now known as the Red Fox Inn, lined
its main street where oxen-pulled wagons raised clouds of dust and the anvil
of the blacksmith beat a steady tattoo. Children's voices and the soft singing
of slaves filled the air, along with the snorting of pigs, cattle, and chickens,
which roamed at will.

Sadly, the Loves had no children, so after Jane's death in 1838, the mansion
was sold to Col. Asa Rogers, his wife, Ellen Lee Orr, and their five children.[4]
Asa, the quintessential Southern gentleman, was a Middleburg merchant who
advertised in 1834 that "Asa Rogers is now receiving from Philadelphia and
New York his spring supply of goods." But Rogers also owned Leven Powell's
old mill and was a Loudoun County magistrate, a member of the state legislature, and a colonel in the Virginia militia. He was noted for treating all men
kindly, including his nineteen slaves. With his son Arthur, an avid horticultur-
ist, he planted fruit trees of all kinds and arbors rich with grapes so that the
property soon became known as Vine Hill.[5]

As winds of Civil War drifted down from Boston to Virginia, Asa, now a man
of almost sixty with five grown children, joined the Confederacy in 1861 with

Vine Hill as it appeared in the early 1900s.

the rank of general. He was far from home when his wife, Ellen, and his daughter Lucy Lee, wife of Episcopal Rev. Otis A. Kinsolving, both died the following year.

A fascinating insight into the character of this Southern gentleman occurred on a brutally hot day in June of 1863. General Rogers had returned to Vine Hill as Union troops under the command of Col. John Gregg stormed through Middleburg and, after a punishing battle at Mount Defiance, forced Confederate forces back through the woods toward Upperville. As evening fell, Asa Rogers opened his home to the Union officers and treated them with the utmost courtesy.[6]

Asa's son Arthur Lee Rogers, after attending Virginia Military Institute, graduated in law from the University of Virginia, married Charlotte Ann Rust, daughter of Gen. George Rust, and also joined the Confederacy. Arthur raised a company of Loudoun artillery, fought at the Second Battle of Manassas,

served on Gen. Stonewall Jackson's staff, and was severely wounded at Chancellorsville. Yet in the waning days of the war, he designed the third and last official flag of the Confederacy. After returning to Vine Hill, Arthur Rogers died of war wounds in 1871.

The war had devastated his father. Forced to sell his home and lands to pay his debts, the old general left for Richmond where a grateful legislature appointed him as state auditor. Years later, in 1887, he returned home to die and rest in Old Sharon Cemetery.

A young, handsome Englishman named Harry Wood-ward arrived in Middleburg about that time. An accomplished and noted actor with winning ways, he soon captured the hearts of both the town and young Fanny Cochran, whom he married in 1898. In one of those delicious turns of fate that so permeate Southern life, the young couple moved into Vine Hill, built by her great-grandfather Richard Cochran almost a century earlier.[7]

222

Fanny immersed herself in founding the Middleburg Chapter of the Daughters of the Confederacy. She and her friends raised funds for a Civil War memorial—the famed "Circle of Stones" at Old Sharon Cemetery—and a building called Confederate Hall that was erected in 1909. Meanwhile Harry Woodward ran the farm and delighted the town by singing and acting on the stage of Confederate Hall, which soon became the social center of town.

Fanny and Harry Woodward had just one child, a daughter named Katherine who was born deaf. Upon inheriting the old house, Katherine, or "Foffy" as she was called, turned it into a shop called "The Beaver Hat," featuring antiques and country furniture to serve the growing tourist market. Middleburg by the mid-1900s had become home to many wealthy Northern horse breeders and political folk from Washington, so quite a few old Virginia family treasures found their way from Foffy Woodward's shop to homes around the Piedmont.

Foffy loved her old home and happily pointed out its eight mantles, which were all hand carved with a penknife! But the kitchen was her pride and joy. It was the first part of the house to be built and had a dirt floor until she took up the rich-toned pine attic boards and had them laid in the basement kitchen.

Unfortunately, she was unable to maintain either the house or the grounds of Vine Hill, and it had long since seen its glory days. For a while it served as a rental property, but then along came a man named George L. Ohrstrom, Jr., who would change its destiny.

George Ohrstrom's father was a horse lover who published a small newspaper called *The Middleburg Chronicle, A Sporting Journal*, which in 1949 became *The Chronicle of the Horse*. He and the late Alexander MacKay-Smith began collecting rare books, paintings, etchings, sculpture, and memorabilia about horses, racing, hunting, and horse history, resulting in an enterprise called the National Sporting Library.

This love of horses was not just an interest, it was a passion that he passed on to his son, George Orstrom, Jr., who in 1968, moved the entire enterprise to the old mansion at Vine Hill. As the circulation of *The Chronicle* expanded to biblical proportions across the international equine community, so too the equine collection eventually outgrew the fourteen rooms of the old mansion.

As a result, two beautiful stone buildings were constructed adjacent to the Vine Hill house, on grounds where Jane Noland and Charles Love once

The history of Vine Hill as a private home changed in 1968 when it was purchased by George Ohrstrom, Jr., who made it the home of The Chronicle of the Horse, *the "Bible" of the equine world. He appears here with his wife, Jacqueline, and the late Alice duPont Mills. Courtesy of Ken Tomlinson.*

rode, where Asa and Arthur Lee Rogers raced off to fight for the Confederacy, and where Harry Woodward jauntily mounted his steed to saunter through town.

A well-designed reception room holds little alcoves for study, and gracious, knowledgeable volunteers greet visitors to these lovely new quarters. Paintings and awards won by famous steeds fill the walls and exhibit cases, while rooms with seemingly thousands of shelves, provide a temperature-controlled environment for one of the most valuable equine book collections in the world. Running the entire length of one wall hangs a panorama, dating from 1821, illustrating the coronation of King George IV of England.

Some say that the National Sporting Library is Middleburg's best kept secret, although it undoubtedly

These two new buildings, which seem to blend into the hillside around Vine Hill, are home to the National Sporting Library. Photo by Jim Poston.

Above, bottom and top: Sunlight streams through the front fanlight door into empty rooms in which the only furniture is a great old bench bearing the date 1696.

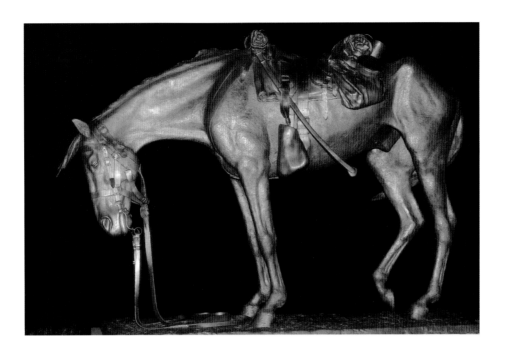

accounts for a good portion of the myriad tourists who pour into town annually. It also serves as an historic research center for scholars and an educational experience to those who are unfamiliar with Hunt Country lore.

But as for the home built by Charles Love for his bride back in 1810? Well, it still sits on the ridge overlooking Middleburg, where a glorious yet incredibly poignant bronze sculpture by Tessa Pullan, entitled "The War Horse," stands upon the green. Donated by the late philanthropist and horse lover Paul Mellon, its inscription reads: "In memory of the one and one-half million horses and mules of the Confederate and Union Armies who were killed, wounded, or died from disease in the Civil War."

The horse's head hangs low, somehow reflecting both the tragedy of that terrible conflict and the weariness of the old mansion. For although its brick walls still stand proudly on the hillside, exhibiting the simplicity and elegance of early nineteenth-century, Federal-style architecture, its interior walls and ceilings, old pine floors, fireplaces, hand-carved mantles,

and spiraling staircase speak of two hundred years of wear and neglect.

Restoring any old home to twenty-first century standards is a major—and very expensive—undertaking. Some small restoration has already begun, however, for the old mansion is currently being leased to the Paul Mellon Foundation. Hopefully, Vine Hill will survive to tell its tales of nineteenth-and twentieth--century life in Middleburg to future generations of historians and horse lovers.[8]

Above: "The War Horse," sculpted by Tessa Pullan, donated by Paul Mellon, and photographed by Jim Poston.

Opposite: This finely constructed circular staircase, which winds up three stories at Vine Hill, once knew the steps of Cochrans and Loves, of Gen. Asa Rogers, CSA, and a handsome English actor named Henry Woodward.

WHAT'S IN A NAME

*O*nce upon a time, as all good stories should start, when people lived in widely scattered small villages or farms, people had just one name. John, or one of its variants, was the most popular for men and appears in almost every language: Johannes in Greek and Latin, Johan or Hans in Germanic lands, Jan in the Netherlands and Scandinavia, Jean in France, Ivan in Russia, Ian in Scotland, Evan in Wales, and Juan in Hispanic countries.

But as small villages grew into towns, it soon became necessary to differentiate one Johannes or Jan or John from another, usually by a description of some sort. Thus surnames were born, and they basically evolved from four different sources.

Kinship and Nicknames: a son of John became John's son (Johnson); a son of Robert might be Robert's son (Robertson); also Robin's son (Robinson) or Dob's son (Dobson).

Occupation: John the farmer or John the blacksmith would be called John Farmer or John Smith.

Place Names: someone who lived near the town well would be known as John atta (at the) well, or Atwell, while a traveler from the English capital was known as John London.

Personal Characteristic: grey-haired or a good runner, one would be identified as John Grey or John Lightfoot.

So Johnson and Farmer, Smith, Atwell, Wells, Grey, and Lightfoot soon became surnames, passed down from father to son for generations. Since the thirteen colonies were settled primarily by English, Scots-Irish, Welshmen, and Germans, Piedmont names still reflect that heritage today. But they also reflect the invasions of Britain by Romans, Anglo-Saxons, Vikings, and Normans.

Since there was no standardization of spelling until the mid-nineteenth century, names were often spelled as they were heard—phonetically. Thus the German "bauer," meaning farmer, became the English Bower or Power, while the French "fils," meaning son, became Fitz as in Fitzhugh. Tayler, Taylor, Tailor, and Tayloe all indicated someone who made clothing. Beans became Binns, and Kerr became Carr.

Many names also succumbed to the English (and Southern) penchant for slurring syllables. Thus "town" became "ton," as in Washington, and Credenhill became Crednal.

So for those who love trivia, here are the origins of some family names and places that have resonated around the Piedmont for a long, long time.

Adams   Kinship: English
A son of Adam was known as Adam's son, then simply Adams.

Albers   Kinship: French
The name Albert in French is pronounced "Al-ber"—the "t" is silent. Thus the child of a man named Albert was called Albers or Albert's son.

Allen   Kinship: Norman/English
When William the Conqueror arrived on English shores in 1066, one of his companions was Aleyn de Fergeant, Count of Brittany. Aleyn soon became Allen, first as a baptismal name and then as a surname in the 1279 rolls.

Armistead   Place: English/Danish
A hermitage, or "hermit stead," was pronounced "armit-stead" in England. Thus someone from such a place or who lived nearby, became known as Armistead. The "stead" dates back to the Viking invasions of England in the eighth century, and the name appears long before 1379 on English rolls.

Asbury   Place: Scandinavian/English
Originally "Askeby" then "Ashbury," meaning a town where Ash trees were prevalent. (The Scandinavian suffix "by," the German "burg," and English "bury," all mean "a town.")

Ball   Kinship: English
A "Ball" was a son of Baldwin. It became a very popular name for animals as well and was used by Chaucer for a horse and for Henry VIII's dog, who was once lost in the forest of Waltham. The Ball family of Virginia became prominent through the maternal heritage of George Washington.

Bedford   Kinship/Place: Old English
The name "Bed" originated as the proper name "Beda," which appears in Somerset County, England, prior to 1000 A.D. Combined with "ford," a place where a river or stream could be crossed, it became Bed's Ford. By 1273, Jordan de Bedford appears in the rolls in County York. There is also a County Bedford, so someone from there would likely assume it as a surname.

Benton   Place: English
The place where a river or road bent often became a settlement or town. Thus someone from a "bent-town" became Benton.

Berkeley   Place: Saxon
The British pronounce their vowels a bit differently than Americans, so the word "bark," meaning birch trees, became "berk." The family probably originated (as did the name) with the ancient Saxons of Barking, around 900 A.D. in County Kent. The Barks (Berks) lived near a lea (meadow) and thus the patronymic "Berkeley," which in England is still pronounced "Barclay."

Beveridge   Place: Norman French
A fascinating name that dates to the Norman invasion of England in 1066, when mundane Saxon names were replaced by more attractive French appellations. Thus "Bev"—from the French "beau"—was added to a rugged crag in Dorset to become a "beautiful ridge," or Beveridge.

Beverley   Place: Norman
See "Beveridge." Beverley ("Bev" plus "lea") was a "beautiful meadow."

Binns   Place: English
The prominent eighteenth-century Binns family, who served for eighty-seven years as clerks of the Loudoun Court, would probably not be overjoyed to hear that their name originated from a field of "beans" in Northhamptonshire.

Bolling   Place: English
A little river runs through County Chester named Bolling, which gave rise to Bollington. Bolling appears as a surname in Somerset as early as 1529.

Breckenridge   Place: German/English
"Brachen," in both Germany and Scandinavia, indicates a wild place, overgrown with thickets and weeds. A "ridge" lies over a valley. Thus a Breckenridge came from a location in England that meets those criteria. I have not located the name, though, in any English place or name references.

Buchanan   Place: German-Scots
Originally from the German "buch" or book, Buchanan became a parish in County Stirling, Scotland, then spread throughout England. The family was allied with the MacCormick clan of Scotland.

Burden   Place/Occupation: English
A township in County Durham, it originally meant the annual obligation or payment required of a tenant to his lord—i.e., days of work, percentage of crops, or silver coin.

Burton   Place: Old English
From the Old English "Boue," a field that lay above a "ton" or town, we get Burton. Since high places were often used as places for defense, a Burton indicates a fortified town. In England, there are at least twenty-nine parishes bearing this name, which appears in tax rolls as early as 1379.

Carlyle   Place: Celtic
Few Celtic names survived the Roman, Anglo-Saxon, Scandinavian and Norman invasions, but Carlyle is one of them. Its journey took it from the Celtic god Lugus, to Luel, to Carleol in 1108, to Cairlell in 1129, and finally to Carlisle and Carlyle. A car, cair, or caer is a hill, which is where churches were almost always located. It is the seat of County Cumberland.

Carr   Place: Saxon/English
Originally "Kerr," which meant a low-lying meadow. Those who lived near a kerr took it as their surname. It appears in the 1273 rolls in both Yorkshire and Lancaster Counties.

Carrington   Place: Saxon/English
From the same root as Kerr and Carr, there was an ancient English village of this name dating to 1067.

Carter   Occupation: English
Literally, one who carts or hauls things from place to place: a mover or, sometimes, a traveling merchant. The Carter influence in Virginia began with two brothers, John and Thomas Carter, vintners of England, who arrived to Virginia in 1649.

Chapman   Occupation: French/English
The French "chape," meaning a hood, led to "chapeau," meaning a hat, thence to a chap maker or chapman: a hatter.

Chinn   Place: French/English
"Chene" means a canyon or deep crevice in France. It was anglicized to Chinn by the seventeenth century in England. Joseph Chinn was one of the first settlers in what is now known as Middleburg around 1728. His home is currently known as the Red Fox Inn.

Chilton   Place: Old English
From "cild" or child of a noble family, who upon reaching maturity was given a farm of his own. Thus Chilton means a "child's town."

Collette   Characteristic/Kinship: French
"Collet" means a collar or neck and came to indicate someone who was straight-laced. But "Collette" was also a girl's personal name and would have been used as a surname (Jean de Collette) for her son.

Cox   Personal characteristic: English
From Chaucer to Shakespeare, stories of young boys whose actions and attitudes, similar to the cock—the strutting barn fowl—abound. The name survives as a testament to "Cock Robin" and boys who emulated the fowl's feisty traits.

Dabney   Kinship: English
Englishmen have always loved nicknames, and, as noted previously, their vowel pronunciations differ from American English. Thus someone named Robert would have a son nicknamed Dob, which was pronounced "Dab." Dabney thus indicated a son of Robert.

deButts   Place: French/English
An English "Butt" and French "Butte" both meant a mound or small hill. Thus a deButts is one who lived on or near such a place. In England, the name had an early significance with archery since bowmen would practice their skills on hillsides.

Denton   Place: Celtic/Middle English
As early as 1086, an old Celtic town named Denbury in Devonshire existed. Later, a "dean" or valley became den and joined with "ton" so that towns called Denton arose in many parts of England. Those in Yorkshire were the largest, but the name Denton appears in many places as early as 1279.

Dudley   Place: Saxon/English
The Old Saxon name "Dudda" gave rise to Dud Lea—a meadow owned by a man named Dudda. Dudley was an important market town in County Worcestershire.

Dulany   Place: Irish
The Gaelic "Dubhshlaine," from dubh, meaning black, and "slaine," a river, was anglicized to Delany in the 1600s. The name became Dulany or Dulaney upon Thomas Dulany's arrival in Port Tobacco, Maryland, in the early 1700s. It originated in Counties Leix and Kilkenny, Ireland.

Evans   Kinship: Welsh
A son of Evan (the Welsh equivalent of John) and a popular baptismal name in Wales.

Fairfax   Personal characteristic: English
Literally, "fair-haired." This name appears as early as 1300, when "fair" meant blonde and "fax" meant hair (not a means of communication).

Fenton   Place: Old English
A "fen" was a marsh or swamp. Fenton (Fen Town) lies in County Cumberland. The surname first appears with Gilbert de Fenton in 1273.

Fletcher   Occupation: Anglo-Saxon/English
Of Anglo-Saxon origin, it took root in Sussex then spread through England. A Fletcher was an arrow maker. The fletchers' guild had a monopoly on wood of the Aspe (Aspen) tree, which was the finest wood for swift missiles.

Furr   Occupation: German
Whether this Furr family of Loudoun originated as "Foer," meaning a forest, or "Fohr," a Fir tree, is unknown. In either case, it indicates a woodsman.

Gibson   Kinship: Norman/English
A son of Gilbert. It's interesting to note that the "l" in many Norman/English names was not pronounced. Thus, for example, Walter sounded like "Water" and Gilbert became "Gi-ber."

Glascock: Occupation: Old English
This originated as "Glascote" in County Warwickshire. "Glas," or glass making, had begun in England by the twelfth century, but the word also pertained to all kinds of materials. There is no reference to glass being manufactured in Warwickshire, however, so most likely when combined with "Cote," a cottage, it simply indicated a place where materials were stored.

Gulick   Place: German/Dutch
Originally "Guelich": someone who came from that city on the Rhine.

Hall   Place: English
A "hall" was a pretentious home, and someone who lived there (or worked there) would take it as a surname, as did Roger de la Halle in the 1273 rolls.

Harrison   Kinship: English
A son of someone named Harry, or Harry's son. Harry was a diminutive for Henry.

Haxall   Place: English
Originally Hawkeswell, this derived from the personal name Hawke. Thus a well owned by Hawke became Hawke's well or Haxall. It appears as early as 1273 in County Suffolk.

Hough   Place: English
A "how" or "hough" was a hill. Thus someone who lived on a hill became Hough. Someone from a town on a hill became a Houghton.

Howell   Kinship: Welsh
This is not a Piedmont name. I include it in honor of Ross Howell, my publisher and a true Virginia gentleman. It originated as Hoel in Wales and first appears in the Pipe Rolls of 1154 and in 1313 as Howel of Waleys.

Humphrey   Personality: Anglo-Saxon
This name has Germanic roots and appears in early English records as both a baptismal and surname. Germanic names combined Teutonic virtues, such as strength, tenacity, and bravery. Humphrey includes two of those: "hum" (a bear cub) and "frei" (free). Thus Humphrey symbolized someone with those attributes.

Janney   Kinship: Dutch
Jan is the Dutch equivalent of John. Janney is a son of Jan.

Keatinge   Kinship: English
A Keatinge is a son of Kit, which is a diminutive of Christopher.

Lacey   Place name: French Norman
Laci was a town in Normandy. Illbert (Gilbert?) de Laci appears in the Domesday Book of 1085, the census of all residents of England after the Conquest.

Lane   Place: English
Though the Lane family was prominent here in the 1700s, their origins may have been humble, for the name simply indicates someone who lived in a narrow passageway.

Lee   Place: English
Though it originally indicated someone who lived near or on a lee or lea (a meadow), Lee is arguably the most popular name in Virginia. It began here with Thomas Lee, who established a great estate in the Tidewater.

Leith   Place: Saxon/Scots
The old Saxon name for a steep slope was "lythe," but in Scotland, a leith was a meadow. So either meaning may apply.

Lemmon   Baptismal name: English
Leman was a man's baptismal name and later became a surname that appears as Lemmon, Leeman, Leaman, and Limon. An English quip once went: "There are two Lemons in the House of Commons but only one Peel."

Littleton   Place: English
Littleton (a small town) appears in at least eight English counties. Used as a surname, it indicates someone who came from such a place.

Loudoun   Place: Scots
The Barony of Loudoun lies in Ayrshire and dates back to the twelfth century. Baron James of Loudoun was the first to use the name.

MacKenzie   Kinship: Scots
The first king of Scotland in 850 A.D. was Kenneth or Kenzie. The prefix "Mac" indicates a son of a man named Kenneth—a noble name indeed.

McCarty   Kinship: Gaelic Irish
The McCarty clan is one of the oldest in Ireland, widely represented in County Cork. "Mc" indicates a son of Carthaigh or Carty.

McCormick   Kinship: Gaelic Irish
A son of Cormac. The clan originated in Ulster.

McGhee   Kinship: Scots-Irish
A son of Hugh (known as the diminutive Ghee) once lived in Ulster on the Antrim coast, where the McGhees (also shown as McGees) were a prominent clan. In Scotland the name is MacGhee.

McMahon   Kinship: Gaelic/Irish
Mahon in Gaelic means "bear," a beast to beware of, as was Brian Boru, ancestor of the McMahons of Ireland. The family is strong in Counties Clare, Monaghan, and Thomond. McMahon was a son of such a man.

Marshall   Occupation: English/Norman
A marshal in England was originally a farrier, or one who shoed horses. In France, a marechal was a member of the cavalry. Both meanings appear in English records, so take your choice.

Mercer   Occupation: English
A "mercer" was a draper or clothes merchant. The "Mercer's Guild" was a prominent organization in England and its members were often wealthy.

Morison   Kinship: Norman/English
A son of Maurice or Morris. It appears in Northampton rolls as early as 1272.

Mosby   Place name: English/Scandinavian
The Christian name Morris combined with the Scandinavian "by," meaning a village, became Moresby in County

Cumberland and then Mosby.

Noland   Characteristic/Kinship: Irish Gaelic
From the Gaelic word "nuall," which meant "shout," became the name of the Chiefs of the Barony of Forth in County Carlow. In early times, they held a hereditary office under the Kings of Leinster and were a noble clan.

Osteen   Place: Germanic
This name could have at least two different roots. Ost, in German, means East. Oster, however, means Easter. While steen, which was originally stein, means stone. So Osteen could indicate either someone who lived near the East stone (or eastern ridge near a town) or near a place called the Easter Stone.

Palmer   Nickname: English
One who carried palms while on a pilgrimage to the Holy Land, was referred to as a "palmer." It was a common surname in England by 1273.

Payne   Baptismal name: French/English/Irish
It's hard to believe that "Pain" was actually a baptismal name, possibly originating from the French word for bread. But it was indeed a birth name that then became the surname Payne. It gravitated from England to Ireland in the fourteenth century where it took root as "Payneston" (Payne's town) in Leinster and Tipperary.

Peyton   Place: French
Another fascinating name that may have arisen as "Paix Town" (peace town) or simply "pey town" (country town) after the Norman invasion. Though its origin is obscure, it is undoubtedly French. It appears as "Payton" in County Hereford in 1594 and as Peyton in County Devon.

Poston   Place: Anglo-Saxon
A tribe of Anglo-Saxons settled an area, circa 1086, called Poscetnetune, which later became the villages of Poston in Dorset and Somerset.

Powell   Kinship: Welsh
The Welsh equivalent of the Irish "Mc" or Scots "Mac," meaning "a son of," is "Ap," but the "A" was dropped. A Powell was thus a son of Paul. Leven Powell arrived in this area in 1759, served with General Washington at Valley Forge in 1778, and founded the Town of Middleburg in 1789.

Randolph   Personality: Scots/Norman English
To the early Picts or Scots, "ran" meant "fair," and "ulph" meant "help," thus a Randolph gave "fair help." It was a popular given name before the Norman invasion of 1066 and first appears as an English surname in 1200 with Richard Randolph, bailiff of Yarmouth. In Scotland, Thomas Randolph was created earl of Murray in 1313.

Rector   Occupation: German
From the German "recht" meaning "right," the original application described someone who was the head or rector of a church, school, or institution.

Rogers   Kinship: German/French
Originally hrodgar, meaning fame and spear in Germany, it became Roger in France and was brought to England by the Normans. Rogers is simply a contraction of Roger's son.

Roszel   Place: Scandinavian/Norman
When the Vikings swept along the coasts of England and France in the eighth century, one "Sveide the Viking" settled along the Normandy coast at a spot he called "Rozel." ("Roz" means castle, as well as "red," and "el" was an ancient word for water). Later generations of the family adopted Rozel as their

surname. One of them, Hugh Bertrand du Rozel accompanied William the Conqueror to England. In America it became Roszel, Roszell, Rossell, and, sometimes, Russell.

Rust   Place/Descriptive: Scandinavian
Another fascinating name. The Vikings were known for their red hair. Their influence survives in names like Russell, Rozier, Rust, and Ross. In the Anglo-Saxon annals for the year 893 A.D., after England had been invaded by Vikings, a description is given of a forest called the "weald," which extended 130 miles all the way from Hampshire to Sussex. These lands were not arable and were used only for swine, but several estates are mentioned there, one of which was Rust Hall in Sussex. Then in the thirteenth century, Rust appears as a baptismal name in County Norfolk. It probably originated from the red clay of the area and like many other similar names is Scandinavian in origin.

Shelburne   Place: Anglo-Saxon/Scots
A "shal" or "shel" to the Anglo-Saxons was a "shelf"; a "burn" to the Scots was a small flowing stream or river. Thus a "shelburn" was a shelf or piece of land overlooking a flowing body of water. In England, "burn" often appears as burne borne or bourne.

Slater   Occupation: Germanic/Middle English
Originally "sclater," meaning one who worked with slate.

Smith   Occupation: German/English
One of the most common names in Germany, Schmidt became equally common in England and America as Smith. There were goldsmiths, silversmiths, iron smiths, blacksmiths, brownsmiths (who worked with copper and brass), plus redsmiths and greensmiths (don't ask me what they did!). In 1901, there were over 900,000 Smiths in England. In America, Longfellow paid tribute to their craft in his poem "The Village Blacksmith."

Spilhaus   Occupation/Place: German
"Spiel" had many meanings: a field drawn by lot, a lookout, a gambler, or a minstrel. Combined with "haus," meaning house, it could indicate the home of a farmer, watchman, gambler, or musician.

Stoke   Place: Latin
The Romans who conquered England in the second century left a heritage, and from their word "stuppa" derives the word "stoke," which means a small place or village. It simply implied a place where a family lived. In fact, of the sixty-six parishes of that name in England in 1901, all but one were combined with a family name such as Stoke Poges or Stoke Bishop.

Swaart: Place/Descriptive: Germanic
Originally Schwartz in the German, it became Swaart in the Netherlands, but retained the same meaning: black. This might have indicated someone from the Black Forest area, or a blacksmith, or someone of swarthy complexion.

Tabb   Occupation: English
A Tabb, a contraction of tabberer, was a musician who played a tambourine. The name first appears in Northumberland in 1273.

Tasker   Occupation: English
An old English rhyme begins: "A tisket a tasket, put it in the basket." Thus a "tasker" was a laborer charged with a specific job. By the fifteenth century, it pertained to a thresher or reaper in many parts of England.

Tavenner   Occupation: English
An inn or tavernkeeper. This heritage is particularly interesting because many of the Tavenner families around the Pied-

mont were devout Quakers who eschewed all liquor and spirits.

Tayloe   Occupation: French/English
A tailor, tayler, tailer, taylor, or tayloe was a cutter of cloth or maker of clothes. Taylor, or one of its variants, became the fourth commonest surname in England, preceded only by Smith, Jones, and Williams. The name originated from the French Tailleur, but the Loudoun Tayloe family holds royal ancestry dating back to Charlemagne and William the Conqueror according to a genealogy prepared for Mr. W. Randolph Tayloe in 1962. (Courtesy of Mr. Julian Roszel and Mrs. Janet Dulany Roszel Tayloe.)

Triplett   Occupation: Anglo-Saxon
A "trip" was a herd of goats or swine and gave root to the names Tripper and Triplett, meaning one who herded those animals (as shepherd is to a sheep herder.) Tripp also became a baptismal and surname that appears as early as 1273.

Turner   Occupation: English
A "turner" was one who worked with a lathe. A skilled occupation, which ranged from making fine drinking vessels to manufacturing tools and simple objects like beads, turners appear in the rolls of 1273, as well as in Chaucer, who spoke of the Miller of Trumpington who could "turn" cuppies.

Twining   Place: English/Welsh
"Twyning," as it was originally spelled, meant a place or town that lay between two rivers.

Washington   Place: Old English
Originally Wesyngton, a manor owned by George Washington's ancestors in County Durham during the twelfth century. The family adopted the manor name as their surname. A later ancestor, Laurence Wesyngton, a prosperous wool merchant, built another home in Northhamptonshire in the sixteenth century called Sulgrave Manor, which became the family's ancestral home. A portrait of George Washington, by Gilbert Stuart, now hangs over the mantle in the Great Hall of Sulgrave.

Welby   Place: Scandinavian/Old English
A "wel" or "welle" was a spring, and "by" at the end of a word indicates a Viking village. Thus Welby was a village around a spring. (Note that when "by" occurs at the beginning of a word, as in "Byford," it means by or near a ford.) There are still towns named Welby in Counties Lincoln and Middlesex, where it first appears as a surname in 1273.

Wiltshire   Place: Anglo-Saxon
A river runs through the county of Wiltshire called the Wylye, and a town called Wilsaeton derived from that name in the year 800 A.D. By the year 870 A.D., the name became "Wiltunscir," which later became Wiltshire.

Woodward   Occupation: English
Someone who looked after the forests of a land owner was a "ward" (or warden) of the woods.

Young   Kinship: Middle English
A nickname to distinguish between a father and son bearing the same name, as in James the Younger or simply James Young. Later, this distinction became Senior and Junior. Hugh le Yunge appears in the 1273 rolls of County Oxford.

NOTES

PREFACE & ARCHITECTURAL NOTES

1 Excerpted from *The Journal of Nicholas Cresswell, 1774-1777*; kindly provided by Mrs. Janet Dulany Roszel Tayloe.

2 This figure came from the Civil War Historical Museum at Harper's Ferry, West Virginia.

3 From *Bingo Night at the Fire Hall* by Barbara Holland, Harcourt Brace and Co., 1997. Reprinted courtesy of Barbara Holland.

4 The word "slave" originated back in the early Middle Ages when northern Germanic hordes swept across Europe. The conquered Slavs of Eastern Europe gave rise to the term "slave."

5 *The Washington Post. Book Review, Jonathan Yardley, July 14, 2002.*

6 Ibid. Walter Percy.

7 This quote is from *Architectural Treasures of Early America* by R.F. Whitehead and F.C. Brown.

ASPEN HILL

1 Chinn was originally the Norman "Cheyne," which means "canyon." The name was anglicized early in seventeenth-century England.

2 Three passengers on the Mayflower were James Chilton and his wife (who both died during the first "sickness") and their twelve-year-old daughter Mary. Mary married John Winslow who arrived at Plymouth in 1621. Whether this family is related to these Chiltons has not been researched. However, the Chiltons were very prominent in early Piedmont records. Col. George Chilton married Ann Lee and was a large landowner in 1759; Sturman Chilton served in the Revolution; Samuel Chilton was the attorney assigned to defend John Brown and his sons at Harper's Ferry in 1861; Joseph Chilton and his wife, Ann Smith, owned the plantation known as Chilton and were grandparents of Judge James Keith, president of the Virginia Court of Appeals.

3 The third possibility seems most likely since all the Aspen Hill property reverted to Sarah Chilton's brother, Cuthbert Powell of Llangollen, upon her death in 1838.

4 We know that there was a house on this property prior to 1666 when it was sold by Burgess Smith to Charles Chinn, because the contract specifically mentions "houses and appurtenances." Also the construction of the house, especially the basement kitchen, is more indicative of eighteenth century rather than nineteenth-century workmanship.

5 Caleb Rector was captured and died in prison; Welby Rector rode with Mosby and was killed near Berryville. The original Rector house is now owned by the John S. Mosby Heritage Area Association.

6 The Tabb family were the owners of Glen Ora, which appears in *Old Plantations and Historic Homes around Middleburg, Volume I*, by this author.

7 See the chapter on Crednal in this volume.

8 Much of the information in this chapter and the quote from the Richmond newspaper was secured from Mr. MacKenzie Tabb III of Richmond, to whom the writer is much indebted.

9 Although the Tabbs had been living at Aspen Hill for several years, Nina did not purchase the property from the Bangs until 1920.

10 Louise Whitney married into the Mellon family. The Whitneys owned Aspen Hill from 1945 to 1964, per Mrs. Minna Reese Whitney Marston.

11 Some believe this building to have been a smoke house, but it does not have the wall vents that were essential for such a building. Due to its location close to the main house, it more likely lodged house servants.

BRIAR PATCH

1 See the chapter on Mercer House in this volume for information on Charles Fenton Mercer.

2 For more information on the DiZerega family, please see the chapter on Mercer House in this volume.

3 Hillcrest shows on the Yardley-Taylor map of 1853 with the DiZerega name, so it was probably part of the 1843 sale of the 1,300-acre Mercer land to Augustus DiZerega.

4 Nothing is known about William Adam. He was apparently not a member of the prominent local Adams family and may simply have been a tenant farmer.

5 Appreciation, as always, is given to Eugene Scheel for this story, which appeared in the Loudoun section of *The Washington Post* on 18 June 2000.

6 Sleepy Hollow has been chronicled in an earlier volume entitled *Old Plantations and Historic Homes*, by this author.

7 Hillcrest had two other owners prior to this time, but neither remained long or impacted the history of the property.

EXNING

1 Valentine Peyton (1686-1751) married Frances Harrison and represented Prince William County in Williamsburg at a time when all of what is now Fairfax and Loudoun Counties were part of Prince William.

2 The children of Valentine and Frances Harrison Peyton were: Robert, Craven, Henry, Eleanor, Francis, John, and Valentine.

3 The Anglican Church was the established faith of the Virginia Colony and thus a powerful force. A vestryman, always chosen from a wealthy family, was an influential member of the community.

4 Of the seventy-five plantation owners around Middleburg, only eleven signed these "Resolutions."

5 Henry Peyton was shot on 12 November 1776 while trying to capture a deserter from the Continental Army.

6 The author has found no definitive proof that Francis Peyton lived at the manor now known as Exning. However, some evidence suggests that he did. 1) Francis's father, Valentine Peyton, owned its eight hundred plus acres and sold 214 of them to his son Robert. The balance would equate to the six hundred plus acres owned by Francis, which lay "southwest of Aldie," per the 1765 Tithe List. 2) In contemporary archives Francis is said to be living "five miles east of Middleburg" and "southwest of Aldie," which is a fairly close, though not exact, approximation to Exning. 3) In another account, Francis is called a "neighbor of Leven Powell's," and Powell owned the mill and stone mill house at the end of Exning. 4) In 1763,

both Powell and Francis Peyton petitioned the Leesburg Court for a road to be put through from their properties to the "Mountain Chapple." 5) Francis Peyton owned twenty-five slaves per the Loudoun County Tithe List of 1758, which indicates a large plantation. Although other locations have been explored as Francis Peyton's home, no other possibility has come to light thus far.

7 Townsend Peyton served in the 57th Regiment, First Battalion, under Capt. Robert Powers, as an ensign or flag bearer, a role typically given to younger boys.

8 Francis Peyton died in 1806; his wife, Frances Dade, died in 1814; in 1802, Francis Peyton, Jr., married Frances Washington Ball; Townsend Dade Peyton married 1) Harriet Colston Beale and 2) Sarah Yates.

9 The close relationship between the Peyton and Lee families is reflected in the number of early intermarriages. During this period alone, in 1831, Susannah Peyton married William Lee, and in 1840, Alfred Lee married Margaret Peyton.

10 Bolling Haxall, who married Lavinia Noland, was the son of Barton Haxall. Bolling's cousin Rosalie Haxall married Powell Noland, son of Col. Burr Powell Noland, CSA, who owned the estate known as Chestnut Hill. He built a home in Middleburg called Burrland for Powell and Rosalie.

11 There may have been a name for Exning prior to this time, but it does not appear in any local records. Exning, in Suffolk, England, was the home of the Haxalls and supposedly the birthplace of St. Etheldreda. It is named for the Exe River.

12 Fannie was the daughter of Dr. William B. Cochran (17th Virginia, CSA) of Middleburg.

13 Bishop Dudley married three times: 1) Frances "Fannie" Cochran of Middleburg who bore him three children; 2) Virginia Rowland Fisher, with three more children; and 3) Elizabeth Aldridge, who at her demise in 1901 had an estate worth $28,000,000, bore Bishop two more children.

14 Anne Haxall and Thomas U. Dudley, Jr., were married in 1901. Bishop Dudley's daughter, Fannie, married Henry R. Woodward, a noted English actor who settled in Middleburg. See the chapter on Vine Hill in this volume.

15 Mount Recovery is known locally as the old Chinn property. After Rowland Farm burned, it was rebuilt and renamed Wolver Hill by Oliver Iselin.

16 The fire at Rowland Farm began on the third floor and thus many of its treasures were saved, including antique furniture and portico columns, which now stand between the kitchen and family room at Exning.

17 Polly Dudley's birth surname was Potter, but she used Walker, the name of her stepfather who raised her. The Dudley's first son, Thomas U. Dudley (1903-48), was a graduate of VMI and Lehigh, and worked as a chemical engineer at DuPont. He died of tuberculosis in Saranac, New York. He married 1) Fairfax Harrison and 2) Helen Quimby. His daughter, Jane Dudley, was raised by her grandmother, Anne Haxall Dudley, at Exning.

18 The other two sons of John Rowland and Polly Dudley are John Rowland, Jr., and Arthur Sayres.

19 The mill was built by Henry Peyton in 1753 and later owned by Leven Powell who named it Sally Mill, in honor of his wife, Sarah Harrison. It has known many owners in the meantime, including Samuel Love, Col. Asa Rogers, and James T. Potts.

20 Exning was sold by Judge Thomas Dudley to Mr. Morency of Middleburg Real Estate Co., who subdivided the property.

THE CARRIAGE HOUSE
1 Pat Rogers's daughter, Mrs. Penny Degegre, is currently joint master of the Middleburg Hunt.

THE LOG CABIN
1 The Gibson family in Loudoun goes back to 1730 when Joseph Gibson was granted 630 acres here. Jonathan Gibson was an influential landowner and member of the vestry of Hamilton in 1759. The Gibsons intermarried with many prominent families, including the Rusts, Carters, Adamses, and McVeighs. Henrietta Powell, daughter of Humphrey Brooke Powell, married Sen. Charles H. Gibson in circa 1870; Dr. James Gibson married Frederica Crabites.

2 William, Henry, and Joseph Gibson served the Confederacy, as did members of many families with whom they intermarried.

3 Fredrica Crabites is a member of the DiZerega family, once owners of Briar Patch, which appears in this volume.

4 See *Apprentices, Poor Children and Bastards of Loudoun County, Va. 1757-1850* by Louisa Skinner Hutchison, Westminster, Maryland: Willow Bend Books, 2000.

5 Ibid. The other children taken in by the Gibsons were: Nan Thomas in 1767; Susannah Burners, 15, in 1787; Lavitha Violett, 8, in 1797; Sally Strip, 7, in 1797; Orpha Wilson, 14, in 1807; and Louisa Cornwall, 10, in 1811.

6 Hugh and Elizabeth Smith's first-born son, Rufus, also became a Loudoun County justice in 1865.

7 In his will, Hugh Smith specifically noted that all his children were to be educated in the Catholic faith. Per family documents kindly provided by Mrs. Pat Smith Boatright of Lancaster, Texas.

8 The sale of land for the Asbury Methodist Church occurred in 1829.

9 Hugh Smith did not die until 1864, but it's interesting to note that his impact on the property and on Middleburg history is such that a century and a half after his demise, The Log Cabin is still shown on Historic Landmark documents as "The Hugh Smith House."

10 Historic Landmark document #53-938 shows The Log Cabin going from Valentine Peyton to his son, Robert, who sold it to Thomas Gibson in 1765; Gibson heirs owned it until the 1820s when it was sold to Hugh Smith, who sold it to Lorman Chancellor in 1859, then Charles Lee in 1869.

11 See the chapter on Old Welbourne in this volume. Note that Erskine Bedford had just restored Old Welbourne and used some of the same barn wood to panel his library.

GROVETON FARM
1 The name "Carter Hall" is not to be confused with magnificent Carter Hall in Clarke County, which was part of the Carter-Burwell estate and was later the residence of Girard Lambert. (See the chapter on Old Welbourne in this volume.)

2 This account of the Battle of Mountville comes from Mr. David M. Frantum of Fairfax, Virginia, to whom the writer is most grateful.

3 There were several intervening owners of Groveton in this forty-year period, but none changed or added to its architecture or history.

4 Jan King Evans's father, Col. Charles Bowler King, was killed at the Battle of Normandy in 1944. He was thirty-eight years old.

5 George Sand's real name was Amandine Aurore Lucie Dupin. She married Casimir, Baron Dudevant, by whom she had two children. After their separation, she became a prolific Parisian writer (1804-76).

6 Belleview is now Prince George Plaza.

7 Louise Evans and Clifford "Okie" Turner own the 250-acre Gritton Mill Farm. They have two sons: Austin and Benjamin.

CREEK HILL
1 Margaret Prichard was the wife of Francis Carter of Groveton. The land purchased by Ezekial Mount was part of the Carter estate.

2 James, John, Mary, Thomas, and another child followed the birth of Stephen Mount.

3 This quote of Bishop Asbury's is found in *The History of Middleburg and Vicinity* by Eugene Scheel: Warrenton, Virginia:

Piedmont Press, 1987.

4 The pews, and pine boards of the Methodist Chapel at Mountville was given to the Mount Zion Church Preservation Association by Mr. and Mrs. Robert Humphrey in 1997.

5 Dr. John Mount married Mary Louise Fitzhugh, and they had two sons, James and Fitzhugh. James was the owner of the Mountville general store.

6 Colonel Gove's family came to Creek Hill after the war to retrieve his body and thanked the Mounts for their care of him.

7 See *Revolutionary Records of Loudoun County* at the Thomas Balch Library. An ensign was usually a young boy appointed to carry the flag of his company.

8 The McMahon's elder daughter, Adela Griswold, was at school this day.

FAIRVIEW

1 The quoted stories in this chapter are excerpted from an interview between Carl Furr and Eugene Scheel in 1977, available at the Thomas Balch Library in Leesburg.

2 Many Germans fled Germany and lived for a while in England mbefore heading for America.

3 William Furr, 60; Richard Furr of Leesburg, 45; Eban Furr, 51, of Middleburg; William Furr, 61, of Bloomfield; and Fenton Furr, 53, of Bloomfield, all signed the Union oath. John and Henry Furr served with the 8th Virginia Cavalry; Dallas Furr of Aldie, and William and Calhoun Furr (twin brothers of Dallas Furr) were killed at Balls Bluff, and Thompson Furr died in 1864 in a Union prison.

4 From "Snickers Gap, Virginia," a poem by Marion Holland. Used by permission of her daughter, Barbara Holland, an author of note who has written extensively about the Piedmont.

5 The known children of Kemp B. Furr were Etta, Edith, Lottie, Violet, Marguerite, Clayton, Warren, Anne, Buckner, Walter, Carl, and Kemp. *Note: He had 3 sons named Kemp; 2 died young.*

6 Forty-five members of the Furr family are buried at Old Sharon or Memorial Cemetery in Middleburg, including Kemp B. Furr (1825-1912); his third wife, Margaret Miley Furr (1861-1949); Walter Furr (1886-1973); and Carl (1888-1981).

7 Carl Furr had thirty-six nieces and nephews, so his estate became involved in some disputes, which unfortunately caused a bit of friction between members of the Furr family, some of whom are still not talking to the others.
The author gratefully acknowledges the kind assistance of Mrs. Bettie Furr and Mrs. Joan Furr.

MERCER HOUSE

1 Charles Fenton Mercer's grandfather John Mercer built a small mill along the banks of Little River in 1748. John Mercer was one of the first large landowners in the area; his deed dates back to 1731. He was also known as "the finest barrister of his time" and represented Cleric and Dr. Charles Greene in the famous case involving Anne Fairfax. Charles Mercer's father, Judge James Mercer of Fredericksburg, owned 5,300 acres in this area, all of which were inherited by his son, Charles Fenton. Per Spotsylvania County Will of James Mercer, dated 26 May 1791.

2 This was a separate building close to the existing miller's house of earlier vintage. The two were later joined together. See the chapter on the Miller's House in this volume.

3 This quote is from Douglas Egerton of LaMoyne College, author of a biography of Charles Fenton Mercer.

4 Mercer's opinion was shared by Pres. Abraham Lincoln, when on 14 August 1862 he addressed colonization with a group of free negroes at the White House by saying, "You and we are different races. We have between us a broader difference than exists between almost any other two races. Whether it is right or wrong, I need not discuss but this physical difference is a great disadvantage to us both. Your race suffers very greatly...by living among us,

while ours suffers from your presence."

The concept of finding a separate home for negroes occurred again in the 1870s when Pres. U. S. Grant, concerned for their welfare, proposed annexing Santo Domingo as a "safe harbor" for them. The plan was vetoed by the U.S. Senate, however.

5 The "Back to Africa Movement" was also known as "The American Colonization Society," which was founded about 1817. For almost two hundred years, freed slaves and their descendants dominated Liberian government, business, and land. Liberians are still sold into slavery and the country has been ravaged by vicious civil war and poverty ever since its inception. It was devastated during the 1990s when over 150,000 people were killed. It remains a land callous to violence where feuding warlords vie for supremacy. (See "Briefing/Africa," *The Washington Times* (18 October 2001): 18.

6 See Eugene Scheel's article on Margaret Mercer, "A Life devoted to Freedom and Opportunity," *The Washington Post* (17 March 2002).

7 For almost two hundred years, freed slaves and their descendants dominated Liberian government, business, and land. Liberians are still sold into slavery and the country has been ravaged by vicious civil war and poverty ever since its inception. It was devastated during the 1990s when over 150,000 people were killed. It remains a land callous to violence where feuding warlords vie for supremacy. (See "Briefing/Africa," *The Washington Times* (18 October 2001): 18.

8 See the chapter on the Miller's House for more information on the Moore family.

9 An advertisement for sale appeared in the Virginia Intelligencer on 4 January 1842 in which Mercer appointed Col. William Ish and Col. Hamilton Rogers of Oakham to handle the sale of his Aldie estate. See Volume I of Old Plantations for additional information on Oakham and the Rogers family.

10 The DiZerega family also appears in this volume in the chapter on Briar Patch, and in Volume I of Old Planatations in the chapter entitled "Sleepy Hollow."

11 See the chapter on Briar Patch in this volume.

12 Emily (born 1868) and Fanny were the daughters of Alfred DiZerega and Alice Almeda Gasquet, who were married in 1864.

13 Emily Irvine DiZerega (born 1907) was the granddaughter of Alfred DiZerega and Alice Alemeda Gasquet. Her mother, Martha Alice DiZerega, and father, William Irvine DiZerega, were first cousins.

THE MILLER'S HOUSE

1 There was a cottage, possibly a log or stone cabin, on this land in 1751 occupied by one Simon Kenton whose son was born there in 1755. Legend has it that the son later saved the life of Daniel Boone, but this has not been verified.

2 John Mercer was the attorney who represented Rev. Charles Green in the infamous debauchery case initiated by William Fairfax in the mid-1700s. It was said that Reverend Green was acquitted only because of "the brilliant defense provided by John Mercer."

3 An old, unsigned letter, kindly provided by Mrs. Sarah Douglass, says, "The Aldie Mill was built by Carles (sic) Fenton Mercer as was the early part of the millers house."

4 For more information on the "Back to Africa Movement" please see the chapter on Mercer House in this volume.

5 This account comes from an interview between Captain Moore's great-great grandson, James Edwards Douglass, during a 1977 interview with historian Eugene Sheel, which is available at the Thomas Balch Library in Leesburg. It is also attested by an old family letter provided by Mrs. Sarah Douglass.

6 The Lacys or Laceys, are an old Loudoun family. Some accounts show her name as Matilda Lacy Beard, which may indicate that she had been married prior to her marriage to Captain Moore although

there is no record of such a marriage.

7 Two of Captain Moore's children were Robert, born 1841, and Alexander.

8 Another marriage between the two families occurred in 1918 when Rosa Lacey Douglass married G. Frederick Moore.

9 From The Journal of Nicholas Cresswell 1774-1777 by Nicholas Cresswell, New York: Dial Press, 1924. Courtesy of Mrs. Janet Roszel Tayloe.

10 Capt. William Douglass married twice: 1) Elizabeth Offit Lewis and 2) Sarah Orrick Chilton. He had at least five daughters: Margaret, Catherine, Elizabeth, Nancy, and Hannah, and a son, Hugh.

11 Per 1870 Loudoun County census records.

12 Marion Skinner (wife of James Edwards Douglass) died in 1893, leaving their son, John, and daughters, Rosanna Lacy, Mary Virginia, and Katherine Fleming. James married his sister-in-law Mary Castell Skinner in 1895. There was no issue from the second marriage.

13 Ibid. Footnote 3.

14 James Love and his wife, Susanna Dillon, settled on a property north of Hamilton called Loveland prior to 1775. His son, Fenton Mercer Love, and his wife, Elizabeth Morris, and their son Morris and wife, Ruth Grubb, all lived there. James Love's great-grandson Ned Douglass lives there today.

15 Much information on the Moore and Douglass families was supplied by Mrs. Sarah Douglass to whom I am most grateful.

MOSBY SPRING FARM

1 Maryland remained under military occupation by Federal troops throughout the Civil War.

2 Frank Key Howard subsequently wrote a book about his experience entitled American Bastille, which was banned by the federal government as soon as it was published.

3 Written by James Ryder Randall, a native of Baltimore, "Maryland! My Maryland!" was adopted as the official song of the state in 1939, seventy-four years after the end of the Civil War. As of now (2003), it is still the official state song.

4 Further exploits of Lt. James Wiltshire may be found in "Mosby's Confederacy," Blue and Gray, 17, no. 4 (April 2000).

5 Colonel Mosby refused to take a penny from the Greenback Raid so his men bought him a new horse in gratitude.

MOUNT BEULAH

1 Hudson, of course, was actually looking for a new trade route to the Orient. His discovery was an accident that proved beneficial to the Netherlands.

2 For more information on the Swaart family, please see the chapter on Valley View in the first volume of Old Plantations by this author.

3 The name is shown as both Swaart and Swart in the old records. The former is the original spelling, however.

4 Oak Hill later became the home of Sen. Henry Fairfax and his wife, Eugenia Tennant. After Senator Fairfax's demise, it was sold to Frank Littletons and is now owned by Thomas deLashmutt.

5 It is unknown whether Mount Beulah dates from the 1790 period or the early 1800s, and it's thus impossible to determine the builder. Its current owner believes the earlier date is most likely.

6 The Pilgrim's Progress was written in 1678 and soon became a "Second Bible" for religious families. Since the name "Mount Buelah" appears on the Yardley Taylor map of 1853, it was obviously given to the property by the Swaarts.

7 Ship Passenger Lists, New York and New Jersey, Carl Boyer; privately published; Newhall, California: 1978. There was also a Henrick Gulich whose wife, Gertrud Wilkens, arrived in 1653. Both Joachim and Henrick Gulick are listed in Knickerbocker Families, New York Genealogical Records.

8 Per Revolutionary War records at the Thomas Balch Library. Unfortunately, his first name does not appear, though judging by the time frame, it may have been a son of James Gulick.

9 James Gulick (1815-64) was the son of William Gulick and Mary Hixson.

10 The A & M Institute was built by four men: Jude William Metzger, Harmon Bitzser, G. Benton, and James Gulick. Oak Hill, in 1841, was owned by Pres. James Monroe's daughter, Maria Monroe Gouverneur.

11 John Franklin Gulick was named for his cousin, John Franklin Allen. The Allens came from Ireland to Pennsylvania in 1729. John F. Gulick retained Red Hill Farm until 1910 when it was sold out of the family.

12 Per an article in the Loudoun Times-Mirror dated 16 September 1897.

13 Charles Franklin Riticor owned a considerable amount of land along Route 15 at this time, which he later sold.

14 The following is synthesized from an interview given to Eugene Scheel by Frank Riticor on 10 March 1977. Available at the Thomas Balch Library in Leesburg.

15 Sen. Henry and Eugenia Fairfax owned Oak Hill from 1885 until his death in 1906 when Mrs. Fairfax sold it to Frank Littleton.

16 In 1926, Mount Beulah was conveyed to Flora Saffer Gulick by her husband, John Franklin Gulick, and in 1953 conveyed to their son, John Allen Gulick.

17 Aldie School was enlarged to serve 250 elementary and high school youngsters in 1915 with an addition that cost ten thousand dollars. It was built to "the most up-to-date and approved lines," and the money was available in full at the command of the school committee, consisting of Mr. Claude Saffer, Capt. C. McCormick, and Mr. Autust deZerega.

18 Mount Beulah is currently in an LLC, owned by several members of the Gulick family. So although John and Stacy Gulick are restoring it and living in it, they are not the sole owners.

MOUNT DEFIANCE

1 Even today, though it has only five acres of its original 366 remaining, the owners of Mount Defiance pay taxes to both Loudoun and Fauquier Counties.

2 See The Battles of Aldie, Middleburg and Upperville by Robert F. O'Neill, Lynchburg, Virginia: H.E. Howard, Inc., 1993.

3 Grace Gibson had divorced her husband prior to her demise so the taxes on Mount Defiance during this period were paid by Burr Powell Noland, Ella Gibson's kin. (Humphrey Brooke Powell's daughter, Henrietta, married Sen. Charles H. Gibson).

4 Gourley Hatcher's name also appears as Ghorley and Gurley.

5 William Hatcher received a grant of three to seven hundred acres in 1775 (the records vary on the number) in the vicinity of Lincoln. His descendents intermarried with the Houghs, Greggs, Piggots, Halls, and Laceys.

6 Mary (Kate) Hatcher married Howard J. Gibson, but her relationship to Gourley Hatcher has not been determined. She died in 1902; Howard died in 1920.

7 For more information on the Humphrey family see the chapter on Creek Hill in this volume.

8 The Rufus Humphreys had two daughters: Cathy and Sandra.

9 Gladys Johnson's family received a land grant in New Jersey in the early 1700s.

10 Excerpted from a letter written by James Young to the Fauquier Democrat, March 1993.

MOUNT HARMONY

1 Information on the early history of Woodwind (now Mount Harmony) can be found on Virginia Historic Landmarks Commission Form File # 53-931, at the Thomas Balch Library in Leesburg.

2 This Breckenridge family was not related to John Cabell Breckenridge (U.S. vice president prior to the Civil War) who hailed from Kentucky and owned Featherbed Farm in the 1850s.

3 This story came from Tom Crouch's grandson, Otto Crouch of Middleburg, who swears it is true. *Note: Otto Crouch died in April 2002.*

4 Betty Fox Miller remarried soon after to James McCormick of Dover House in Aldie where she still lives. (Jamie McCormick died 9 May 2002 at the age of eighty-nine.) See Dover House in Volume I of *Old Plantations.*

5 Carol Miller is a partner in Armfield, Miller, Ripley Realty Company in Middleburg.

6 Phil Thomas is owner of Thomas and Talbot Realtors of Middleburg. He sold the property in 1967 to Hildegarde and John Mitchell, who conveyed it a year later to their son Walter Mitchell.

7 The Dukes purchased Mount Harmony in 1992 and sold it in 1997 to the Feneises.

NOLAND FERRY HOUSE

1 Philip Noland, gentleman, was granted a large section of land by Thomas, Lord Fairfax, at the head of Little Hunting Creek in 1728. Philip and his wife, Elizabeth Awbrey, had six children, including Awbrey; Philip, Jr.; Thomas; Elizabeth; and Molly. Thomas, Elizabeth, and Molly all married into the Luckett family who owned many beautiful homes and plantations around the Piedmont, including Dresden and Featherbed Farm.

2 The Awbreys were also wealthy landowners of property and islands around the Potomac River.

3 This quote is from the Noland Family Papers, courtesy of Mrs. Horace Figuers.

4 This may have been one of Sally Hemings's sons. It's interesting to note that although most slaves of that time did not have surnames, the Hemingses did.

5 From *John Adams* by David McCullough, New York: Simon and Shuster, 2001, p. 110, tells of Jefferson's journey through Virginia, then of his crossing the Potomac at Noland's Ferry into Maryland to Philadelphia.

6 George Washington kept a meticulously accurate diary and noted his stay at Noland's Ferry House in 1783.

7 The writer is grateful to Mrs. Claree Noland Doty of La Jolla, California, and the family of Paul Innes Noland for information on members of the Noland family who headed west.

8 For information on the Berkeley family please see the chapters on Stoke, Exning, and Creek Hill in this volume. The story of Charlotte Haxall Noland can be found in Volume I of *Old Plantations* in the chapter on Foxcroft.

9 Mr. Wayne Brookins now lives in Petersburg, Virginia, and kindly provided this information.

10 Mrs. Emily Figuers, a beloved member of Loudoun County society for many years, died, as this book went to press, on 3 March 2003.

OLD WELBOURNE

1 Thomas, Lord Fairfax, inherited the land from his mother, Lady Culpeper, but since he was living in England at the time, he appointed his friend Robert "King" Carter as his land agent.

2 Annapolis was named for Princess Ann of Denmark.

3 *Life and Times of the Rev. Walter Dulany Addison.* Philadelphia: George W. Jacobs & Co., 1895.

4 Daniel was the son of Thomas Dulany who died in Baltimore in 1738. Daniel's first wife was Charity Courts who died in 1711 sans issue.

5 Rebecca Smith was the daughter of Col. Walter Smith and Rachel Hall. For more information on the Hall family see the chapter on Crednal in this volume.

6 The children of Daniel and Rachel Dulany were Daniel Dulany II, Walter, Dennis, Rebecca, Rachel, Mary, Margaret, and Lloyd.

7 Several members of the Dulany family either served in the British Army or fled to England.

8 Benjamin Tasker Dulany was the son of Daniel Dulany II and Rebecca Ann Tasker.

9 Elizabeth's parents, Daniel and Penelope French of Claremont, Fairfax County, Virginia, both died leaving her care to George Mason.

10 The deed in Leesburg Courthouse shows this grant to be 503 acres. There were later acquisitions however, for records show that John Peyton Dulany owned one thousand acres.

11 This letter is in the Welbourne Plantation Papers, courtesy of Mr. Nathaniel Morison.

12 Mrs. Lewis was a widow at this time. Her brother-in-law was Sen. Joseph Lewis, whose widow, Elizabeth, married George Carter of Oatlands Plantation. (See the chapter on Oatlands in Volume One of *Old Plantations.*)

13 Old Welbourne was used as a tenant house during the intervening years.

14 This was Julia Dulany's second marriage. The first, to her cousin Samuel Welby deButts, ended with his early death. For more information on the Roszel family see the chapter on Shelburne in this volume.

15 Whether the brick mansion at Old Welbourne was built circa 1850 by the Roszels or by John Peyton Dulany for his daughter is unknown. Dulany was a very wealthy man, and the Roszels were also well-to-do. The Roszels lived at Old Welbourne for three generations yet the property remained in the hands of the Dulany family and was eventually heired to Col. Richard Henry Dulany's son Richard Hunter Dulany in the early 1900s. It is, therefore, more likely that the mansion was erected by John Peyton Dulany.

16 Per records of the Methodist Museum in Baltimore collected by Julian Roszel and kindly provided to the writer by Stephen Roszel.

17 See the chapter on Denton in this volume for more information on the Stephen Roszel family.

18 Richard Hunter Dulany, son of Richard and Rebecca A. Dulany, married Eva Randolph of Grafton in 1877. Their daughter, Dorothy Willing Randolph, married Beverly Mason.

19 The appraisal of Peyton Randolph's estate in April 1776 (York County) showed a total wealth of £1,578 in furnishings and £2,883 in slaves.

20 From an article on Welbourne in the *Loudoun Times-Mirror,* 1982, by Eugene Scheel.

21 Mrs. William Beverley Mason, Jr., and her brother, R.H. Dulany Randolph, sold Old Welbourne in 1959.

22 Erskine was the son of Louise Lott Banks and Dean Erskine Bedford of Fallston, Maryland.

23 Gerard Lambert was a native of St. Louis, Missouri, but he loved the South and so wanted to be a Virginian that he legally changed his middle name from Barnes to Burwell. The Burwells, who intermarried with the Carters, date back in local history to the late 1700s and are remembered through the old Burwell Mill and beautiful Long Branch plantation in Clarke County.

24 Lily Lambert had a daughter, Lily Bedford Raines, by her first marriage; then Lily and Erskine Bedford had three children: Daphne Bedford Wooten, Dean Erskine Bedford, and Cintra Cricket Bedford Whitner. Erskine's second wife, Nancy Gerry Bedford had two children by her first marriage: Bryan Benitz and Cynthia Benitz McClory, who were both at University at the time of their mother's remarriage. They did, however, spend most holidays and summers at Old Welbourne and are an integral part of the family.

25 Trinity Church was built by Erkine Bedford's friend and fellow horse lover, Paul Mellon. *See the following endnote.*

26 Cricket was named for her great-grandmother, Rachel Lowe (Lambert) Clopton whose nickname was Cricket. Rachel and

Gerard Lambert had three children: Gerry, Lily Lambert McCarthy, and Rachel "Bunny" Lambert Mellon, wife of Paul Mellon.

27 Louise Whitner was named for her great-grandmother, Louise Lott Banks of Brooklyn, New York, and Fallston, Maryland, a petite and fearless horsewoman.

28 The Bedford Fund, co-founded with Dr. Joe Rogers, is a subsidiary of the Westmoreland Davis Memorial Foundation designed to provide legal, tax, and estate planning resources to rural landowners.

29 In addition to the main house, there are nine other outbuildings on the grounds of Old Welbourne, including barns, stables, silos, a tenant house, cottage, and pool house.

30 Appreciation is given to Mrs. Janet Dulany Roszel Tayloe for this story.

31 Another Dulany home on Welbourne Road was named Pelham in honor of Maj. John Pelham, CSA, who visited Welbourne Plantation and singlehandedly held off ten thousand federal troops with one cannon on the foggy December 13th morning in 1862 at Fredericksburg. Gen. Robert E. Lee called him "The gallant Pelham."

WELBOURNE PLANTATION

1 John Peyton Dulany's parents were Benjamin Tasker Dulany, justice of the Fairfax Court, and Elizabeth French, the beautiful and wealthy ward of George Washington. Mrs. Dulany owned 2,000 acres including Old Welbourne, Welbourne, and Crednal. It was said of this young heiress that "half the world was in her pursuit."

2 James Lewis died in 1796. The property was purchased by the Dulanys from his wife, Joanna Wales Brent Lewis, and son Thomas Lewis. James's brother, Joseph Lewis, was a U.S. senator whose wife was Elizabeth Greyson. Upon the senator's demise, Elizabeth married George Carter, Sr., of Oatlands.

3 Julia married her first cousin Samuel deButts and after his death, Rev. Samuel Roszell. Mary Ann married Carlyle Whiting, a banker who once owned Oakley Plantation in Upperville, but lived primarily at Richland in Stafford County.

4 Per Loudoun County Land and Personal Property Assemements and Taxes for 1859.

5 From an article by Eugene Scheel in the *Loudoun Times-Mirror* (16 August 1979). This lack of shoes was not due to poverty, but to lack of a shoemaker, since footwear of the time was handmade.

6 The name of this hamlet prior to the war was Union, but was changed to Unison when hostilities began in 1861.

7 Pelham lies just down the road from Welbourne.

8 President Lincoln's Emancipation Proclamation applied only to states in the Confederacy, where it had no legal standing. It did not apply to northern and western states that supported the Union and was therefore a political move designed to defeat the Confederacy. Note that during the Lincoln-Douglas debates, Lincoln repeatedly called for "shipping the negroes back to Africa" and repeatedly insisted that blacks and whites could not live together in harmony.

9 Dr. Robert Lemmon bought land along Gun Powder River in Maryland in 1777. The family was ardently Baptist, and Lemmon Hill in Salisbury was for over a century a hallowed place for members of that faith. Per Lemmon family papers, courtesy of Mr. Stephen Roszel.

10 Rebecca died at age nine; Frances married Nathaniel Holmes Morison; Isabel married Winthrop Gardiner of Long Island, New York; Mary married George H. White and lived at Pelham; Grace married H. Gwynne Tayloe; Janet Southgate married R. Julian Roszel; Ethel married George Gaither; Elizabeth never married; and Neville married Thomas Atkinson.

11 In her handwritten diary of 1906, Ella Noland MacKenzie of Glen Ora refers several times to the hunts, parties, and balls at Welbourne. Courtesy of Mr. J. McKenzie Tabb of Richmond.

12 The Morisons' had three children: Southgate Lemmon married Anne Tennant; Nathaniel Holmes married Sally Harris, who inherited Stoke; and Frances Dulany Morison married John P. Tyler of New York and England.

13 See the chapter on Stoke in this volume for background on the Harris family.

14 George Harris Morison married (1) Lucy Reed and (2) Hope Moore; Eleanor Truax Morison married Dr. Travis R. Jacobs of Connecticut; and Nat Holmes Morison married (1) Alice Ames and (2) Sherry Weymouth.

15 "Jass" was the original spelling of Jazz. It changed after 1930 when "white folks" adopted it as a music form.

THE OLD CHURCH HOUSE

1 For additional information on the evolution of black music see *Many Thousands Gone* by Ira Berlin, Williamsburg, Virginia: William and Mary College, 1999.

2 Gullah resulted from the combination of an English vocabulary and a West African grammatical structure.

3 This quote is by historian James Weldon Johnson, from a book called *Black Manhattan,* New York: Da Capo Press, 1930.

4 In 1923, the black community near Welbourne, named Willisville, wanted a new church but could not afford it. Mary Dulany Neville designed a French-style country chapel for them, and she and Fanny Dulany Lemmon paid to have it built. It is still in use today.

5 It's interesting to note that Lincoln emancipated only those slaves in the Confederate states—the Emancipation Proclamation did not pertain to those in the Union.

6 This quote is from *The Collected Stories of Richard Yates* by Richard Yates, New York: Henry Holt, 2001.

7 The relationship between the former slaves and the Dulanys of Welbourne was both warm and respectful as evidenced by their loyalty to the family after the war.

8 This is not the same as Bryn Mawr College in Pennsylvania.

9 The specific quotes come from *Max Perkins: Editor of Genius* by A. Scott Berg, New York: E. P. Dutton, 1978.

10 Elizabeth met Max Perkins through her roommate at school who became the wife of Max Perkins. Their relationship was apparently a stormy one, however.

11 Information on the life of Elizabeth Lemmon and other stories were provided by William Tayloe, owner of the Old Church House, and is gratefully acknowledged.

12 The Tayloe family dates back to John Tayloe who in 1750 built Mount Airy, near Warsaw, Virginia, which has been called the "most impressive Colonial mansion in Virginia." It has never gone out of family ownership.

CREDNAL

1 The history of Crednal's ownership went through the female line as follows: Robert "King" Carter's second wife was Elizabeth Landon Willis (Willis from her first marriage). It was the Landons who owned Credenhill in England. Elizabeth and Robert Carter's daughter married William Harrison; Sarah Harrison married John Manley; Penelope Manley married Daniel French; Elizabeth French married Benjamin Tasker Dulany; Louisa Dulany married Richard deButts; and Richardetta deButts married John Armistead Carter.

2 A letter written by Richard deButts's mother, Mary Ann deButts, in 1813 says, "Richard has received from his wife's Father and Mother a farm worth £1500." It would appear that Richard purchased the farm known as Crednal, but after his marriage to Louisa Dulany, the Dulanys refunded the purchase price.

3 Elizabeth French and Benjamin Tasker Dulany had twelve children, all of whom received large land grants. John Peyton Dulany who married Mary Ann deButts acquired the thousand acres now known as Old Welbourne, while Louise and her husband, Richard

deButts, settled at Crednal.

4 Mary Millicent deButts died young.

5 Samuel Welby Carter (1815-39) married Julia Ann Bladen Dulany in 1833.

6 Edward Hall was a son of Richard and Sarah Cowman Hall. He married Louisa Dulany deButts in 1820. Their children were: James Hall who married Rosa Gunnell; Eliza Hall married Robert Carter; Henry A. Hall married Susan Grayson; and Sarah M. Hall married Richard Earle deButts in 1844.

7 After being deprived of her Maryland home and property, Sarah Cowman Hall moved to Cumnor near Marshall, Virginia, with her two daughters and younger son, Thomas Samuel Hall. Per family papers graciously provided by Stephen Roszel.

8 Mary Burwell Armistead's relative, Col. George Armistead, was commander of Fort McHenry in 1814 when Francis Scott Key was so moved by the sight of the American flag being embattled by the British that he wrote "The Star Spangled Banner." Colonel Armistead rescued the flag, which was turned over to the Smithsonian by his family in 1907.

9 Per the census of 1850 for Loudoun County, Virginia.

10 The name of this hamlet north of Crednal was originally Union. It was changed to Unison immediately after the outbreak of Civil War.

11 The majority of landowners in Loudoun County also opposed secession, so Senator Carter was representing his constituents as well as his own opinion.

12 Information about Welby Carter's service to the Confederacy comes from Civil War military records in Richmond, Virginia, and family letters published in *The Dulanys of Welbourne* by Margaret Ann Vogtsberger, Berryville, Virginia: Rockbridge Publishing Co., 1995.

13 Armistead Carter appealed to Gen. Jubal Early who agreed to support a petition to set aside the court martial of Welby Carter. But the petition was not successful possibly because the end of Civil War was approaching. Some believed at the time—and some family members still believe—that unjust accusations by Gen. Thomas Rosser led to his conviction.

14 Rev. Samuel Skinker killed himself with a shot through the head at Glen Welby when his love was rejected in 1863. Per *Samuel Skinker and his Descendants* by Thomas Skinker, privately published, 1923.

15 *The Diary of a Confederate Staff Officer* by Capt. James Keith Boswell, privately published. Boswell, a military engineer, was one of Gen. Thomas "Stonewall" Jackson's most trusted and able officers. He adored Sophia deButts and wrote in his diary, "I have loved you for years. I never loved another and never can. Your bright image has been with me in the crash of battle and your influence has ever been for good."

16 The deButts Bible was made available through the kindness of J. MacKenzie Tabb III of Richmond.

17 The children of Welby Carter and Sophie deButts Carter were Mary, Fannie, Sophie, John Armistead, Richard Welby, Harry, Nina, Rebecca, and Juliet.

18 Per historian John Gott, in an article written in 1966 on the fiftieth anniversary of the United Daughters of the Confederacy.

19 Welby Carter died in 1889. Sophia deButts Carter survived until 1928.

20 Sophia deButts Carter (daughter of Richard Welby and Sophia deButts) married Malbon Richardson, lived at Corotoman, and died in 1931; Fanny married Arthur C. Marshall of England, died 1945; Nina married J. MacKenzie Tabb, died 1950; Mary married H. Gordon Moore; Rebecca married Paul Whitin of Massachusetts, died 1970; Juliet married Peter Wood of Baltimore, died 1946; John Armistead married Ashley Dempsey, died 1931; Richard Welby died 1928. The Tavenner Papers show a ninth child, a son Harry, but there is no further information on him so he may have died young.

21 This "receipt" was provided by J. MacKenzie Tabb III of Richmond, along with much other information pertaining to the Carter, Tabb, deButts, and allied families, for which the author is very grateful.

22 Thanks for this story go to Mrs. Janet Dulany Roszel Tayloe.

23 Ibid.

24 Anna and Stanley Dees, a Washington attorney, have two grown children: Claire, who as a young girl was so intrigued by Crednal's history that she wrote a comprehensive report that was kindly made available to this author, and a son, Clark.

25 The Dees were not aware of the flag, which had been placed there and at other sites, by a group of visiting Civil War reenactors.

26 The writer gratefully acknowledges the contributions of the Stanley Deeses, Mrs. Janet Dulany Tayloe, Mr. David Boyce, Mr. N.H. Morison, and Mr. J. MacKenzie Tabb and other members of the Middleburg community to this history of Crednal.

POOR HOUSE FARM

1 From *Piedmont Virginian,* by Claire Kincannon, 31 March 1976

2 This was not the first almshouse. Loudoun County established one at Arcola in 1789 and a second in Leesburg in 1806.

3 William Burson built the home for Judith and William Dorsey but put his own initials on the chimney.

4 Loudoun County paid $3,479 for the house and 229 acres in 1822.

5 See Eugene Scheel's *Loudoun Times-Mirror* article on the Poor House, 16 August 1979.

6 The Overseers had purchased additional acreage around the Poor House over the years so that its original 229 acres accrued to 420 by 1947.

POT HOUSE

1 Jane Ball Kyle, wife of John Kyle, was shot through the head with a Revolutionary bullet and quickly buried in the orchard of Locust Hill. Her ghost was said to roam the property until Charlotte Noland had her body exhumed. For the full story, see the chapter on Locust Hill (now Foxcroft) in Volume I of *Old Plantations and Historic Homes.*

2 Joseph Lane was described as a "'dandy' who wore silk clothes and ruffled shirts" by Philip Vickers Fithian, a fellow Princetonian (from the Fithian Papers at the University of Virginia).

3 President Monroe was godfather to one of William Benton's sons.

4 William Leith purchased Farmer's Delight with 182 acres for $7,260.50 from John Kyle in 1839. Kyle's second wife was Winifred Leith, aunt of William Leith. Theodoric married Ann Gregg and lived at Turkey Roost; Howard Leith married Martha Gregg of Farmer's Delight.

5 Louise Evans Turner is the daughter of Mrs. Benjamin Evans of Groveton, which is chronicled in this volume.

ROSE HILL

1 Maine entered the Union as a free state and Missouri as a slave state in 1820.

2 Washington, Jefferson, and Madison had served as U.S. presidents at this time, and Monroe followed in 1831. All told, eight Virginians were elected president.

3 Amos Denham had six known children plus two who died in infancy and were buried in the apple orchard. Charles born 1813; Amos born 1820; Mary born 1817, married William Henry Cassady; Margaret married Malcolm Horton, 1832; Amy Ellen married Andrew Balmain, 1839; and Sarah born 1826.

4 Amy Denham received one-third of the property as her dower, including the house and seventy-two acres. The rest of the property was sold. After Thomas Glascock purchased the property, he

bought all of its original land.

5 The name also appears as Glasscock in many old records.

6 Several members of the Rose Hill families served the Confederacy, including Capt. Alfred Glascock, _____ Fletcher, and Luther Slater.

7 Rockburn was built by John G. Scott prior to the Revolution.

8 Thomas Glascock is said to have twenty-four slaves in the 1860 Loudoun County census.

9 This information comes from Eugene Scheel, Loudoun County historian.

10 This quote is taken from an article in *The Century* (a popular magazine in the 1880s) that was reprinted in *The Washington Post*, 22 April 2001, "Still Bearing the Southern Cross," by Joshua Michael Zeitz.

11 Tom Glascock's daughter, Tacie Glascock, married Robert Fletcher in 1877 and died in childbirth in 1878. Her daughter was Tacie Fletcher.

12 Slater received a patent for 355 acres near Tuscarora in 1729, and another for 1,080 acres near Noland's Ferry in 1730.

13 Mount Bleak and several hundred surrounding acres on both sides of Route 17 were purchased by the late Paul Mellon and given to the state of Virginia as a park.

14 Bedford Slater died in an automobile accident at eighteen.

15 Thomas Slater married Hylton Rucker. George Glascock Slater married Katherine Gochnouer, a.k.a. Kitty Slater, a well-known horsewoman and writer in the Hunt Country. She died in 2000. Her father, Dr. Gochneour, and his family had long been prominent in the Upperville area.

16 Tacie Slater's other grandson, Robert Slater, owns the 325-acre property across from Rose Hill known as Plum Run Farm. His son, Rucker Slater, is a mortgage banker in Middleburg and also lives on the Plum Run property.

SHELBURNE

1 The name appears as Roszell, Roszel, and Rossel.

2 Stephen Roszell actually came to Loudoun with his father, Peter, and mother, Ann Gray Roszell, who stayed in Loudoun for ten years before leaving in 1772 for Spotsylvania County, Virginia. Peter was the son of Charles Roszell of New York. Their antecedents go back to the Viking settlements in Normandy where their family chateau of Rozel still stands. A Roszel ancestor was a nobleman in the court of William the Conqueror.

3 For more information on the Chilton family, see the chapter on Aspen Hill in this volume.

4 Stephen Chilton Roszell served for eight years in the Virginia Assembly and married Ann Dove who left her considerable estate in 1839 to Methodist missions. Along with his parents, he is buried in the old family cemetery.

5 Some sources claim that the stone house dates back to 1719, but that is unlikely because the survey done at the time of its conveyance to Stephen Roszel only mentions land, not buildings or appurtenances.

6 The glebe given to Shelburne Parish was 465 acres—an extremely generous gift from a parishioner named Joseph Combs.

7 The original 1778 Loudoun County Militia List is in the Richmond collection. A copy is available at the Thomas Balch Library in Leesburg. Stephen Roszel appears under both Col. William Tripplet's and Colonel Peyton's militia commands.

8 Lord Shelburne was secretary of colonial affairs and opposed American independence, so he sent an emissary, one Richard Oswald, to France to meet with Franklin to negotiate the Treaty of Paris.

9 From *Wealth and Democracy* by Kevin Phillips, New York: Broadway Books, 2002, p. 8.

10 From *The Diary of Nicholas Cresswell 1774-1777* by Nicholas Cresswell, New York: Dial Press, 1924, p. 165.

11 In 1802, the General Assembly of Virginia abolished all the land holdings of the former Anglican Church (which was renamed the Protestant Episcopal Church) and allowed former owners who had donated the lands to reclaim them. Many churches and glebe lands, however, had simply been appropriated earlier, as had the stone church on the Roszell property, which was given along with two acres to the Methodist church in 1842.

12 Stephen George Roszel's sons were Stephen Edmondson, Stephen Chilton, Stephen Wesley, Stephen Calvert, Stephen Asbury, Stephen McKendree, and Stephen Cherub. Only his third son, George Washington, was not named Stephen, and he was born mentally retarded. Stephen George also had three daughters: Mary Ann, Octavia Owen, and Sarah Ann.

13 From *Minutes of the Annual Conferences of the Methodist Eposcopal Church*, vol. 111, 1845.

14 See *From Frontier to Suburbia* by Charles P. Poland, Marceline, Mo.: Walsworth Publishing Co.

15 This was written for a reporter for the *Alexandria Gazette* in 1858 upon hearing Rev. Stephen G. Roszel speak at the new Methodist Church in Middleburg. From *History of Middleburg and Vicinity*, by Eugene Scheel, 1987.

16 This story comes from *The Journal of the Philomont Historical Society*, Mr. Edward Robishaux, ed., to whom I am most grateful.

17 John Cunningham Dice and his wife, Sally Roszel, were the great grandparents of Sen. Charles Robb of Virginia.

18 From the Roszel Family Papers, compiled by Richard Julian Roszel, Jr. Courtesy of Mrs. Janet Dulany Roszel Tayloe and Mr. Stephen S. Roszel.

19 "Seldom Seen" was originally part of Landon Carter's Field #6. Today it is called Heronwood and is noted for its great white oak tree, which dates back before 1853.

20 Stephen S. Roszel VI married (1) Page Nelson Dabney and (2) Susan Hull. He has four children: Dabney, Stephen S. VII, Susan, and Thomas. Stephen S. was born in 1953, married Sandra Kallenberg, and their son, Stephen VIII, was born in 1980.

21 Roger Roszell is director of music at the Church of St. Agnes in Arlington. At the time of this writing, his choir is leaving for a tour of Italy culminating in a performance for Pope John Paul II, in Rome. Quite an achievement for an American musician.

DENTON

1 James N. Hathaway married Mary Ann Adams on 23 November 1844.

2 Four thousand dollars in 1853, though a fortune at the time, is roughly equivalent to $80,000 in today's terms. Note the value of the entire property in 1893 *See endnote 5, below.*

3 The four children of James Hathaway and the two Adams sisters were Charles G., Mollie V., Lovinia, and Anne.

4 This story had been told many times over many years, but it was verified to James Young by two visitors to Denton: the grandson of Maj. John S. Mosby and the grandson of James Hathaway.

5 This lawsuit—Hathaway v. Hathaway, 1893 Fauquier Record, Book 84, p. 508—resulted in the total property, worth $24,942.61, being divided three ways: Lot 1 (the home lot) and 126 acres to Mollie V. Fant, two hundred acres on the south side of Route 708 to Charles Hathaway, and 180 acres south east of Route 708 to Fountain Beattie.

6 For more information on the Roszel Family please see the chapters on Shelburne and Old Welbourne in this volume.

7 The four children of George Asbury Stephen Roszel and Sarah deButts were Richard Julian, Stephen Samuel, Rosa Earle, and Sarah deButts.

8 For more information on the Hall Family, see the chapter on Crednal in this volume.

9 The two Tines children, Annabelle and Lester, followed the

Roszel family to Delaware in the 1930s.

10 Prohibition laws, commonly known as the Volstead Act, were repealed in 1933.

11 Sam and Rosa Roszel later moved to Front Royal and finally back to Middleburg where they lived on Washington Street until their demise. They are both buried at Old Sharon Cemetery.

12 The maples were cut down and Washington Street was paved and curbed. Route 15 was widened rather than Route 50.

13 The Youngs also had a son, Robert, who lives across the road from Denton.

14 Sally Fendall Harrison Young is related to all the Harrison and Lee families. Both her father and grandfather were Virginia Commonwealth attorneys.

STOKE

1 Maj. William Noland, son of Thomas Noland and Elizabeth Luckett, was born at Noland Ferry House in 1796 and died in Aldie in 1851. He served as a member of the Virginia General Assembly. See the chapter on Noland Ferry House in this volume.

2 Charles Fenton Mercer, neighbor and friend of the Nolands and Berkeleys, owned much of the land (including 768 acres he sold to them) and the mill in Aldie. Though he never married, many children were named in his honor.

3 Mathew Rust served as a lieutenant in the Revolution and was related to famed Gen. George Rust of Fauquier County.

4 Martha Triplett was the daughter of Col. Simon Triplett of Sleepy Hollow, which has been chronicled in Volume I of *Old Plantations and Historic Homes*.

5 Norborne Berkeley was actually the owner of Stoke at this time, but he conveyed it to his brother Charles on 27 March 1863, complete with slaves, appurtenances, and outbuildings. Charles conveyed it to Richard and Molly Cox at a later date, and the Coxes' heirs sold the property to Colonel Harris in 1907.

6 This letter written by Mary Berkeley Cox, parts of which have been excerpted for this book, was found among the Berkeley Family Papers at the Thomas Balch library in Leesburg.

7 Richard Cox was originally the paymaster for the Confederate Army and an aide de camp to Gen. Robert E. Lee. He later served as treasurer of the Confederacy. The brothers all served in the 8th Virginia Regiment: William Berkeley was a major, Pickett's Division; Edmund was a lieutenant colonel; Norborne was a colonel; and Charles Fenton was a lieutenant.

8 William Berkeley owned thirty-five slaves per the 1860 Loudoun County census, and many of his letters to his wife concerned them.

9 Evergreen was the estate of Edmund Berkeley (Molly's brother) and lay halfway between Aldie and Warrenton.

10 William, Norborne, and Charles Fenton Berkeley were all imprisoned at Johnson's Island for several months. Upon being paroled, they immediately rejoined their regiments. It is not known where Edmund was imprisoned.

11 It probably seemed like twenty thousand troops to Mrs. Cox, but this number is greatly exaggerated.

12 Charles Fenton Berkeley, however, died just a few years later in 1871, at the age of 38.

13 This quote is from an undated letter written by Colonel Cox to his sister-in-law, Cynthia Berkeley. From the Berkeley Papers.

14 The annual Eleanor Truax Harris silver trophy is still awarded annually in her memory by the Garden Club of Virginia.

15 The five Harris children were Eleanor, Martha, Mary Virginia, Floyd, and Sarah (Sally).

16 The children of George Morison and his first wife, Lucy Reed, are George Southgate, Hatley Norton, and Cameron Dulany. George Morison's second wife is Hope Morison.

17 Charles Berkeley was married at Stoke in 1861.

18 "Jass," the original spelling of jazz, indicates that the music

predates 1930, when the term became famous and its spelling changed.

19 See the chapter on Welbourne in this volume.

TRAPPE SPRING

1 The Peace of Albany in 1723 decreed that Indian tribes would stay west of the Blue Ridge and settlers to the east. However, just as settlers pushed westward, legends indicate that Indian raids continued in the Piedmont long after 1723.

Dr. John H. Boucher of Silver Spring, Maryland, recently visited Trappe Springs. Believing himself to be the descendant of Peter Boucher, he has spent years researching the genesis of this story, but with few records to rely on, the murder still remains a legend.

2 See *John Marshall and the Heroic Age of the Supreme Court* by R. Kent Newmyer, Louisiana State University Press, 2002.

3 See *Maps and Notes Pertaining to the Upper Secion of Fauquier County*. Warrenton, Virginia: Warrenton Antiquarian Society, 1954.

4 This Rawleigh was the son of Thomas Colston, son of Rawleigh I.

5 There are other explanations for the name Trappe, but this seems the most likely (and certainly the most romantic). See "View from the Trappe" by Eugene Scheel, *Loudoun Times-Mirror*, 27 August 1981.

6 Oscar Littleton (son of Thomas) served in the Revolution. Edgar and Francis Littleton both served in the 17th Virginia Infantry, CSA. Intermarriages occurred between the Littletons, Furrs, Fletchers, Carters, Montegues, and Fraziers.

7 Mrs. Greenough is the mother of Randy Waterman, past master of the Piedmont Hunt.

8 The Snowden manor house has not been restored and is currently used as a guesthouse by the Zilucas.

9 Although neither Paul nor Louise Ziluca has heard the ghost, their son tells of his own frightening experiences, and a previous resident of Trappe Spring, Mrs. Tancia Herd, confirms the stories of apparitions and unexplained sounds in the night.

VINE HILL

1 Jane was the daughter of Thomas Noland and Elinor Luckett Noland. For additional information on the Noland family see the chapters on Noland Ferry House and Mercer House in this volume. Also refer to the index, since the Nolands intermarried with other prominent families around Loudoun County.

2 Charles Love was the son of Samuel Love, Jr., and Jane Jones, and grandson of Samuel Love who had five slaves and tithed in Cameron Parish in 1775. Per Tavenner Papers at Balch Library.

3 Although many mansions had been built around Middleburg by this time, the only other "great home" of the 1810 era within the town of Middleburg was Noble Beveridge's home on Washington Street, across from the Red Fox Inn.

4 The children of Asa Rogers and Ellen Lee were Arthur Lee, John Dalrymple, Lucy, Laura, and Hugh. Hugh was named for Asa's father, Hugh Rogers of Stone Hill, just east of Middleburg.

5 Children of a later generation sometimes referred to Vine Hill as Vinegar Hill, probably because the fruit was turned into apple vinegar and bottled for local use.

6 Thomas Jefferson also exemplified this Southern courtesy when he offered hospitality to British and Hessian officers who had been captured at Saratoga and marched to Charlottesville. See *John Adams*, by David McCullough. New York: Simon and Schuster, 2001, p. 314.

7 Fanny (Frances) was the daughter of William Cochran, and granddaughter of Richard Cochran, the builder of Vine Hill.

8 The author is grateful to Mr. Ken Tomlinson and Ms. Lisa Campbell of the National Sporting Library for their kind assistance.

BIBLIOGRAPHY

Angle, Paul M. *The Civil War Years.* New York: Doubleday & Company, Inc., 1947.

Boorstin, Daniel J. *The Americans: The Colonial Experience.* New York: Random House, 1958.

Boswell, Capt. James Keith. *The Diary of a Confederate Staff Officer: Capt. James Keith Boswell.* Privately printed.

Boyer, Carl. *Ship Passenger Lists, Pennsylvania and Delaware.* Newhall, Cal-ifornia: C. Boyer, 1980.

Bruce, Philip A. *History of Virginia: Virginia Biographies.* The American Historical Society, 1924.

Bulloch, James D. *The Secret Service of the Confederate States in Europe.* New York: Thomas Yoseloff.

Chappelear, B. Curtis, Esq. *Maps and Notes on the Upper Section of Fauquier County, Va.* 1954.

Charles Lewis Files, The. Leesburg, Virginia: Thomas Balch Genealogical Library.

Cresswell, Nicholas. *The Journal of Nicholas Cresswell, 1774-1777.* New York: Dial Press, 1924.

Dees, Elizabeth Claire. *The Carters of Crednal.* 1980.

Egerton, Douglas R. *Charles Fenton Mercer and the Trial of National Conservatism.* Jackson: University of Mississippi Press, 1989.

Edwards, Betsy Wells. *Virginia Country: Historic Homes of the Old Dominion.* New York: Simon and Shuster, 1998.

Encyclopedia Americana. 1963 Edition, volumes 2, 18, 28.

Fauquier County, Virginia 1759-1959. Warrenton, Virginia: Fauquier County Bicentennial Committee.

Fenn, Elizabeth A. Pox. *Americana: The Great Smallpox Epidemic of 1775-1782.* Hill and Wang, 2001.

Garnett, James Mercer. *Honorable Charles Fenton Mercer.* Richmond, Virginia: Whittet & Shepperson, 1911.

Gurganus, Allan. *Oldest Living Confederate Widow.* New York: Alfred A. Knopf, 1989.

Hutchison, Louisa Skinner. *Apprentices, Poor Children and Bastards of Loudoun Co. Va. 1757-1850.* Westminster, Maryland: Willow Bend Books, 2000.

Johnson, James Weldon. *Black Manhattan.* New York: Da Capo Press, 1930.

Journey Through Hallowed Ground. Washington, D.C.: National Register of Historic Places.

Life and Times of the Rev. Walter Dulany Addison. Philadelphia: George W. Jacobs & Co., 1895.

Lee, Marguerite DuPont. *Virginia Ghosts.* 1930.

Legends of Loudoun. Thomas Balch Library. Leesburg, Virginia: privately printed.

Loudoun County Families and History. Thomas Balch Library. Leesburg, Virginia: privately printed.

Loudoun County Birth and Death Records. Leesburg, Virginia: Leesburg Courthouse and Thomas Balch Library.

Lundgren, Richard J.A. *Genealogy of the Carters of Crednal.* Privately printed, 1991.

Lussier, Paul. *Last Refuge of Scoundrels.* New York: Warner Books, 2001.

McCullough, David. *John Adams.* New York: Simon and Schuster, 2001.

Middleburg Cemeteries Loudoun County, Va. Compiled by the Thomas Balch Library. Westminster, Maryland: Willow Bend Books, 2000.

O'Neill, Robert F. *The Cavalry Battles of Aldie, Middleburg and Upperville.* Lynchburg, Virginia: H.E. Howard, 1993.

Phillips, John T. II. *The Bulletin of the Historical Society of Loudoun County, Va.* Leesburg, Virginia: Goose Creek Productions, 1997.

Phillips, John T. II. *The Historian's Guide to Loudoun County, Va., 1757-1766.* Leesburg, Virginia: Goose Creek Productions, 1996.

Phillips, Kevin. *Wealth and Democracy.* New York: Random House, 2002.

Poland, Charles Preston, Jr. *From Frontier to Suburbia.* Marceline, Missouri: Walsworth Publishing Co., 1976.

Scheel, Eugene. *The History of Middleburg and Vicinity.* Warrenton, Virginia: Piedmont Press, 1987.

Sims, C.F. *The Origin and Signification of Scottish Surnames.* Baltimore: Genealogical Publishing Co., 1989.

Skinker, Thomas. *Samuel Skinker and his Descendants.* Privately published, 1923.

The Smiths of Virginia. Courtesy of Mrs. Patricia Boatright, Lancaster, Texas: privately published.

Story of Middleburg, Virginia 1787-1958, The. Middleburg, Virginia: The Middleburg National Bank, 1958.

Tavenner Papers, The. Leesburg, Virginia: Thomas Balch Genealogical Library.

Templeman, Eleanor Lee and Nan Netherton. *Northern Virginia Heritage.* New York: Avenel Books, 1975.

———. *Virginia Homes of the Lees.* Privately published, 1985.

Trotta, Lee C. *The Lees in Virginia, Again!* Reston, Virginia: privately published, 1992.

Virginia Regimental Histories, The, 1st Edition. Lynchburg, Virginia: H.E. Howard, Inc., 1991.

Vogtsberger, Margaret A. *The Dulanys of Welbourne.* Berryville, Virginia: Rockbridge Publishing Co., 1995.

Whitehead, R.F. and Frank C. Brown. *Architectural Treasures of Early America.* New York: Arno Press, Inc., 1977.

Winik, Jay. *April 1865: The Month that Saved America.* New York: Harper Collins, 2001.

Yates, Richard. *The Collected Stories of Richard Yates.* New York: Henry Holt, 2001.

INDEX

Page numbers in **boldface** type indicate photographs.